BEYOND
COMPUTOPIA

Japanese Studies
General Editor: Yoshio Sugimoto

BEYOND COMPUTOPIA

Information, Automation and Democracy in Japan

Tessa Morris-Suzuki

KEGAN PAUL INTERNATIONAL
London and New York

First published in 1988 by Kegan Paul International Limited
11 New Fetter Lane, London EC4P 4EE

Distributed by
Associated Book Publishers (UK) Ltd
11 New Fetter Lane, London EC4P 4EE

Routledge, Chapman and Hall Inc.
29 West 35th Street
New York, NY 10001, USA

Set in Times
by The Eastern Press Ltd
and printed in Great Britain
by Dotesios Printers Ltd
Bradford-on-Avon, Wiltshire

The publishers gratefully acknowledge the assistance of The
Japan Foundation in the publication of this volume.

ISBN 07103–0293–2

Contents

Contents

List of Figures

List of Tables

Acknowledgements

The individuals and organisations who have helped me with this study are so numerous that it would be impossible to name them all. Particular thanks, however, are due to Professors Seiyama Takurō and Tahara Eiichi of Ōita University, at which I held a visiting research fellowship while gathering material for this book. I was concurrently a visiting researcher at the Kyūshū Keizai Chōsa Kyōkai, and my thanks go to Mr Imamura Akio and to all the staff of that institution for their assistance and hospitality. I am grateful to Messrs Koizuka Fumihiro of the Mainichi Newspapers, Watanabe Eiki of the Japan Socialist Party, and Shimomichi Naoki of the *Shakai Shimpō*, and to Ms Murota Yasuko of the *Asahi Shimbun* for their help in arranging the interviews upon which sections of this book are based; and, as always, to Messrs Shimamoto Shūji of Shogakkan Publications, Toshikawa Takao of *Korea Report* and Ogawa Taku of Eva Press International for their unfailing assistance and kindness.

The University of New England provided financial support for my research, and my colleagues in the Economic History Department have given continual support and encouragement, and occasional light relief. Mrs Judith Dodd and Mrs Naomi Bell gave invaluable help in typing a sometimes difficult manuscript.

I could not conclude without acknowledging a deep debt of gratitude to the late Professor Ron Neale, with whom I discussed many of the ideas contained in this book, but with whom, sadly, I shall not be able to discuss its final form.

Note: Names in this text are given in the normal Japanese order: family name first and given name second, except in quoted references where the western order is used in the original.

1 Introduction

In recent years, an unceasing stream of books, newspaper articles, conferences and television programmes have drawn our attention to profound technological changes which are transforming the structure of the world economy. The automation of factory and office work is increasing; communications networks are being radically reshaped; new areas of productive knowledge such as biotechnology and artificial intelligence are being developed; information-based industries are expanding. Some writers have welcomed these developments as ushering in an age of greater affluence, leisure and intellectual creativity, while others see them as posing profound threats to economic welfare and to political freedom; but almost all agree that they are changes whose implications we ignore at our peril.

From these writings, two important themes emerge. The first is that we are in the midst of an 'information revolution', whose outcome will be the emergence of an 'information age' or 'information society'. At a conference on the topic held in 1983, for example, the British Minister of Science and Technology, Kenneth Baker, told his audience that 'technology today is changing faster than ever before and no area more so than information technology. In turn, this promises to change society every bit as radically as the industrial revolution of the nineteenth century',[1] while a 1979 symposium held under the auspices of the European Economic Community produced the prediction that 'in the 1980s the information society could become the most important policy question in organisations and governments alike'.[2]

Since that date, a growing number of governments have certainly turned their attention to various issues identified under the rubric of the information revolution. But what *is* the information revolution; what *is* an information society? Daniel Bell, perhaps the best-known western writer on the subject, states that the axial principle of the newly emerging social order (which he originally called 'post-industrial society' but more recently has begun to term 'information society') 'is the centrality of theoretical knowledge and its new role, when codified, as the director of social change'.[3]

By contrast with the traditional Marxian view of socio-economic development, which predicted a transformation from capitalism to socialism, Bell identifies a number of changes at work in all industrialised societies, whether capitalist or socialist. The most important of these are seen as being the growing bureaucratisation of society and the associated dominance of a rationalist, science-based, technocratic ethos. These developments are linked to a metamorphosis in the nature of economic activity, which, in Bell's words, is becoming less a 'game against nature' than a 'game between persons'.[4]

In practice Bell's vision of the information society embraces the growing role of organised theoretical research in industry, the increasing importance of information as a source of value, the shift of employment from agriculture, industry or services to the 'information sector', the computerisation of society and the fusion of computer and communications technology. Yet, although it can be agreed that these are all important elements in contemporary economic and social change, the precise way in which these elements relate to one another remains obscure. As one United States academic puts it: 'whether knowledge led to computer development or computers led to a preponderance of information is difficult to conclude; they seem caught up in a circle and dependent on each other'.[5]

Indeed, for all the wealth of research on specific aspects of the information revolution, theoretical attempts to grasp and analyse the phenomenon as a whole remain few and far between. We ourselves, it might be said, seem to be caught up in a circle of change whose origins, dimensions and implications are beyond the scope of our vision.

A second theme common to many writings on the information revolution is that this wave of change is being accompanied by a gradual shift in the centre of gravity of economic activity away from the old industrial cores (the United States in particular) and towards new centres of dynamism, most notably Japan.[6] One writer after another has pointed to Japan's high and accelerating rate of automation, to increasing Japanese dominance of technologically advanced industries such as microelectronics, and to the fact that Japan, from being an imitator or follower in industrial technology, is emerging as a leader in crucial fields of research (including research into artificial intelligence).[7] It is, indeed, no coincidence that the term 'information society' was itself coined in Japan.

The emergence of Japan as a major rival to the United States in certain fields of advanced technology has evoked a variety of responses. On the one hand, since the mid-1970s there has been a growing tendency for academics, business analysts and others to argue that western nations (by which they usually mean western governments and/or management) should learn the 'secrets' of Japanese success – frequently seen as involving a far-sighted and coordinated approach to development on the part of government and business, harmonious labour relations, consensus decision making, and a strong emphasis on lifetime training within the enterprise.[8] On the other, a growing number of writers have reacted to exhortations to 'learn from Japan' by arguing that Japan's success represents not so much a model for emulation as a sinister conspiracy based on 'the web of plots and secret agreements, the concerted acts and duplicitous manoeuvres . . . that have served Japan's goals ever since World War II'.[9]

Here again the contours of the issue often remain confused. Since the nature of the information revolution is itself ill-defined, it is difficult to establish whether or not this revolution is more advanced in Japan than in other countries. Language barriers have made it difficult for those outside Japan to penetrate Japanese debates on the nature and consequences of technological change, and the material available to English-speaking readers has therefore tended to be dominated by the rather tired stereotypes of Japan so eagerly propagated by Japanese management, and so readily accepted by their counterparts in the west: stereotypes of social harmony, group cohesion, hard work and loyalty to the enterprise.

My purpose in writing this book is neither to offer any specific lessons from Japan's experience, nor to add to the warnings of the 'Japanese menace' to western technological hegemony. Instead, the perspective here will be a somewhat different one. Although, for example, the percentage of Japanese workers employed in the information sector is considerably smaller than the comparable figures for the United States (I shall say more about this in

3

Chapter 8), there is evidence that many of the technological and social changes commonly associated with the information revolution are occurring at a particularly rapid rate in Japan. Moreover, these changes have become the focus of a great deal of research and debate within Japanese government and business circles, academia and mass media. For these reasons, the patterns, possibilities and problems common to many advanced industrial countries are becoming particularly clearly visible in Japanese society. My intention, therefore, is to use the study of Japan as a means of outlining a theory of information society which will be radically different, both from that of Daniel Bell and from the ideas put forward by most Japanese theorists of the subject.

In order to do this, it is first necessary to review the idea of an information society as it exists in Japan at present, and to examine a variety of means by which government and business in Japan are attempting to convert this idea into reality. Rather than attributing the emergence of these ideas and policies simply to the spread of computerisation or to the growing complexity of human knowledge, I shall suggest that the origins of the contemporary information revolution are to be found primarily in the crisis which faced business enterprises – in Japan and elsewhere – during the late 1960s and early 1970s. I shall argue that the responses of business and government to this crisis are bringing about the emergence of 'information capitalism', which differs in significant ways from the industrial capitalism of earlier eras. The second half of the book will look at the implications of information capitalism for the nature of work in Japan, and at the possibilities for its transformation.

Although this book contains some personal verdicts on social trends in Japan, these verdicts are not intended to be seen in a comparative perspective, implying that Japanese society is either superior or inferior to other industrial societies. Instead, they are political judgements which arise from a theoretical stance critical of the corporate structures which characterise all advanced capitalist economies. Many readers will disagree with this stance. But I hope that, by taking it as a starting point, this book may contribute in some way to a freer exchange of data and ideas, not just between Japanese and western managers or government officials, but between all those caught up in the exhilarating, bewildering and often alarming social change of the information age.

Notes

1 Kenneth Baker, 'Towards the Information Society' (keynote speech presented to the Hong Kong Computer Conference, 1983) in R. C. Barquin and G. P. Mead (eds.), *Towards the Information Society*, Amsterdam, New York and Oxford, North Holland Publishing Co., 1984, p. 3.
2 N. Bjorn-Anderson, M. Earl, O. Holst and E. Mumford (eds), *The Information Society: for Richer, for Poorer*, Amsterdam, New York and Oxford, North Holland Publishing Co., 1982, p. xii.
3 Daniel Bell, 'The Social Framework of the Information Society' in Tom Forester (ed.), *The Microelectronics Revolution*, Oxford, Basil Blackwell, 1980, p. 501.
4 Daniel Bell, *The Coming of Post-Industrial Society*, London, Heinemann, 1974, pp. 116–17.
5 Mary Louise Biunno, 'Industrial Policy for a Post-Industrial Society: an Alternative for the United States' in A. Bruce Boenau and Katsuyuki Niiro (eds.), *Post-Industrial Society*, Lanham, New York and London, University Press of America, 1983, p. 135.
6 E.g. R. Hofheinz, Jr. and K. E. Calder, *The Eastasia Edge*, New York, Basic Books, 1982; Robert B. Reich, *The Next American Frontier*, New York, Times Books, 1983.
7 E.g. M. Mclean (ed.), *Mechatronics: Developments in Japan and Europe*, London, Francis Pinter, 1983; E. A. Feigenbaum and P. McCorduck, *The Fifth Generation: Artificial Intelligence and Japan's Computer Challenge to the World*, London, Michael Joseph, 1984; Jerry Fox, 'Japan's Electronic Lesson', *New Scientist*, 20 Nov. 1980, 517–20.
8 E. F. Vogel, *Japan as Number One: Lessons for America*, Cambridge, Mass., and London, Harvard University Press, 1979; B. Boatwright and J. Sleigh, 'New Technology: the Japanese Approach', *Department of Employment Gazette* vol. 87, no. 7, July 1979; P. Marsh, 'Japan's Recipe for Industrial Success', *New Scientist*, 15 Nov. 1980, 430–2; J. Northcott, M. Fogarty and M. Trevor, *Chips and Jobs: Acceptance of New Technology at Work*, London, Policy Studies Institute, 1985, pp. 106–38; Trevor Barr, *The Electronic Estate*, Ringwood, Australia and Harmondsworth, Penguin Books, 1985, ch. 11.
9 M. J. Wolf, *The Japanese Conspiracy*, Sevenoaks, New English Library, 1984. See also Russell Braddon, *The Other Hundred Years War, Japan's Bid for Supremacy 1941–2041*, London, Collins, 1983.

2 The Technocrats' Utopia: Plans for an Information Society

For centuries, visionaries and revolutionaries alike have dreamed of worlds where material goods are abundant, and where human energy, no longer exhausted in a constant struggle for physical survival, can instead be directed to innovation, imagination and creativity.

Sir Thomas More, in his archetypal Utopia, designed a society in which men and women work no more than six hours a day; where health, relaxation, conversation and learning are valued more than material possessions; and whose citizens 'be not greatly desirous and fond of [labour]; but in the exercise and study of the mind they never weary'.[1] This Utopia was based upon the redirection of human values from material to spiritual aims. But, with the emergence of capitalism, a further catalyst – the force of science – came to be harnessed to the dream of liberating the human spirit from the bonds of physical labour. As early as the mid-seventeenth century the English radical Gerrard Winstanley could prophesy that 'when . . . Freedom is established . . . there will knowledge cover the earth as the waters cover the sea'[2] and 'there will be plenty of all Earthly Commodities, with less labour and trouble than now'.[3] And Winstanley's vision was to reappear with even greater power two centuries later in Karl Marx's glimpses of society's ultimate communist transfiguration:

> [The] historic destiny [of capitalism] is fulfilled . . . when the development of the productive powers of labour . . . have flourished to the stage where the possession and preservation of general wealth require a lesser labour time of society as a whole, and where the labouring society relates scientifically to the process of its progressive reproduction;

hence where labour in which a human being does what a thing could do has ceased.[4]

But although these themes in themselves are familiar ones, it is still a little startling to rediscover them, not in the writings of radical or Utopian thinkers, but in the normally sober and prosaic reports of economic planning agencies or government committees on industrial policy. It is, however, precisely such a vision of a community where manual labour will be reduced, where 'materialistic value thinking . . . will give place to time value thinking',[5] and where there will be a 'blossoming of intellectual creativity',[6] which lies at the heart of recent Japanese governmental and semi-governmental pronouncements on the imminent coming of the 'information society' (*jōhō shakai* or *jōhōka shakai*).

The outlines of this Utopian image of the society of the immediate future have emerged, with growing clarity, from a number of reports published since the late 1960s. Of these, five particularly significant and well-publicised documents form the basis for the sketch of the information society concept which I shall present in this chapter. They are: *Japan's Information Society: Themes and Visions* (1969)[7]; *Policy Outlines for Promoting the Informisation of Japanese Society* (1969)[8]; *The Plan for an Information Society* (1971)[9]; *Signposts to a Prosperous Information Society* (1981)[10]; and *The Information Society and Human Life* (1983)[11]. Of these, the first and last were produced by advisory bodies attached to Japan's Economic Planning Agency, while the 1969 Policy Outlines and the 1980 report were compiled by the Industrial Structure Council, an influential think-tank which operates under the auspices of the Ministry of International Trade and Industry (MITI). The 1971 *Plan for an Information Society* is not strictly speaking a government publication, but was presented to MITI by the privately funded Japan Computer Usage Development Institute (JACUDI), and is regarded in some quarters as being essentially an attempt by Japanese computer companies to lobby government support for their industry.[12]

Besides these official or quasi-official reports, there are also a number of independent academics whose writings have obviously exerted a powerful influence on government thinking about the information society. The most famous are Hayashi Yūjirō, a Professor of Tokyo Institute of Technology and adviser to the Economic Planning Agency, who is widely credited with the

7

invention of the phrase 'information society', and Masuda Yoneji, President of the Institute for the Information Society and one of the principal authors of JACUDI's Information Society Plan. Hayashi's best-known work, *The Information Society: from Hard to Soft Society*[13] was published simultaneously with the first government reports on the subject, while Masuda's *Information Society as Post-Industrial Society* (1980)[14] has been translated and widely read in the English-speaking world.

The ideas contained in works such as those of Hayashi and Masuda are not only echoed in the government reports on the information society. They have also influenced other very important policy statements, including Economic White Papers and the development plans of the Industrial Structure Council from the late 1960s onwards. Even though these White Papers and plans may not actually use the same terminology, we shall see that their underlying thinking is often very close to that of the information society theorists.

The Economic Basis of the Information Society

The term 'information society' is one which is more often used than defined, and indeed part of its popularity is probably due to a comfortable elasticity of definition which allows the user, like Humpty Dumpty, to make the phrase mean 'just what they want it to mean – neither more nor less'. Where definitions are given, they are sometimes reminiscent not so much of meaningful analysis as of the purple prose of the advertising slogan. JACUDI, for example, tells us that 'The information society may be termed "a society with highly intellectual creativity where people may draw future designs on an invisible canvas and pursue and realise individual lives worth living"'.[15]

But all this is not to say that the concept is a vacuous one. In fact its history suggests several strands of meaning which have become intertwined as the idea has matured and developed. The first three significant statements of this idea, all of which were published in May 1969, defined it in three distinct ways. In the Industrial Structure Council's *Policy Outlines*, 'informisation' – the process by which the information society is created – is equivalent to 'computerisation'. So the information society is defined as 'a society in which the progress of computerisation will give people access to reliable information, free them from clerical work, and thus bring about the blossoming of human creativity'.[16] But Hayashi Yūjirō, in *The Information Society*, uses the same words in a rather different sense. For him, the most significant economic tendency of modern societies is for prosperity to reduce the importance of human physical needs and to amplify their psychological and emotional needs. This influences the type of goods which consumers demand. Greater and greater emphasis comes to be placed on fashion, style and quality, and, as a result, a larger and larger share of the price of goods is attributable, not to material or labour costs, but to 'information costs' – research and development, design and so on. In Hayashi's view therefore, the information society is characterised by the fact that 'the importance of information processes relative to material processes increases'.[17]

The third 1969 publication, *Japan's Information Society*, manages to incorporate something of both of these approaches. While its general definition of 'informisation' is almost identical to that of Hayashi, and it too places great emphasis on the diversification of demand and the expansion of consumer choice, its concrete predictions resemble those of the Industrial Structure Council. The coming of Japan's information society, we are told, will be marked by the computerisation of commerce, finance and manufacturing and by the expansion of information industries such as software production.[18]

Most subsequent reports have taken a similar line, and the commonly accepted picture of the information society has come to be one in which two central elements are integrally connected. On the one hand, *methods* of production and distribution will be transformed. Computer-related technologies will result in higher levels of automation and in faster flows of information between office, factory and consumer. The consequence, it is argued, will be substantial increases in efficiency and productivity. On the other hand, however, the *content* of production will be simultaneously transformed. Products will become more 'information intensive', in the sense that innovation, planning design and marketing will come to represent an increasing share of their value.

These two basic elements of the information society contain a number of more specific ideas which appear (with varying emphasis) in all the recent writing on the concept:

1 In the information society, the application of computer technology to production, office work, commerce and banking will lead to the rapid automation of many areas of work;

2 The development of computer-based automation is inseparable from the development of communications networks. Just as human thought would have little function without the human capacity to communicate thought through speech, so the automation of certain mental functions requires the creation of means by which computer can communicate, both with computer and with human user;

3 New communications technology will open up new ways of performing work and enjoying leisure;

4 Information-producing industries such as the software industry and mass media will become more important;

5 There will also be a rapid growth of 'knowledge-intensive' industries, i.e. of areas such as computer and robot production, telecommunications and biotechnology, which require large inputs of research;

6 The simpler basic industries which survive will also gradually become more knowledge intensive, using increasingly sophisticated forms of innovation and product differentiation to market their goods.

Since 1969 there have been great changes, both in the world economy and in the state of the art of information technology, so it is hardly surprising that the original information society concept should have been modified in a number of ways. In particular, whereas the early reports spoke of a single process of computerisation and automation, later ones see the process as being subdivided into phases of increasing complexity. The Industrial Structure Council's 1980 report, for example, introduces a two-stage model of informisation.[19]

The first stage of the information revolution, according to this analysis, occurred in Japan between the late 1960s and the end of the 1970s. It was characterised by the rapid growth of 'knowledge intensive industries', and by the growing application of computer technology to the automation of three major areas of activity: factory production, office work and distribution (including warehousing, banking, retailing and so on).

In the second stage of informisation, which the Industrial

Structure Council envisages as starting in the 1980s and ushering in a fully-fledged 'high-level information society' (*kōdo jōhōka shakai*) by the 1990s, two crucially important things will happen. In the first place, computerisation will begin to link together the previously separate areas of planning, control, production and distribution into 'total systems'. As a result of this, a much more flexible relationship will be established between demand and supply, and the age of mass production will give way to an age in which the small-scale manufacturing of a wide variety of goods becomes the mark of the most advanced levels of industrial technology:

> in the 1980s, in order to meet increasingly diversified human needs, a major issue for the continued growth of industry will be the discarding of the old format of mass producing standardised goods, and the development of technologies for the automatic production of small batches of varied products. For this purpose it will be necessary to integrate information management and to create total systems controlling everything from the receipt of orders, through the planning and production processes, to the delivery of goods.[20]

The main technological advance which will make this process possible will be the integration of computer-based management information systems (MIS), computer-aided design (CAD) and computer-aided manufacturing (CAM) into a wholly automated productive system. Figure 2.1 shows how this is envisaged by the Industrial Structure Council.

The other major feature of the second phase of informisation will, it is argued, be the spreading of the effects of computer technology far beyond the confines of factory or office, to affect such areas of everyday life as commuter transport, health care, housework and recreation. Computer-communications systems might be used, for example, to order the groceries, make holiday reservations or take classes in French or philosophy. In this context, information will become not only an increasingly important factor of production but also an increasingly important consumer product. And it is here that we encounter an area of innovation which is seen as critical to the emergence of the information society: the sophisticated digital communications network, through which

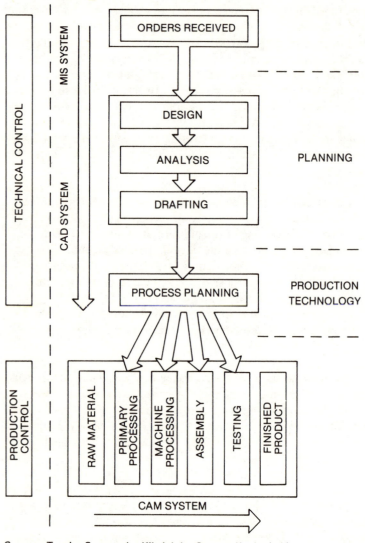

Source: Tsusho Sangyosho Kikai Joho Sangyo Kyoku (ed.)
Yutaka Naru Johoka Shakai e no Dohyo, p.165

Figure 2.1 *Model of an Automated Manufacturing System*

voice, visual symbols and electronic data can be conveyed at high speed to offices, factories and households throughout the country.[21] This communications system, clearly, would not only provide consumer information but would also play a central role in the anticipated integration of planning, manufacturing and distribution by business corporations.

As the idea of the information society has become clearer, so statements on its historical significance have become more outspoken. In its 1969 report, the Industrial Structure Council argued: 'The industrial revolution of the eighteenth century gave birth to modern industry in place of agriculture. But the future information revolution will not mean that information production succeeds industrial production. Rather, in raising the industrial level of contemporary society and enhancing human welfare, it constitutes a "revolution within the system".'[22] By the 1980s, however, fine distinctions between the nature of the industrial and information revolutions seem to have been forgotten. The 1983 report on the *Information Society and Human Life* stated that 'the development of human society has proceeded through three types of societal technology: hunting, agricultural and industrial. . . . information technology can be called the fourth societal technology.'[23] And the Industrial Structure Council itself, with subtle change of emphasis, was claiming that 'the impact of informisation on society as a whole will be as extensive and profound as that of the industrial revolution, and that it will have a correspondingly decisive effect on the future of human society'.[24]

A New Social Order

The Utopian flavour of the information society reports is most clearly evident, not in their predictions of changes in the industrial structure, but in their suggestions of the effect which these changes will have upon work, leisure, social relationships and human values. The authors of the various reports go much further than simply predicting the increased automation of housework, medical care and so on, and consistently put forward quite dramatic claims for the impact of informisation upon the social order.

Informisation does not merely contribute to increased

productivity, reduced resource consumption and reduced energy consumption in the industrial field, it is also effective in solving social problems and broadening the realms of human activity. Moreover, through its impact on each individual's life it also influences the cultural values of the nation.[25]

The transformation of human values in the information society is a concept which has been particularly eloquently expounded by Masuda Yoneji. According to Masuda, reduced working hours in the information society will be reflected in an increased preference for the cultivation of leisure over the accumulation of material possessions. The decline of materialism will express itself in a growing demand, not for goods but for services, more particularly for the new information services whose consumption will contribute to a perpetual process of self-education. As *The Information Society and Human Life* (composed under Masuda's chairmanship) puts it:

> While our sense of values in industrial society centered around the consumption of goods, in the information society this will give place to the importance of time value. With this change in our sense of values, the question will arise on how we can utilise this time, extending throughout a lifetime, and the need for self-actualisation will assume greater importance. Considered in the light of human need, it means that more emphasis will have to be given to our need for self-actualisation, in the sense that we will want to pursue new possibilities throughout this lifelong time process.[26]

Like More's Utopians, it seems that the citizens of the information society are to 'embrace chiefly the pleasures of the mind, for them they count the chiefest and most principal of all'.[27]

Closely connected with the concepts of declining materialism and increasing self-actualisation is the theme of creativity. A point repeatedly stressed in the information society reports is that 'informisation' – by expanding leisure time and automating monotonous manual labour – will create a fertile soil for the flowering of human creativity.

With regard to the industrial structure in the information society, the proportion of intellectual labour will increase, compared with other types of work, and greater creativity will be called for, with an intensification of knowledge-demand.[28]

. . . the home computer will not only promote the rationalisation of life [*seikatsu no gōrika*]. . . . It will [also] provide information to assist the use of free time for research, education and creativity at home, and so bring about lifetime fulfilment.[29]

Lastly, the information society is depicted as a world of harmony and social cohesion: 'human relations will . . . be transformed, and instead of competing with and restricting others, better relationships will be established through synergetic voluntary cooperation'.[30]

This concept of synergy closely follows the thinking of Masuda, who sees the information society as a classless and conflictless community where government will be small and simple and 'the dominant form of maintenance of public order replacing resort to the law will be the *autonomous restraints exercised by the citizens themselves*'.[31] The reasoning behind this optimistic prediction is not precisely spelled out in the information society reports, but it appears that the vision of future social harmony rests partly on the anticipated transformation of human values, and partly upon the effects of specific technological changes. The development of new communications networks, for example, is seen as having great potential for allowing the growth of decentralised regional information and entertainment networks which would strengthen the participation of individuals in and identification with their community.[32]

Throughout much of the writing on the information society, the Utopian goals of human creativity, social harmony and diminishing materialism are presented as the spontaneous outcome of techno-logical transformation. Occasionally, however, there are sugges-tions that the natural emergence of these qualities will need to be reinforced by education. JACUDI (in a passage which, read in the context of Japanese history, has a slightly sinister ring) outlines an information society education policy where, alongside computer education, 'ethics should be introduced . . . based on new ethical

15

standards. Amongst other things, self-control under one's own initiative, and active service to contribute to the society are important as formation [*sic*] of such ethics.'[33]

Problems of the Information Society

In arguing that the official writings on the information society contain Utopian features I am not, however, suggesting that they present a wholly idyllic picture of the future, or that they ignore possible problems involved in the adoption of new technologies. All the reports, in fact, include a clear recognition of certain dangers implicit in the emergence of the information society, and all share a wide measure of common ground in their analysis of the nature of these dangers.

Firstly, there is the risk that new information technologies may erode the privacy of individuals and organisations.[34] The development of complex and possibly interconnected data systems containing information on tax returns, health and education records, bank deposits and so on contains obvious and widely recognised potential for abuse. The problem of increasing computer crime is also discussed in the reports. To avert these dangers both the Industrial Structure Council and the Social Policy Council recommend the strengthening of legal systems governing access to information, and argue that these systems should balance the desirability of the 'democratisation of information', on the one hand, against the need for privacy and security, on the other.[35]

Secondly, there is the possibility of 'information pollution': the deluging of society with a mass of irrelevant, misleading or poorly comprehended information. This is regarded as a potential future source of alienation, neurosis and other social disorders.[36] Some of the reports also recognise the risk that, since certain individuals will be better equipped than others to adapt to the environment of the information society, a growing gap could appear between the 'information elite' who are actively involved in the design and development of new technologies, and the mass of relatively powerless information consumers.[37] To meet these problems, a variety of educational policies aimed at increasing 'information literacy' and public acceptance of computerisation are suggested.[38]

Rather surprisingly, the Japanese reports place comparatively little emphasis on the issue which, in other industrialised countries, has been regarded as the greatest danger of current technological change: unemployment. JACUDI's *Plan for an Information Society*, for example, disposes of the question of unemployment in a single paragraph appended to a much more lengthy discussion of the problems of computer privacy,[39] while the Industrial Structure Council reassuringly observes that

> In the past, waves of technological innovation have caused unemployment and other frictional phenomena in the short term, but in the long term, by giving rise to new industries and creating new employment opportunities, they have absorbed the decrease in employment and as a consequence working conditions have been improved and the level of welfare raised.[40]

This tone of confidence is undoubtedly derived from Japan's experience in the 1950s and 1960s, when rapid technological change was accompanied by low and generally falling rates of unemployment. Even in the 1970s Japan's unemployment rates remained low by international standards in spite of exceptionally rapid automation. In the light of this history, the information society reports suggest that some measures to promote re-training, combined with the maintenance of Japan's traditional employment system, will be sufficient to prevent unemployment from reaching unacceptable levels.[41] Noting the relatively insignificant level of Japanese unemployment during the last decade, the Industrial Structure Council's 1981 report observes:

> It can be considered that the major factors in this phenomenon were our positive national attitude to the introduction of innovations, and our country's distinctive employment practices. The latter have meant that there has been no direct connection between the rationalisation of industry through new technology and reductions in employment levels. In this respect the situation is very different from the environment which nurtured European fears of unemployment.[42]

But the most significant aspect of the approach of the official reports to the problems of the information society is that these problems are regarded, not as inherent contradictions of contemporary economic and social development, but rather as peripheral difficulties which may be solved or controlled by prudent government action. This attitude is most strikingly exemplified by the Economic Planning Agency's Social Policy Council, which accepted the importance of possible malignant features of the information society, but argued that these needed to be 'discussed on an appropriate occasion at some later date', and was then content to compose its report 'on the premise that the various negative aspects which are likely to accompany the information society will be overcome by introducing appropriate counter-measures'.[43]

The general impression, therefore, is that, given some elaboration of legal controls on access to information, certain alterations to the education system, and policies to promote the re-training and mobility of labour, a prosperous, harmonious and life-enhancing society is virtually within our grasp. With this assurance, the information society reports have little hesitation in recommending very substantial government commitment to the promotion of automation, the expansion of information-processing industries and advanced communications networks, and the stimulation of scientific and technological research,[44] all of which are seen as hastening the realisation of their vision of a radiant future.

The Information Society Concept: a Preliminary Critique

The Japanese government reports on the information society, then, do far more than merely charting the course of various contemporary trends in technology and the industrial structure. Instead, they bring together a whole range of observations, predictions and speculations – from relatively down-to-earth comments on the spread of the automation or recommendations on increased funding for the computer industry, to sweeping images of revolutionised human values, expanded intellectual creativity and transcendent social harmony. These elements they weave together into a complex and alluring whole: a vision of an information Utopia. Our task in this book will be to examine that vision, and to unravel the threads of fact from fantasy, insight from ideology.

Many of the predictions made in the information society reports have a validity and importance which, I believe, cannot be denied. Here it is important to remember that the reports are not mere forecasts of future developments: they are also policy documents drawn up by influential advisory bodies. To the extent that their recommendations are put into practice (and we shall see in the next chapter that they often have been), the reports help to shape the society whose future they predict. Their emphasis on the rapid proliferation and profound impact of computer technology, on the emerging structure of the communications system, and on the increasing importance of technological research in industry is amply justified by contemporary trends in Japanese industry. It seems plausible, too, to suggest that these developments will have certain beneficial social effects: automation *can* be used to reduce dangerous, unpleasant or monotonous work; computer systems *may* increase the efficiency of medical services; 'knowledge-intensive' industries *are* in general less environmentally polluting than conventional heavy industries. There are, however, some very significant ideas implicitly or explicitly contained in the information society reports which need to be examined and challenged.

The first of these is the assumption, most succinctly expressed in the Industrial Structure Council's 1981 report, that 'technological innovation is the fountainhead of social progress'.[45] The whole notion of the information society is, in fact, founded on the view that social evolution progresses through a series of stages, with each stage being determined by the principal forms of technology applied by society to the creation of wealth. (It is, incidentally, surely no coincidence that this model of human development has origins which go back to the nineteenth-century German historical school, whose impact upon the study of history in Japan has been particularly great.)

If we contrast this model of history with the Marxian model, which postulates a transformation from feudalism to capitalism – or even with the Rostowian stages of 'traditional society', 'pre-conditions for take-off', 'take-off' and so forth – it becomes clear that its outstanding characteristic is its technological determinism. In this vision of evolution the motive force flows almost wholly in one direction.

When epoch-making technological innovation occurs,
changes take place in the existing society and a new society
emerges. The steam engine precipitated the industrial
revolution, bringing about changes that led to a new
economic and political system: the capitalist system and
parliamentary democracy. The information epoch resulting
from computer-communications technology will bring about
a societal transformation just as great or even greater than
the industrial revolution.[46]

In all but the crudest of the Marxian models, on the other hand,
the relationship is a two-way, dialectical one. Technology not only
shapes society, but is in turn moulded by the structures of economic
and political power which exist in that society. Herbert Marcuse
and others have taken this analysis one step further, and observed
that, in a very real sense, technology is itself an integral and
inseparable part of social structure.[47] As the American historian
of technology David Noble observes:

technology is . . . a social process; it does not simply stimulate
social development from outside but, rather, constitutes
fundamental social development itself. . . .
Since those who comprise society are at the same time the
human material of which technology is composed, technology
must inescapably reflect the contours of that particular social
order which has produced and sustained it. And like any
human enterprise, it does not simply proceed automatically,
but rather contains a subjective element which drives it, and
assumes the particular forms given it by the most powerful
and forceful people in society, in struggle with others.[48]

In later chapters I shall argue that the technologies of the
information society cannot be studied except in their social context,
as the products of corporate capitalism. The refinement and
application of these technologies were motivated by a need to
overcome frictions within the corporate structure (frictions which
were very severe in the case of Japan). Even more importantly,
these technologies continue to be applied within a clearly defined
economic system, one dominated by large, profit-seeking, corporate organisations strongly supported by a pro-business political
environment. As a result, the potential of new technology is

circumscribed. Alternative applications (the decision, for example, whether the most advanced robot technology is to be used primarily in manufacturing, in the home or in assisting the ill, elderly and disabled) are not freely chosen on the basis of some abstract concept of social equity. Instead, they are very largely determined by the economic motivation and relative power of competing and unequal interest groups in society.

Examining the information society concept from this perspective, some of the social benefits predicted in the Japanese government reports are called into question. Firstly, I feel that the optimistic approach to employment – in which unemployment is seen as a transient phenomenon whose threat is easily outweighed by the promise of shorter working hours, better working conditions and more creative employment – is an inadequate one. It fails to take sufficient account of the very profound impact which new information-related technologies already appear to be having, not only upon the amount of work available, but also upon the organisation and content of work. Where the Industrial Structure Council sees traditional Japanese employment practices as providing a safeguard against unemployment in the information society, I would argue that those employment practices (from whose scope many workers are already excluded) are most unlikely to survive the present wave of technological change.

Secondly, I would question the reports' assertion that the new technologies of the information society will promote social interaction and harmony. This again seems to be based on a philosophy of technological determinism: if machinery makes it possible for human beings to communicate with one another, the argument runs, human beings will do so. But in reality it is evident that human interaction is based on much more than mere technical possibility. Here we will need to consider the way in which the new technologies influence economic and social connections between individuals, and there is evidence to suggest that this influence may run more strongly in the direction of social atomisation than of community solidarity.

My purpose, therefore, is to challenge the Utopian image of the information society presented by certain sections of Japan's business, bureaucratic and academic elites. It is not, however, simply the Utopian nature of their predictions which requires criticism. Utopias can be said to have had a positive function in history, often providing the oppressed with a vision of the world as it might be, and so acting (in Hata and Smith's words) as 'a scale to criticise reality and as an ideology for social change'.[49] Rather, the problem of the information society reports is that they represent a technocrats' Utopia, a public justification for the policies desired by economically powerful groups. In this sense they are closer to the 'conservative Utopias' which Hata and Smith describe as providing 'a very convenient basis for the ideology of the ruling class'.[50]

However, while the conservative Utopia traditionally offered an idealised image of society as it is at present or was in the past, the information society concept is, I shall argue, a 'neo-conservative Utopia'. By this I mean a vision of the world transformed not by the revolutionary action of the oppressed but by the benign guidance of the ruling elite. Many sections of the political and economic elites in Japan and other industrialised countries are well aware that capitalism implies a state of constant growth and change, and that the only way to ensure the perpetuation of their own power is to accept and control those processes of change. The concept of the information society encapsulates this objective. It offers the image of a world in which material abundance and spiritual fulfilment will be achieved, not through the painful restructuring of the social order, but through the spontaneous evolution of the existing system itself: an image of a transformed society in which, nevertheless, the fundamental structures of power will be conserved and strengthened.

Notes

1   Sir Thomas More, *Utopia*, London, J. M. Dent & Son, 1951, p. 94.
2   G. H. Sabine (ed.), *The Works of Gerrard Winstanley*, Ithaca, N.Y., Cornell University Press, 1941, p. 564.
3   Ibid., p. 526.
4   Karl Mark, *Grundrisse*, London, Penguin/New Left Books, 1973, p. 325.
5   *The Information Society and Human Life: the Outlook for the People's Lives in the Information Society* (Report of the General Policy Committee of the Social Policy Council), Tokyo, Social Policy Bureau, Economic Planning Agency of the Japanese Government, 1983, p. 50.
6   Japan Computer Usage Development Institute, Computerisation

Committee, *The Plan for an Information Society: a National Goal Towards Year 2000*, English translation published in *Change*, July/Aug. 1972, 31.

7 Keizai Shingikai Jōhō Kenkyū Inkai, *Nihon no Jōhōka Shakai: Sono Kadai to Bijon*, 1969; summary published in *Zaikei Shoho*, nos. 822–4, Nov. 1969.

8 Sangyō Kōzō Shingikai Jōhō Sangyō Bukai: *Nihon Shakai Jōhōka Sokushin no tame no Seisaku Yōkō*, 1969; summary published in 'Sutāto shita Jōhōka Seisaku', *Ekonomisuto*, 24 June 1969, 53–6.

9 *Plan for an Information Society*, op. cit.

10 Tsushō Sangyōshō Kikai Jōhō Sangyō Kyoku (ed.): *Yutaka Naru Jōhōka Shakai e no Dōhyō* (Sangyō Kōzō Shingikai Jōhō Sangyō Bukai Tōshin), Tokyo, Computer Age, 1982.

11 *Information Society and Human Life*, op. cit.

12 Tsugawa Kei, 'Jōhōka Shakai no Kyokō to Genjitsu' in *Keizai Hyōron*, (special edition); 'M. E. Kakumei to Rōdō Kumiai', 25 June 1983, pp. 50–1.

13 Hayashi Yūjirō, *Jōhōka Shakai: Hādo na Shakai Kara Sofuto na Shakai e*, Tokyo, Kodansha, 1969.

14 Y. Masuda, *The Information Society as Post-Industrial Society*, Tokyo, Institute for the Information Society, 1980.

15 *Plan for an Information Society*, op. cit., p. 8.

16 'Sutāto shita Jōhōka Seisaku', op. cit., p. 53.

17 Hayashi, *Jōhōka Shakai*, p. 70.

18 *Nihon no Jōhōka Shakai*, op. cit.

19 *Yutaka Naru Jōhōka Shakai*, pp. 46–9.

20 Ibid., p. 68.

21 *Yutaka Naru Jōhōka Shakai*: pp. 99–101; *Information Society and Human Life*, pp. 21–2; *Plan for an Information Society*, p. 22.

22 'Sutāto shita Jōhōka Seisaku', p. 53.

23 *The Information Society and Human Life*, pp. 5–7.

24 *Yutaka Naru Jōhōka Shakai*, p. 46.

25 Ibid.

26 *Information Society and Human Life*, p. 51. See also Y. Masuda, *The Information Society*, p. 127.

27 More, *Utopia*, p. 92.

28 *Information Society and Human Life*, p. 52.

29 *Yutaka Naru Jōhōka Shakai*, p. 79.

30 *Information Society and Human Life*, pp. 51–2.

31 Masuda, *The Information Society*, p. 141.

32 *Plan for an Information Society*, p. 32.

33 Ibid., p. 32.

34 *Yutaka Naru Jōhōka Shakai*, pp. 102–6; *Information Society and Human Life*, pp. 38–9; *Plan for an Information Society*, pp. 31–2.

35 *Yutaka Naru Jōhōka Shakai*, pp. 104–5; *Information Society and Human Life*, p. 39.
36 *Yutaka Naru Jōhōka Shakai*, pp. 107–8; *Information Society and Human Life*, pp. 37–8.
37 *Plan for an Information Society*, p. 32.
38 *Yutaka Naru Jōhōka Shakai*, pp. 107–8; *Information Society and Human Life*, p. 38.
39 *Plan for an Information Society*, p. 32.
40 *Yutaka Naru Jōhōka Shakai*, p. 107.
41 Ibid.; *Information Society and Human Life*, pp. 49–50; *Plan for an Information Society*, p. 32.
42 *Yutaka Naru Jōhōka Shakai*, p. 107.
43 *Information Society and Human Life*, pp. 1–2.
44 *Yutaka Naru Jōhōka Shakai*, Pt 2, chs. 1–4; *Plan for an Information Society*, ch. 4.
45 *Yutaka Naru Jōhōka Shakai*, p. 52.
46 Masuda, *The Information Society*, p. 66.
47 H. Marcuse, 'Some Social Implications of Modern Technology', *Studies in Philosophy and Social Science*, ix, 1941.
48 D. Noble, *America by Design: Science, Technology and the Rise of Corporate Capitalism*, Oxford, Oxford University Press, 1979, p. xxii.
49 H. Hata and W. A. Smith, 'Nakane's *Japanese Society* as Utopian Thought: a Theoretical and Methodological Critique', Paper presented to the Asian Studies Association of Australia's Fourth National Conference, Monash University, 10–14 May 1982, p. 34.
50 Ibid.

3 The Plans in Action: Information Society Policies in Japan

There is, perhaps, a danger in looking at documents like the information society reports, of falling for what might be called 'the conspiracy theory of Japan'. This view, currently popular among certain sections of the western media and business worlds,[1] tends to attribute to Japan's leaders and people extraordinary cohesion, consensus and far-sightedness, and to interpret any officially inspired attempts at futurology as evidence of complex Japanese strategies for world economic domination.

In fact, of course, the reports on the information society do not represent a consensus view on Japan's future development (there is no such consensus view), and their publication has been greeted even in official circles with everything from extreme enthusiasm to profound scepticism. These documents are really part of the well-established (and not uniquely Japanese) tradition of using small groups of experts – often consisting of bureaucrats, academics and businessmen – to examine problems and try out new ideas: ideas which may then be adopted or ignored by government, depending upon their political expediency and upon the reactions which they evoke from media, lobby groups and the public.

In this chapter we need to examine the impact which the reports have had upon government in Japan, and the extent to which their proposals have been translated into active policy.

'Information Society' as a Political Slogan

It seems to me that one of the most significant functions of the information society concept has been its suitability as a political slogan, a phase which may be used at once to describe certain contemporary trends and policies and to conjure up diffuse images of prosperity, progress and technological sophistication.

During the late 1950s and much of the 1960s, a similar role was performed *par excellence* by the phrase 'high economic growth' (and, from 1960, by the supporting concept of 'doubling the national income'). 'High economic growth' implied actual policies designed to foster high levels of investment and rapid industrialisation, but also, in general terms, conveyed a promise of more money, more consumer goods and the enhancement of Japan's status in the world economy. The emphasis on high growth met with criticism both from those within the establishment who were dubious about its feasibility and from those on the political left who questioned its benefits for the working class (and therefore tended to prefer the phrase 'high capital accumulation'). However, until the late 1960s its appeal was sufficiently wide for it to provide a constant unifying principle at the core of the ruling Liberal Democratic Party's economic policies.

However, by the late 1960s (for reasons which we shall explore in the next chapter) this principle was beginning to lose its cohesive force. Japan's business and political leaders were starting to recognise the necessity of discovering new directions for economic expansion and new ideologies which would endow those directions with political content and credibility. Out of the intense debate and soul-searching of this troubled period, three main policy alternatives emerged.

The first, and the policy most closely resembling the earlier strategy of high growth, suggested the revitalising of the Japanese economy by means of massive public works programmes which would rectify the gross unevenness in the geographical distribution of Japan's industrial capacity. This approach was most cogently argued by Tanaka Kakuei, whose *Plan for the Remodelling of the Japanese Archipelago*,[2] published in 1972, called in almost Biblical terms for the levelling of mountains and the raising of valleys, reshaping Japan's recalcitrant terrain to provide space for networks of highways and express rail routes, for vast industrial estates and for new cities of hundreds of thousands of inhabitants.

A second approach, favoured by those on the liberal wing of the Japanese establishment, was a shift in emphasis from economic growth to the relatively neglected area of welfare, transforming Japan into a 'welfare state' along the lines of other industrialised democracies such as the Scandinavian countries.[3] The impact of this idea on government is reflected, for example, in the fact that the Five Year Plan put forward by the Economic Planning Agency in 1973 listed as two of its principal objectives 'the creation of a rich and balanced environment' and 'a guarantee of affluent and stabilised living conditions'.[4] The third alternative was the information society concept.

Although the Japanese government has never made an explicit choice among the three models of the future, a survey of the direction of policies since that time produces a fairly clear picture of the implicit choices which have been made. The Tanaka plan has had relatively little impact on economic policies since 1972, and only certain aspects of the plan – such as the extension of the *Shinkansen* super-express railway – have reached fruition. Its ideas are now regarded as being mainly a matter of historical interest. The welfare society concept has, as we have seen, had greater effect, and reference to the objectives of improving the quality of life, raising the level of welfare provisions and increasing social investment have become regular features of most major pronouncements on economic policy.

Typically, however, the phrase 'welfare society' is hedged around with adjectives such as 'efficient' or 'vigorous', and the promise of higher social spending is accompanied by a caution that this must in no way impede the progress of industrial growth. This reflects a deep-seated fear on the part of Japan's business leaders of diverting funds from private investment and of importing the supposedly alien bacillus of idleness. The Seven Year Economic and Social Plan presented by the Economic Planning Agency in 1979 made this very clear. The creation of a welfare society is a major object of the plan, but this is to be a 'Japanese-type welfare society' in which 'the Government provides an appropriate level of public welfare, while still respecting the Japanese spirit of self help, compassion in human relations and the social framework of mutual assistance'.[5]

The commitment of the Japanese government to the information society concept, by contrast, seems to have become steadily more articulate and unfettered, and its principles have repeatedly been incorporated into industrial plans and White Papers. The 1971 interim report of the Industrial Structure Council, for example, focused attention on the need for Japan to transform its industrial structure from one based on traditional heavy industries to one based on 'knowledge intensive' industries, including high-technology manufacturing, information production and the services sector.[6] Little by little, indeed, the 'welfare society' idea itself seems to have been subsumed and incorporated into the vision of an information society; the Industrial Structure Council's 1978 report lists as its main priority 'the perfection of the people's welfare and life', but its practical proposals are not so much an increase in welfare spending as an expansion of high-technology industries and infrastructure, including service and fashion industries, nationwide information networks and research and development projects.[7]

The Nakasone administration embraced the idea of an information society with particular enthusiasm. Nakasone's policy speech at the opening session of the Japanese Diet in February 1984 defined the promotion of an information society (together with administrative and fiscal reform) as one of three major reforms designed to lay 'new foundations as we approach the 21st century'. The government, stated Nakasone, would 'seek to establish a national consensus on what we want of the information society and to respond appropriately in a broad range of fields including frontier technology research and development, expanded international cooperation, broader use of information technologies, the diverse development of the software industry, and the question of balancing the right to know and the right to privacy'.[8]

Although it has hardly succeeded in creating a 'national consensus' on the meaning and structure of the information society, the government certainly had some success in arousing popular interest in and enthusiasm for the concept. This is evident, not only from the large number of books, newspaper articles and television programmes on aspects of the information society which have appeared in Japan over the past decade, but also from the popularity of events such as the International Technology Expo held in Tsukuba in 1985, where over 20 million visitors were presented with exhibits of computer technology, robotics, advanced communications systems and biotechnology, demonstrating (in the words of the official guidebook), 'how science and technology can foster man's dreams and hopes for the future'.[9]

By the mid-1980s, then, the idea of the information society appeared to be the most credible successor to the concept of high growth as the central motif of Japan's economic and industrial policy, and the process of transforming slogan into reality had already begun.

The Machine Information Law

Let us begin by looking at policies directed at realising the information society reports' image of integrated, fully automated production systems. The clearest tangible evidence of the Japanese government's commitment to this objective is provided by the Special Machine Industry Promotion Temporary Measures Law of 1978 (mercifully abbreviated by most Japanese writers to the acronym *Kijōhō*, or Machine Information Law).

To appreciate its importance this law needs to be seen in its historical context as one of a series of measures used by the Ministry of International Trade and Industry (MITI) to select specially significant areas of industrial production for encouragement and promotion. The logic behind these measures is that certain key sectors can act as 'engines of industrial development',[10] propelling the entire economy in a desired direction.

The first two laws of the series were the 1956 Machine Industry Promotion Temporary Measures Law (abbreviated to *Kishinhō* or Machine Promotion Law) and the 1958 Electronics Industry Promotion Temporary Measures Law (*Denshinhō* or Electronics Promotion Law). These became cornerstones of Japanese industrial development policies during the 'miracle' years of the 1960s. The Machine Promotion Law not only stimulated the expansion of general machinery production, but also, by enhancing the supply and quality of locally made equipment, indirectly encouraged the growth of a host of other industries – most importantly, the motor vehicle industry.[11] The Electronics Promotion Law, meanwhile, helped to launch Japanese industry on its highly successful entry into the world market for consumer electronic goods: radios, television sets, cassette recorders and so on.[12] Both laws were designed to speed and protect the early growth of vulnerable new areas of industry, and were originally intended to last for seven years; though both were subsequently extended to enable their respective industries to weather the effects of trade liberalisation in the late 1960s.

In 1971, the second phase of the evolution of these policies was reached when the two earlier measures were replaced by a single Special Electronics and Machinery Industry Promotion Temporary Measures Law (the *Kidenhō* or Electronic Machinery Law). Underlying this law was the concept of fusing together the electronic and machinery industries to produce a new generation of complex productive equipment based on the technology of microelectronics. Under the Electronic Machinery Law, which operated from 1971 to 1978, some US$400 million in low-interest loans was provided by government institutions to encourage the development and manufacturing of products such as numerically controlled machinery and industrial robots.[13]

The Machine Information Law of 1978 takes this process one step further. Its purpose is described as being the 'integration of machinery, electronics and information' with the objective of 'meeting the increasingly diverse and sophisticated needs of our people by the enhancement of national life, the improvement of citizens' welfare, the creation of a society in which life is worth living etc.'[14] Like the three earlier laws, the Machine Information Law is couched in very wide-ranging terms, allowing MITI a relatively free hand in filling in the finer details of industrial development policies. Its implications are therefore best understood by examining the way in which its provisions have operated in practice.

Under the terms of the law, MITI, in close consultation with the representatives of the major enterprises involved, drew up 62 detailed development plans – some relating to a single industry, others covering more than one industry. These plans can be divided into two categories. The first category, which might be placed under the heading of 'progress plans', involved the research and development of new technologies and the expansion of capacity. The main areas covered by these progress plans were the production of advanced forms of microprocessors, computers and computer components, software, automated manufacturing systems, and the new materials required by the expanding high-technology industries. The second group of plans were concerned with 'rationalisation': that is, their objectives were to reduce manufacturing costs, cut the consumption of energy and raw materials, lower pollution levels and improve industrial health and safety. These 'rationalisation' plans covered a wide range of industries, from steel production to paper milling and from food processing to nuclear power generation.[15]

Firms were helped to achieve the plans' target by means of government-financed low interest loans and partial exemption from the provisions of Japan's Anti-Monopoly Law. Small firms in industries affected by the plans could obtain special credit guarantees, while firms installing computer controlled production systems were offered substantial tax concessions.[16]

The essential link between the first and second category of plans is that in most cases the rationalisation of the industries in the second category can only be carried out by use of the computers, computer software and other automated equipment whose development is to be promoted by the first category of 'progress plans'. The Machine Information Law, in other words, provides not only government support for the formation and expansion of the new industries of the information society, *but also* government assistance in *creating a market for the products of these industries*.

It is a little difficult to judge how far the recent proliferation of office and factory automation in Japan has been in direct response to government measures like the Electronic Machinery Law and the Machine Information Law. There can be no doubt, though, that the 'integration of machinery, electronics and information' is proceeding apace, and to some extent at least MITI's promotional policies must, therefore, be considered a success. Between 1978 and 1981 alone, the output of the Japanese computer industry increased 61 per cent in value terms (from just over Y910 billion to almost Y1,480 billion), while that of the information processing industry increased 75 per cent (from Y460 billion to Y806 billion).[17] A survey of corporations in the major metropolitan areas, conducted in 1983, found that 24.8 per cent were already using industrial robots and 66.5 per cent were using office computers.[18]

A small but growing number of firms in Japan's traditional heavy industries have introduced flexible manufacturing systems which allow computer-controlled factories to manufacture automatically a range of relatively complex products. One of the best-known examples is Toshiba Tungaloy's Kawasaki factory, where machine tool parts are produced by a computerised system which can operate unattended for prolonged periods of time. The introduction of this system has had dramatic effects on the cost of production: Toshiba's factory employs 16 workers, as compared with 70 in other plants with a similar output. The number of machines used in production has been reduced from 50 to 6, and their rate of utilisation increased from 20 per cent to 70 per cent.

Similar results have been reported from other machine, engine and car plants using flexible manufacturing systems.[19]

Communications and the New Media

While the Machine Information Law has helped to speed the transformation of production within individual enterprises, a series of policy measures is simultaneously laying the foundations of the communications network which will link the factories, offices and households of the information society. In common with several other advanced industrialised countries, Japan has already begun operation of teletext and videotex services. The former, which use existing TV signals to transmit a range of visual information such as news and weather updates, share price lists, travel services and so on, were initiated with the introduction of the NHK (Japanese Broadcasting Corporation) teletext system in 1983.[20] The videotex service – similar in appearance though different in operation from teletext – uses telephone lines to link television screens to database computers, providing a more flexible and interactive system through which, for example, the user may place orders, make travel reservations or play quiz games. Japan's videotex system CAPTAIN (Character and Pattern Telephone Access Information Network System) has been in experimental service since 1979 and in public operation since 1984. Like similar systems elsewhere, however, it has encountered some teething problems: lack of appropriate software meant that, at least in the experimental stages, there was relatively little use of the system by private individuals and households, and the businesses supplying information through the CAPTAIN system have, significantly, tended to shift their emphasis towards meeting commercial demand for 'producer information' rather than personal demand for 'consumer information'.[21]

Cable television (CATV) networks have expanded rapidly in Japan since the mid-1970s. By 1983 there were estimated to be around 3.3 million homes subscribing to CATV. In most cases, however, this system (which links televisions to a common antenna by coaxial cable) has merely been used to improve reception of regular TV channels in areas suffering from interference. But the launching of a series of communications satellites, commenced in

1983, will (despite initial hitches) eventually open the way to a more adventurous use of the system to provide a multiplicity of nationwide pay TV services similar to those in operation in the United States.

A number of experiments with two-way CATV systems – through which, for example, viewers can respond to questions displayed on their TV screens or can even take part in programmes using video cameras installed in their houses – have been conducted. Perhaps the best known is the Hi-Ovis project, initiated in the town of Higashi Ikoma, near Nara, in 1976. Participants in this project are offered access to services which include video request channels, a community information service and an interactive community broadcast service. The experiment, funded by MITI, is designed to provide a detailed impression of users' responses to the broadcast media. The indications so far are that participants valued the video request services and made considerable use of programmes which offered information on local events. There was, however, considerable resistance to use of the interactive facility built into the Hi-Ovis network.[22]

However, the cornerstone of new media is the 20-year project by the Nippon Telegraph and Telephone Company (NTT) for an Information Network System (INS), which welds together the diverse forms of auditory, visual and data communications into a single web of nationwide information channels. This web is made of glass: more precisely, of hair-like glass fibre-optical cables, along which large volumes of information will travel in digital form. New and more complex communications satellites will also enable the system, among other things, to convey data at very high speeds and to carry single messages in several directions at once. Commercial INS services began in April 1988: by 1995, it is anticipated that telephone, telex, data facsimile and video systems will have been integrated into this single network which, at a cost of some Y25–30 trillion (almost US$130 billion), will have wholly replaced the old copper-cable, analogue telephone system.[23] Japanese communications experts believe that Japan will probably be the first country to complete an integrated service digital network of this type.[24]

Some idea of the possibilities (and problems) which may be generated by the INS can be gleaned by considering the experimental INS model operated in the Tokyo suburbs of Musashino and Mitaka from 1984 to 1987. This system offered various combinations of services (including telephone, facsimile, videotex, telewriting, data terminals and video conferencing) to some 1,990 users. Examples of the practical uses devised for the experimental system are listed below.

1 Home shopping – with 23 department stores and supermarkets providing information on goods which may be ordered through the INS.
2 Links between company offices: one firm, for example, used the teleconferencing system to conduct meetings between staff in its Mitaka branch and the downtown company headquarters.
3 'Telecommuting' – with some enterprises providing employees with terminals enabling them to perform word-processing at home or work on documents which could be transmitted to the office by means of the facsimile system.
4 Municipal services: the Mitaka City government created a service which issued, at high speed direct to users, documents such as residence certificates and tax payment vouchers.
5 Education: a private school used the facsimile link with students' homes as a quick means of correcting arithmetic assignments.[25]

Interestingly, though, the experiment suggested that companies and public institutions were the main users of the system. Individuals and households, by contrast, were often unable to find ways in which the communications system could be made to serve their needs. As the Director of NTT's Model Service Systems Bureau observes: 'It seems that it will take quite a while before the home users fully understand how to gain the maximum benefit for I.N.S. services.'[26]

Similar experiments, combining an adapted INS service with cable television, are being set up under the 'Teletopia' scheme, sponsored by NTT and the Ministry of Posts and Telecommunications. Meanwhile, MITI, not to be outdone in the race towards the information society, is financing a rival but almost identical scheme for 'new media communities' in a number of regional cities. All of these projects are now in the early stages of operation, and will provide a fuller picture of the potential usage and social impact of the new communications media.[27]

The Development of New Technologies

At the heart of the information society concept lies the idea of perpetual innovation. In an industrial society, there is a continuous cycle of production and consumption, creation and destruction: goods must be consumed in the production of more goods, and this consumption in turn re-creates demand for the output of the recurring productive process. But information cannot be consumed; it can only constantly be amassed and expanded. New information, or to be more precise, new technological information which may be applied to the production of commodities, comes to be seen as the vital resource for economic development. The nation which is most successful in creating and applying innovative technological knowledge is therefore expected to have a powerful position in the international economic hierarchy. It is not surprising, then, that all the information society reports should have identified the promotion of scientific and technological research as an essential step toward the fulfilment of their vision of the future.

The level of Japanese investment in research and development (R&D) is not, at present, exceptionally high by international standards. In 1981, Japan's expenditure on R&D activities amounted to 2.65 per cent of total national income – slightly lower than the figure of 2.68 per cent for the USA, and substantially below West Germany's 3.04 per cent and the Soviet Union's 4.85 per cent.[28] The contribution of government to R&D expenditure is particularly low in Japan – only 22.5 per cent of research funding being provided by the government, compared to around 43 per cent in the case of West Germany and 47 per cent in the case of the United States.[29]

However, some qualifying comments need to be made about these figures. Firstly, US and Soviet research involves a far larger military component than Japanese research. Of course, much contemporary industrial technology has its origins in military research, and such expenditure therefore does not imply an unmitigated diversion of funds from non-military commercial purposes. However, it is perhaps true that a greater share of Japanese R&D has direct applicability to the civilian industrial sector.

Secondly, Japanese investment in R&D is increasing very rapidly. From 1976 to 1981 the proportion of national income directed to research rose more sharply in Japan than it did in other major industrialised countries (see Figure 3.1). Since this period was also one in which the Japanese economy was growing faster than the other economies illustrated on the graph, the increase in absolute terms was particularly great.

An important motive for this increased attention to research lies in the changed international status of Japanese industry. Until the

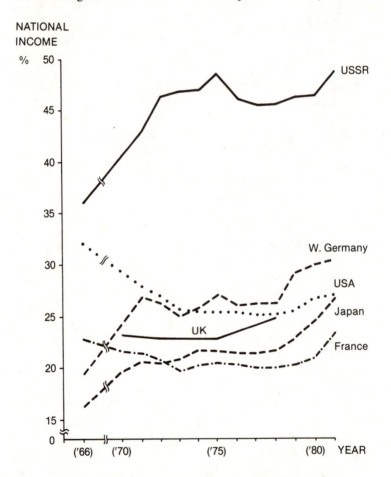

Source: Kagaku Gijutsu-chō Keikaku Kyoku, <u>Kagaku Gijutsu Yōran</u> (Indicators of Science and Technology), 1983, p.4

Figure 3.1. *Research and Development Expenditures as a Percentage of National Income*

late 1960s, the level of Japan's industrial technology remained, at least in several significant sectors, below that of its most advanced industrial competitors, and technological development could largely be achieved by importing foreign scientific knowledge. But as sector after sector of Japanese industry has caught up with or overtaken its foreign rivals in technological terms, so reliance on imported innovation has become increasingly difficult.

However, beyond this, increased R&D expenditure since the mid-1970s also reflects a very specific government policy of fostering the domestic development of the so-called 'next-generation technologies'. The thinking behind this policy, as explained by one MITI official, is as follows:

> Japan has absolutely no natural energy resources. So in order to feed our hundred million inhabitants, we have no alternative but to add value to the products which we sell. It is necessary for us to have bargaining power. For this purpose, it is essential to enhance our technology. So we must take positive steps to develop and nurture the potentially highly influential next generation of industrial technologies.[30]

Just as the Machine Information Law and its predecessors involved not simply government financial aid to industry, but also very close government–private enterprise cooperation in detailing the desirable directions of future industrial development, so the next-generation technology policies use the combined financial and intellectual resources of government and private business to shape the future evolution of technology.

The most ambitious of these policies is the 'Next-Generation Basic Industrial Technology Research and Development Project' announced by MITI in 1981. This project is aimed at filling gaps in the area where Japan's research effort is generally regarded as being at its weakest: basic industrial research. During the ten years from 1981 the government planned to allocate some Y100 billion (about US$500 million) to the development of three areas of new technology: new synthetic materials; biotechnology; and the next generation of microelectronic circuitry. Each of these fields of technology is subdivided into several more specific research projects which are being worked on simultaneously by competing private and government laboratories.[31] A large share of this research is being conducted in Japan's new 'science city' of Tsukuba, north-east of Tokyo, where MITI and numerous private companies have established research laboratories. The list of the 67 private corporations involved in the scheme – which includes names like Ajinomoto, Fujitsu, Hitachi, Kyoto Ceramics, NEC and Toshiba – reads like a Who's Who of the leading high-technology enterprises in Japan.[32] According to MITI, by the summer of 1983 the project had already yielded 488 research reports and 175 patent applications, most of them in the field of advanced integrated circuitry.[33]

The 1981–90 New Generation Technology Project is not the first of its kind in Japan. Between 1979 and 1983 MITI contributed one-third of the finance to the Y70 billion (US$117 million) Next Generation Computer Basic Technology Project, whose principal object was to promote research into high level software technology, including improved Japanese language-processing technology.[34]

However, unquestionably the most famous Japanese research initiative has been the Fifth Generation Computer Project, launched in 1982 and expected to reach completion in 1991. The object of this exercise is the development of a machine capable of inference as well as sequential logic, constructive learning as well as passive information storage, and intelligent interaction with human beings – including those human beings who are not literate in the present-day cumbersome computer languages.[35] Conflicts between MITI and the Ministry of Finance, which takes a rather disapproving view of these expensive and ambitious policies, has resulted in a shedding of some of the project's early aspirations, such as the incorporation of vision and human speech comprehension into the computer. However, during the first two years of the project alone MITI was successful in obtaining over Y3.1 billion (US$15.5 million) in government funding for the project, and the first phase was completed without major setbacks in March 1985.[36]

The 'next generation technology' projects shed the most interesting light on the processes of technological and social change. In the information society reports we saw how the image of a Utopian social order was projected as being the spontaneous outcome of inexorable and impersonal technological evolution. But as we look more closely at that evolution itself, and examine the ideas which inform research ventures such as the Fifth Generation Computer Project, it becomes evident that the technology itself is being designed to fit a preconceived model of an ideal future society.

As Motooka Tohru, chairperson of that project's preparatory committee explained:

> What MITI initially asked our committee to do was to envision the information society of the 1990s and the computer which would be needed in that society, point out anything the government should do to help develop the computer, and also propose a specific research and development setup for this purpose. . . .
>
> As for the society of the 1990s, to begin with, we envisioned an ideal society in that decade rather than merely predicting the society. Then we discussed what information systems and computers would be required to work towards realising the ideal society.[37]

Seen from this perspective, the development of science ceases to be an exogenous force shaping society, and becomes instead the means to an end – the end of engineering the ideal society. But if the outlines of the information society are not in fact determined by technology, how have they been defined? Why is it that the concept of an information society has gained such ready political acceptance, and has had such marked impact on official thinking and on practical policy-making in Japan during the past decade? It is to these questions that we must now turn.

Notes

1 For example, Marvin T. Wolf, *The Japanese Conspiracy*, Sevenoaks, New English Library, 1984.
2 Tanaka Kakuei, *Nihon Rettō Kaizōron*, Tokyo, Nippon Kōgyō Shinbunsha, 1972.
3 See H. Kitamura, *Choices for the Japanese Economy*, London, Royal Institute of International Affairs, 1976, ch. 4.
4 Ibid., p. 84.
5 'New Seven-Year Economic and Social Plan: Yen 240 Trillion for Public Works Investment', *Information Bulletin* (Ministry of Foreign Affairs, Japan), 1979, pp. 31–3.
6 Sangyō Kōzō Shingikai, *70 Nendai no Tsūshō Sangyō Seisaku*, Tokyo, 1971.
7 Sangyō Kōzō Shingikai, *Sangyō Kōzō no Chōki Bijon*, Tokyo, 1978.

8 *Japan Times*, 7 Feb. 1984.
9 Japan Association for the International Exposition, *Tsukuba Expo '85 – Official Guide Book*, Tokyo, 1985.
10 Tsūshō Sangyō Shō Kikai Jōhō Sangyō Kyoku: *Kijōhō no Kaisetsu*, Tokyo, Tsūshō Sangyō Chōsakai, 1979, p. 11.
11 Ibid., pp. 21–2; see also Rōdō Undō Kenkyū Sho (ed.), *Kompyūtā Gōrika to Rōdō Undō*, Tokyo, San Ichi Shobō, 1980, pp. 15–16.
12 *Kijōhō no Kaisetsu*, op. cit., pp. 21–2.
13 Ibid.; Kenmochi Kazumi, 'Sangyō Seisaku no Kaiten to Jōhōka no Shōgeki' in *Keizai Hyōron* (special issue), 'ME Kakumei to Rōdō Kumiai', 25 June 1983, 56–64.
14 *Kijōhō no Kaisetsu*, op. cit., p. 10.
15 Ibid., pp. 97–111.
16 Ibid., pp. 111–22.
17 Namiki Nobuyoshi (ed.), *Gijutsu Kakushin to Sangyō Shakai*, Tokyo, Nihon Keizai Shinbun Sha, 1983, p. 178.
18 Keizai Kikaku Chō Chōsa Kyoku (ed.), *Kigyō no Ishiki to Kōdō*, Tokyo, Ōkura Shō Insatsu Kyoku, 1983, pp. 61–4.
19 Nikkei Mechanical (ed.), *Robotto Kakumei*, Tokyo, Nihon Keizai Shinbun Sha, 1981, pp. 94 and 117–24; see also M. Eugene Merchant, 'Production: a Dynamic Challenge', *IEEE Spectrum*, vol. 20, no. 5, May 1983, 36–9.
20 H. Kaneko, 'New Media Business', *Oriental Economist*, March 1983, 22–6.
21 Ibid.; also K. Komahashi, 'New Media in Japan', *Oriental Economist*, July 1983, 8–12; *Far Eastern Economic Review*, 3 Dec. 1982, 79–80.
22 Kaneko, 'New Media Business'; Komahashi, 'New Media in Japan'; L. Georghiou, 'Public Acceptance of New Communications Technologies in Japan' in PREST (ed.), *Public Acceptance of the New Technologies: New Communications Technology and the Consumer*, Manchester, PREST, 1985; K. Ikeda, 'Hi-Ovis Seen by Users – Use and Valuation of Japanese Interactive CATV', *Studies of Broadcasting*, no. 21, March 1985, 95–120. Ikeda notes that although about 30% of a sample of Hi-Ovis users watched the programmes offered by the service, less than 5% made use of the interactive functions available to them. 'Even in the programme "introductory lecture on personal computer", to which the most use of the interactive facility was recorded, the rate of use was only 4.3%.' Ibid., p. 104.
23 N. W. Davis, 'NTT's Information Network System', *Oriental Economist*, June 1984, 18–21; note: all currency conversions are given at the January 1986 rate of 200 yen to the US dollar.
24 *Far Eastern Economic Review*, 3 Dec. 1982, p. 79.

25 Nishiwaki Tatsuya, 'INS Jikken kara no Repōto', paper presented
    to the NTT International Symposium, Tokyo, 20–21 May 1985;
    T. Murakami, 'Inception of INS Experience', *Japan
    Telecommunications Review*, vol. 27, no. 1, Jan. 1985, 2–16.
26 Murakami, 'Inception of INS Experience', 15.
27 PREST, *Public Acceptance of the New Technologies*, pp. 23–5.
28 Kagaku Gijutsu Chō Tōkei Kyoku, *Kagaku Gijutsu Yōran 1983*,
    p. 4; *Japan Reports*, March 1986.
29 Kagaku Gijutsu Chō Tōkei Kyoku, *Kagaku Gijutsu Yōran 1983*,
    p. 10.
30 Quoted in Mori Shigeki, 'Sentan Gijutsu Kaihatsu no Nerai' in
    Watanabe Eiki and Mori Shigeki (eds), *Sentan Sangyō Shakai no
    Yume to Genjitsu*, Tokyo, Rokufū Shuppan, 1984, p. 16.
31 Ibid., pp. 24–5; see also Ministry of Foreign Affairs, *Information
    Bulletin 1982*, pp. 56–8.
32 Mori, 'Sentan Gijutsu Kaihatsu no Nerai', p. 28.
33 Ibid., p. 25.
34 Kenmochi, 'Sangyō Seisaku no Kaiten to Jōhōka no Shōgeki', p. 61.
35 See E. A. Feigenbaum and P. McCorduck, *The Fifth Generation*,
    London, Michael Joseph, 1983; *ICOT Journal*, June 1983;
    N. W. Davis, 'Recent Fifth Generation Computer Components
    Development', *Oriental Economist*, July 1984, 6–7.
36 *Sydney Morning Herald*, 14 Aug. 1984.
37 'At the Start of the FGCS Project – Discussion', *ICOT Journal*,
    June 1983, 13–14.

4 The Information Society: Beyond Ideology

In this chapter I shall try to show that the development and application of the new information technologies was not the product of an impartial, politically blind unfolding of pure scientific progress. Instead, the direction of technological advance was mainly determined by a variety of problems which confronted corporations in industrialised economies from the second half of the 1980s onward. And the enthusiasm with which Japanese government and enterprises embraced both the new technologies and the concept of an information society becomes understandable when we examine the particular configuration of problems which assailed the Japanese economy.

The 'Economic Miracle'

Throughout the 1950s and 1960s, the Japanese economy had grown at a rate which was remarkable even by the standards of that period of resurgent capitalism. Japan's GNP growth rate in the sixties ran at an annual average of over 10 per cent, compared with 3.9 per cent for the USA, 4.7 per cent for West Germany and 2.8 per cent for the UK.[1] The central feature of this growth process was heavy industrialisation. While industrial output as a whole increased over threefold between 1960 and 1970, output of chemicals and steel increased fourfold and output of machinery more than fivefold.[2] The reasons for this phenomenon are complex, but there are a number of factors which are both significant and relevant to the theme of this book. By outlining each of the factors, it is possible to build up a picture of the structures which sustained rapid industrial growth from the mid-1950s to the early 1970s. We can then go on to observe how, one after another from the late sixties onward, these mainstays of growth weakened or collapsed. As we shall see, the concept of the information society was developed precisely in order to meet the challenges posed by the disappearance of essential economic, social and political stimuli to heavy industrial growth.

I The relationship between agriculture and industry

One particularly important factor in the 'economic miracle' was the ability of Japanese management to restrain wage rises at a time of substantial industrial expansion. In Japan, during the late 1950s and 1960s, although real wages rose *faster* than in any other major industrialised country except Italy, they rose far more *slowly* than did the productivity of the Japanese industrial workforce. This is illustrated in Table 4.1.

By contrast, in most other countries, wage and productivity rises remained more or less in step. (The main exception again is Italy, which experienced a wage explosion in the 1960s.) The low level of Japanese wage rises in relation to the nation's industrial expansion is explained partly by a variety of social factors (discussed below) and partly by the political reverses experienced by the labour movement from the late 1940s onwards. The establishment of pro-management 'second unions' in a number of enterprises and the defeat of the 1960 Mitsui Miike strike were particularly important turning points in this respect. By 1972, the average

Table 4.1. *Growth Rates of Wages and Productivity (%)*

	Annual average growth of industrial productivity 1953–72	Annual average growth of real wages in manufacturing 1953–75
Japan	8.9	5.4
USA	2.7	1.5
UK	3.0	3.4
West Germany	5.0	5.3
France	5.4	4.0
Italy	5.0	7.0

Sources: A. Boltho, *Japan: an Economic Survey*, p. 9; J. D. Hey, *Britain in Context*, p. 157

Japanese manufacturing worker was earning almost three times as much as in 1953, but producing about five times as much. The consequences of this are easily imagined: by the early 1960s, the share of profits in national income had reached a higher level in Japan than in almost any other capitalist country.[3] These profits provided an important source of capital to be invested in new equipment, so raising productivity still further.

Yet a glance at the figures in Table 4.1 also raises an immediate question. If productivity was rising so much faster than wages, who was buying the ever-growing mass of goods churned out by the factories? Why did post-war Japanese growth not rapidly peter out into over-production and stagnation? Part of the answer to this question lies in Japan's success in capturing a growing share of an expanding overseas market. Between 1960 and 1970, exports as a proportion of GNP rose from 9 per cent to 13 per cent.[4] But another, and perhaps more important, answer lies in the special structure of Japan's post-war society. During the 1950s and early sixties particularly, average family incomes in Japan rose considerably faster than average industrial wages (7.2 per cent as against 5.1 per cent a year from 1952 to 1964).[5] A major reason for this trend is that a large share of Japan's growing industrial workforce was drawn from farm families. Many of these new industrial workers, rather than uprooting their entire families from the rural environment, remained on the farm and commuted either to full-time or to seasonal (*dekasegi*) industrial work. Agriculture, meanwhile, was frequently left in the hands of other members of the family, giving rise to the often-described phenomenon of 'San-chan Nōgyō' – farming by the 'three *chans*', i.e. *Kaa-chan* (Mummy), *Baa-chan* (Grandma) and *Jii-chan* (Grandpa). This in turn was made possible by the introduction of light machinery, chemical fertilisers and pesticides, which removed some of the most back-breaking and time-consuming toil from Japanese farming. Between 1963 and 1970 alone almost five million farmers took up non-agricultural employment, but around 15 per cent of them continued to list farming as their main job.[6]

Many of those who moved from farming to industrial work were employed in the lower part of Japan's well-known 'dualistic' employment structure. That is to say, they were employed as temporary or casual workers or in small enterprises, which often acted as subcontractors to large, modern corporations. While full-time male workers in the larger firms were commonly unionised, and received higher wages and certain fringe benefits, workers in smaller firms (under 100 employees) were usually unorganised, had little or no job security and received wages which, in the early 1960s, were on average less than half of those paid to workers in the largest firms (over 1,000 employees).[7]

Japanese industry, in other words, gained enormous benefits from the rather unusual way in which it was able to take advantage of the non-capitalist farm sector. It obtained a large and flexible source of wage labour, which helped it to hold down wages and so increase profits; and, by tapping the wealth created by increases in agricultural productivity it acquired an expanding market for its products: both for capital goods such as machinery and for the consumer goods which soon transformed the interior of many Japanese farmhouses. As one cynical observer puts it: 'Under high economic growth, the introduction of machinery removed the hard labour from farming. And in order to purchase that machinery, the farmer was forced to perform hard labour in the lowest regions of industry.'[8]

II The population pyramid

From Japanese industry's point of view, therefore, there were special advantages to be derived from the fact that Japan, at the beginning of the 'miracle', was still a relatively poor and agrarian nation. One advantage was the pool of labour which existed in the agricultural sector; another was the structure of the Japanese population.

In the period immediately after Japan's defeat in the Second World War, the life expectancy of a new-born child in Japan was just 52 years, and diseases such as typhoid and tuberculosis were widespread. As in other countries with a large agrarian workforce and high death-rate, the birth-rate was also relatively high: 35 per 1,000 population in 1947.[9] But the post-war economic recovery and medical advances (particularly the introduction of streptomycin in the early 1950s) dramatically altered the health of the Japanese population. By the early 1960s, life expectancy at birth had risen to 70 years, and by 1977 it had reached 75[10] – one of the highest levels in the world. At the same time, with improved life expectancy, liberal post-war abortion laws, rising incomes and urbanisation, the birth-rate fell precipitately: to 19 per 1,000 population by 1964.[11]

All of this had very marked effects on the structure of the Japanese population. During the 1960s, the children born in the years of high fertility were coming on to the labour market, but the numbers both of very young and of very old were relatively small. This meant that (looking at the population over all) a large group of working-age people was supporting a much smaller number of dependants, and that Japanese industries could tap a particularly abundant supply of young workers. This was of vital importance to an economy where new industries were developing rapidly: young workers could be trained in the skills most needed by the expanding areas of the economy.

III Social attitudes

In recent years it has become fashionable to try to explain Japan's economic 'success' in terms of some mysterious ingredient in the country's traditional culture: most often by the notions of group-consciousness, vertical social relations or the absence of individualism. Zen and child-rearing practices, family structure and Confucian culture,[12] each in turn has been put forward as the secret of the economic miracle. The problem with these theories is not so much that they cannot be sustained, as that they are too easy to sustain. The phenomena with which they deal are so vague and all-embracing that they can be made to explain almost anything. Thus Confucianism, for example, which earlier generations of social observers readily accepted as a reason for the economic stagnation of the east, has since 1970 been unhesitatingly converted into a reason for its economic dynamism.

In general, Eric Hobsbawm's view that 'economic explanations of economic phenomena are to be preferred if they are available'[13] seems more plausible. But there is one rather more specific psychological factor which *does* seem to be important in understanding the cause of high economic growth in Japan. This was the consciousness of increasing material prosperity which was felt by a sizeable section of the population. The sense of prosperity was not entirely an illusory one. As we have seen, real wages in Japan were rising faster than in most other industrialised countries. And the social effects of this rise were almost certainly magnified by the fact that the relative affluence of the late fifties and sixties was contrasted, in people's memories, with the exceptionally bleak years of the war and American occupation. By 1965, 51 per cent of households owned refrigerators, 90 per cent owned television sets and 98 per cent owned washing machines.[14] For a population in which many people had experienced homelessness and malnutrition in the immediate post-war period, acquisition of these consumer items represented a real gain.

The sense of affluence had several important effects. Firstly, it helps to explain why the Japanese electorate returned conservative, business-oriented governments to power throughout the 1950s and 1960s, so providing the political environment for the rapid expansion of Japanese corporations. Although Japan lagged behind other industrialised countries in terms of its welfare provision, housing standards and social infrastructure (sewerage, surfaced roads, parks, playgrounds and so on), the government's almost exclusive concentration on rapid industrial growth provoked only limited criticism before 1965.

Secondly, unplanned and largely unexpected increases in material wealth seem to have been an important cause of another distinctive feature of Japanese society in the fifties and sixties: the tendency for workers to save a large share of their wages. In 1960, Japanese households on average saved 19.2 per cent of their disposable income. The figure for the United States was 4.7 per cent.[15] The economist Komiya Ryūtarō suggests that an important reason for this was simply that wages were rising so quickly that life-styles could not follow them.[16] In other words, it took time for people to become accustomed to the fact that their income had increased, and that they could now afford goods which, a few years ago, would have been beyond their reach – indeed, even beyond their imagination. In the meanwhile, a large share of their increased earnings were deposited in banks, which then recycled them into industrial investment, once again replenishing the sources of rising productivity and profits.

IV Access to ready-made technology

The effects of this investment on economic growth would not have been nearly so great if a large share of it had not been directed to the introduction of new, more productive technologies. Outsiders may, in the early stages, have mocked Japanese copying of western ideas. But access to a large number of ready-made foreign technologies meant considerable savings in time and money for corporations which wished to modernise their equipment or begin the manufacture of new goods.

The Second World War, like other wars before it, had stimulated development of a host of new technologies, many of which were of use in production as well as destruction. The application of this new knowledge to industry had led to dramatic developments in electronics, petrochemicals, transport machinery and so on in the United States and western Europe immediately after the war. By the second half of the fifties, when Japanese companies were beginning to have the capital necessary for major imports of technology, there was a large supply of tested and tried foreign know-how available for them to choose from. Between 1957 and 1969 Japan imported 6,326 individual items of technological knowledge, most of them from the United States, and 80 per cent of them related to the three key industries: machinery, metals and chemicals.[17]

V The world economic order

Japan's high growth was also deeply dependent upon the economic order which the United States successfully imposed on the capitalist world from the end of the Second World War to the final years of the Vietnam War. One aspect of this order was the exchange stability and relatively open trading system created by the Bretton Woods Agreement and the General Agreement on Tariffs and Trade (GATT). These gave Japan, during the first phase of rapid growth, access to the expanding markets of the developed world, while Japan itself was still able to use a variety of import controls to protect its 'infant industries'. From 1963 onwards, foreign pressures forced the Japanese government to liberalise restrictions on one import item after another, but by that time Japanese industries were becoming highly competitive and the economy was beginning to enjoy the benefits of an increasingly undervalued currency.

A second immensely important facet of the *pax Americana* was the growth of US (and other foreign) aid to and investment in the less developed world. Japan, as the most industrialised nation in Asia, found itself well placed to provide the manufactured goods required for foreign-financed development projects. In fact, in the early stages of Japan's post-war heavy industrialisation, Asian countries provided the major foreign market for goods such as cement and steel.[18] Multinational investments by other developed countries also opened up large new sources of low-cost raw materials which were vital to Japan's industrial growth. The real prices which Japan paid for its imports, around half of which consisted of industrial raw materials, fell sharply in the late fifties, and then remained roughly stable until the oil crisis of the seventies (see Figure 4.1).

The End of the Miracle

The five factors discussed in this chapter were not independent contributions to high growth but were intimately interconnected, working with and reinforcing one another in such a way that, if

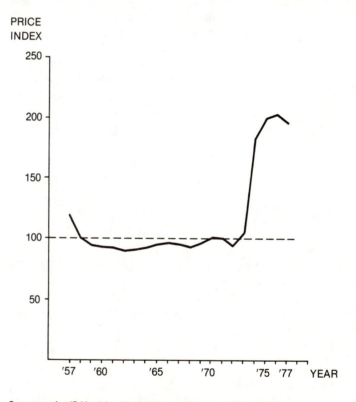

Source: Andō Yoshio, <u>Kindai Nihon Keizaishi Yōran</u>, Tokyo, Tokyo Daigaku Shuppan-kai, (2nd edn.), 1979, p.169

Figure 4.1 *Index of Prices of Japanese Imports* (1970 = 100)

any one factor had been absent, none of the others would have operated as powerfully as it did. But when the end of high growth came, it arrived not because of the disappearance of a single one of these factors, but because, within the short span from 1965 to 1975, they *all* began to crumble.

The crisis which confronted the Japanese economy (and other capitalist economies) at this time is often identified, rather simplistically, with the first 'oil shock' of 1973. More careful analysts of the Japanese crisis sometimes trace it back to the 'Nixon shock' of 1971, when the US, attempting to solve its massive balance-of-payments deficit, imposed import restrictions on certain Japanese goods and floated the dollar. But most commentators appear to have little hesitation in accepting Nakamura Takefusa's view that '[i]t was not forces from within the country that brought on the collapse of rapid growth, but forces from abroad'.[19]

I would argue, on the contrary, that high growth was already doomed as early as 1968 or 1969, and that the first signs of its demise appeared *within* Japan. What is more, many Japanese business people and economists recognised these signs.[20] The concept of an information society, which began to be popularised at precisely this time, was in fact a tentative proposal for a solution to the crisis which Japanese industry faced from the late 1960s onward.

I Agriculture and labour shortage

As a symbolic starting point to the crisis, we might choose the year 1965: the year in which the incomes of farm households overtook those of non-farm households. The flow of labour from agriculture to industry was not, of course, an inexhaustible one. As rural living standards rose and the number of impoverished and under-employed farmers declined, there was less and less incentive for people to move from agricultural to industrial employment. In 1963, the net outflow of labour had amounted to 700,000 people. By 1968 it was down to 575,000.[21]

II Population and labour shortage

The situation was made more serious (from the employers' point of view) by other consequences of increased material wealth. As the effects of falling birth-rate and rising life expectancy worked their way through the population, the percentage of people in the working age-groups began to decline relative to the percentage of elderly people. Japan's dependency index (that is, the share of children and retired people in the population) reached its lowest point in 1970, and then began to rise gradually.[22]

At the same time, there was a sharp rise in the number of young people entering senior high school and college. In Japan's 'academic record society' (*gakureki shakai*) it was after all natural that many people should wish to invest their increased incomes in obtaining for their children that (supposed) passport to upward mobility, the university degree. Consequently, between 1965 and 1975, the number of school and college graduates entering the workforce each year fell by 430,000.[23]

One further point needs to be made about these trends: it is important to remember that Japanese companies at this time (particularly large Japanese corporations) were not unsophisticated entities like the enterprises of the early Industrial Revolution, which waited on the fluctuation of market prices for information about the shortage or excess of labour and raw materials. On the contrary, they had large planning departments and a wide range of tools for forecasting the future. And the picture which their forecasts of the 1970s and 1980s painted for them was not an encouraging one. The falling Japanese birth-rate was certain to reduce the proportion of people in the working age-groups. The decline in the outflow of labour from agriculture was irreversible, and the tendency for more and more young people to remain in the education system seemed likely to continue.

It was the small firms in the bottom half of the dualistic wage structure which experienced the pressures of labour shortage most acutely. The effects of this can clearly be seen in Figure 4.2. But the narrowing wage gap between large and small firms had consequences which were felt right through the Japanese economy. Many large firms depended upon smaller ones for supplies of parts and components, and had therefore indirectly benefited from the low costs of production in their subcontractors. When wages in the subcontracting firms rose, so did the prices of the goods which they supplied to the larger parent firm. Besides, the impact of rising wages soon began to be felt by the large firms themselves. As the comfortable gap between productivity and wage rises abruptly narrowed, labour shortage was translated into increased costs and falling profits (see Table 4.2).

Not all industries were equally affected by these problems, of

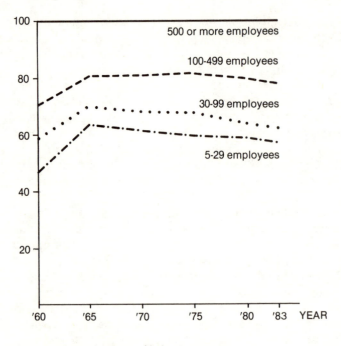

500 or more employees

100-499 employees

30-99 employees

5-29 employees

Source: Japan Institute of Labour,
Japanese Working Life Profile 1985, p.29

Figure 4.2 *Wage Differentials by Size of Establishment – Manufacturing* (Wages in Establishments with 500+ Employees = 100)

course. It was in the expanding 'engine' industries that labour shortage hit hardest. The highest wage rises occurred in the general machinery sector (which included Japan's booming car industry), closely followed by the electrical machinery sector.[24] Now, both these are assembly-line industries which employ a particularly large number of skilled and semi-skilled manual workers. Like all industries involving sophisticated technology, complex processes and a fine division of labour, they have also tended to develop large managerial hierarchies which require substantial clerical support. So it is not surprising to discover that unusually sharp wage rises occurred in occupations such as welding, automobile and electrical equipment assembly and certain types of office work (see Figure 4.3). This fact, as we shall see, formed an important

Table 4.2. *Labour Costs and Profits of Major Manufacturing Corporations, 1967–72*

	Ratio of labour costs to net sales	*Ratio of profits to net sales*
1967	11.0	6.1
1968	11.1	5.8
1969	11.2	6.1
1970	11.3	6.0
1971	12.0	3.8
1972	12.6	4.0
1973	—	—
1974	12.1	3.3
1975	12.3	1.1

Source: Nihon Ginkō, *Keizai Tokei Nenpō*, Tokyo, Nihon Ginkō Chōsa Tōkei – Kyoku (various years)

part of the background to the emergence of the information society concept.

II The rejection of economism

These internal economic contradictions were accompanied by a change in public attitudes to the philosophy of growth. As memories of extreme poverty faded, and as the distortions produced by the government's income-doubling policy grew more evident, people in Japan became less tolerant of poor working conditions, low levels of welfare spending and worsening pollution.

One symptom of disillusionment was the wave of student demonstrations which swept Japan during the late sixties. Beginning from a variety of relatively insignificant discontents (fee rises, financial maladministration and so on), these protests rapidly converged to become a wholesale rejection of the values of capitalism, a declaration (as one student put it), 'of uncompromising struggle against a violent state structure which is remote from and indifferent to the people'.[25] In 1967–68 alone, 167 Japanese colleges were occupied, and the authorities were even forced to postpone entrance exams to that pillar of the establishment, Tokyo University.

However, although the actions of student groups were the most spectacular sign of social unrest, it was probably a quieter, more

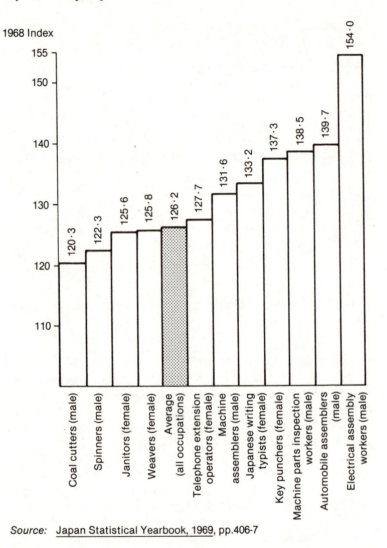

1968 Index

Bars (left to right):
- Coal cutters (male): 120·3
- Spinners (male): 122·3
- Janitors (female): 125·6
- Weavers (female): 125·8
- Average (all occupations): 126·2
- Telephone extension operators (female): 127·7
- Machine assemblers (male): 131·6
- Japanese writing typists (female): 133·2
- Key punchers (female): 137·3
- Machine parts inspection workers (male): 138·5
- Automobile assemblers (male): 139·7
- Electrical assembly workers (male): 154·0

Source: Japan Statistical Yearbook, 1969, pp.406-7

Figure 4.3 *Wage Rises in Selected Occupations, 1966–68*
(1966 = 100)

amorphous but more widespread form of protest which caused the
greatest concern to the Japanese government. Since the fifties, a
group of citizens from the fishing town of Minamata in Kyūshū had
been attempting to gain compensation for crippling neurological
disorders which they claimed were the results of pollution from a

local factory. In 1968, the government officially admitted that 'Minamata disease' was caused by mercury discharged from the factory into sea water and ingested by people who ate locally caught fish. By this time, a second outbreak of the disease had already appeared in north-eastern Japan. There were also reports of smog-induced asthma in expanding cities and of poisoning by other industrial effluents including cadmium and PCBs (polychlorinated biphenyls).[26] These widely publicised cases caused both shock and alarm, as people became aware (often for the first time) that they too were vulnerable to the destructive effects of uncontrolled heavy industrial growth. Environmental damage combined with rising inflation (running at over 9 per cent a year by 1970) to undermine public support for existing economic policies.

This changing political mood had consequences which the government could not ignore. From its formation in 1955 until the general election of 1963, the Liberal Democratic Party had consistently gained over 50 per cent of the vote for the House of Representatives, but from the mid 1960s that share fell steadily to 48.8 per cent in 1967, 47.6 per cent in 1969 and 46.8 per cent in 1972.[27] At local government level there was an even sharper swing away from the ruling party. In 1967 a left-wing academic, supported by the Socialist and Communist parties, won the Tokyo gubernatorial election, and by the early seventies most of the major city governments were in the hands of the opposition parties.[28] It was no coincidence that, from 1967 onward, Economic White Papers began to stress not only the objective of industrial growth but also the objectives of welfare improvement and environmental protection, or that the Japanese government's first significant anti-pollution law dates from the same year.

IV Trade in technology

It seems clear that the internal economic and political pressures which had appeared by 1969 would in any event have made it impossible for the Japanese government to continue unchecked on the path of high growth based on heavy industry. But external events certainly hastened the end of the 'miracle'.

The problems of external economic relations which Japan faced from the late 1960s were in part the inevitable consequences of Japan's new status as a major industrial power. As the technological gap between Japan and other advanced countries narrowed, the range of technologies available for import from abroad shrank. Besides, American and European companies were now more cautious about selling or leasing their know-how to their increasingly successful Japanese competitors. Although Japan's imports of technology continued to rise quite sharply in value terms, the country's changing situation in the world's technological hierarchy was symbolised by the still sharper rises in technology *exports* (see Table 4.3).

V A changing world order

At the same time, Japan's success in capturing world markets for its industrial goods aroused protectionist sentiments abroad. The 'Nixon shock' of 1971 represented the beginning of a new phase in which Japanese firms would face a growing range of formal and informal trade barriers. And their competitive position was made

Table 4.3. *Japan's Technological Balance of Payments, 1965–82 (US$ million)*

Year	Receipts (A)	Payments (B)	Ratio (A)/(B)
1965	17	166	0.102
1966	19	192	0.099
1967	27	239	0.113
1968	34	314	0.108
1969	46	368	0.125
1970	59	433	0.136
1971	60	488	0.123
1972	74	572	0.129
1973	88	715	0.123
1974	133	718	0.157
1975	161	712	0.226
1976	173	846	0.204
1977	233	1,027	0.227
1978	274	1,241	0.221
1979	342	1,260	0.271
1980	378	1,439	0.263
1981	537	1,711	0.314
1982	527	1,796	0.293

Source: Kagaku Gijutsu-Chō Tōkei Kyoku, Kagaku Gijutsu Yōran (Indicators of Science and Technology), 1983, p. 114

still more insecure by the readjustments in exchange rates which followed Nixon's announcement of his New Economic Program. The international value of the yen rose rapidly, from Y360 to the dollar at the beginning of 1971 to Y308 in 1972 and to Y240 by 1977, raising the price of Japanese goods on world markets.[29]

The breakdown of the Bretton Woods system and the rising tides of protectionism can be interpreted as symptoms of the end of a quarter-century of almost unchallenged US dominance of the capitalist world system. But there was another aspect of this restructuring of the world order which also threatened the equilibrium of Japan's trade. As the industrialisation policies of certain Third World countries (particularly in Asia) began to produce results, Japanese firms found themselves facing new competition in their export markets for basic industrial goods such as textiles, steel and ships. Wage rates for skilled workers in Japan were now anywhere from 4 to 14 times the level of wages in Japan's Asian neighbours, and this obviously made it difficult for Japanese firms to compete with these countries exports of basic, labour-intensive goods.

The 1973 oil crisis, therefore, was not the beginning of the end of high growth, but rather the final blow which toppled the already tottering edifice of the 'economic miracle'. With the outbreak of the fourth Middle East War in 1973, the Arab oil-producing nations suspended shipments to nations regarded as supporting Israel, and increased the price of oil fivefold. Japanese companies now began to count the cost of a policy, introduced in the late 1950s, of encouraging the use of imported oil rather than domestically produced coal as a source of energy. By 1973, 77 per cent of Japan's energy was derived from imported oil, and the crisis added some US$14 billion to Japan's import bill, aggravating inflation and triggering the most severe economic recession since the Second World War.[30]

Yet, paradoxically, the oil crisis can be said to have had at least one positive effect on the Japanese economy: it created a mood of crisis (in fact, almost of panic) in which government and enterprises were able to speed the introduction of the radical changes necessary to deal with the crisis of collapsing growth – among them, policies for promoting the creation of the 'information society'.

The Convergent Solution

Against this historical background, the information society concept no longer appears as a recognition of inevitable technological progress. Instead, it becomes clear that it was an idea, devised by bureaucrats, academics, businessmen and politicians, as a solution to a specific crisis of capitalism. JACUDI's *Plan for an Information Society*, written just after the 'Nixon shock', at a time when Tanaka's construction-based recovery policies were at the height of their influence, makes this point quite explicit:

> Japan's economy is gasping under structural depression, and in order to solve this problem it has been stressed that investments should be led by the government rather than the private sector. The treasury has three alternatives.
> (a) Construction investments centering on dwellings and roads.
> (b) Recreation investment directed to leisure.
> (c) Computerisation to increase information and knowledge.[31]

The report then goes on to make a forceful plea for a redirection of funds from the first two objectives to the third. Only in this way, it suggests, can various potential 'disasters' including 'shortage of intellectual personnel, widening information gaps, pollution and traffic problems, and excessive urban population' be solved.

JACUDI and other bodies were, I think, successful in popularising the information society idea, not so much because it offered a clearly superior solution to any one of these impending disasters, but because it could plausibly be presented as the *convergent* solution – that is, as the single plan whose implementation would ameliorate all (and aggravate none) of the major problems threatening the Japanese economy in the 1970s.

I Computerisation and labour shortage

In response to dwindling supplies of young, docile and trainable labour, the information society plans offered the solution of computer-based automation. The development and application of modern computer technology, which had originated in the 1930s and 1940s, entered a new and accelerated stage in the 1960s.

The introduction of integrated circuits from 1965 onwards made possible great advances in speed and capacity and equally rapid reductions in cost. By the time the first information society reports appeared, in 1969, there were already 6,700 computers in use in Japan and some 87,000 in the United States.[32]

The enthusiasm with which corporations adopted computer technology, and the large sums which they invested in the search for new and more powerful forms of that technology, were closely related to the rising cost of labour (a problem which, although particularly acute in Japan, was by no means limited to that country). Unlike earlier types of mechanisation, which involved the application of non-human energy to physical tasks, computerisation implies the application of non-human energy to certain types of mental labour: specifically, memory and logical reasoning.

By combining these two capacities, the computer made possible the automation of a whole range of relatively skilled work. On the one hand, office computers removed much of the human labour from areas such as calculation of payrolls, the filing of documents and even from complex tasks of planning and design. (The combination of computing and typewriting in the word-processor was a development of special significance for Japan, since it enormously simplified the handling of the thousands of characters needed to write the cumbersome Sino-Japanese script). On the other hand, when the computer was applied to manufacturing, it opened up the way towards an entirely new stage in the advance of automation. By the late 1960s it had already revolutionised production in many industries (such as oil refining) which depended upon continuous flow processes. But, as miniaturisation progressed and capacity expanded, computer technology began to be grafted on to manipulative machinery to produce the robot: a machine which could perform a complicated series of movements in response to a variable program of commands. Rapid advances in robotics from 1965 onward led to the automation of many skilled assembly-line jobs such as cutting, welding and spray-painting.

The importance of computerisation, in other words, was that it took effect precisely in those areas of work where the pressures of labour shortage and rising wages were most acutely felt: office work and skilled assembly-line labour. This helps to explain the eagerness with which the Economic Advisory Council urged the wider introduction of computers in Japanese industry.

Considering advances in manufacturing technology from the viewpoint of improved productivity, the computer clearly has a great role to play. It does not simply increase productivity by raising the level of process technology and control procedures. Rather, it goes beyond the traditional framework of 'using brain power to increase output' and makes possible a 'quantum leap in quality levels'.[33]

Within five years of the publication of this report, the number of computers in use in Japan had increased almost fivefold, to 30,100, while the number of robots produced annually by Japanese industry had risen from 600 to 2,500.[34]

II Demand in an age of finite resources

On the one hand, the idea of an information society infers the application of information technology to production; on the other, it means the growing importance of information both as a consumer and as a producer good. Whereas the first aspect offered a solution to the problem of labour shortage, the second could be presented as a suitable response to the changing social environment of Japan.

The production of information does not deplete natural resources or create waste to damage the environment. So the proponents of the information society were able to depict a future in which continued growth and technological advance would be compatible with a more harmonious balance between human beings and nature. JACUDI, in particular, emphasised this point, making it the first and most forceful of their arguments for the information society:

The Computerisation Committee stands on an historical viewpoint that it is necessary to promote the change from industrialisation, which is the extension of old concepts, to new informisation by the plan for an information society, *because world resources are limited*. . . . [T]he Club of Rome warned that we will . . . [face] ruin in the next one hundred years because of scarcity of food, drain of resources, pollution of the environment, congestion in the urban areas; all of which will be accelerated by the increase of population and economic growth. . . . It is our urgent need to change from industrialisation to informationalisation, regardless of the level of industrialisation, or the wealth of accumulated resources.[35]

These words were not just rhetoric. From the point of view of business, the environmental crisis and the growing public rejection of consumerism contained real economic, as well as political, dangers. High growth had been sustained by the ability of firms to find customers for a seemingly never-ending stream of consumer durables – first radios and bicycles; then television sets, washing machines and refrigerators, later colour TVs, stereos and cars: the greatest number of goods for the greatest number of people. But the changing political mood of the late 1960s suggested that, in a nation of crowded cities and limited housing space, demand for these material symbols of prosperity might not be inexhaustible.

There was another difficulty. Computer-based automation was intended as an antidote to the upward spiral of wages. But it was precisely these wage rises which gave workers the wealth necessary to buy more manufactured products. If wage pressure was eased, what would happen to the demand for consumer goods?

There are in essence two ways in which corporations can go about persuading people to buy more goods. One way is to try to stimulate demand for new, more expensive variants of certain existing types of goods. Planned obsolescence in automobile production and the replacement of black-and-white by colour TVs are examples of this approach, which we might term 'intensive demand creation'. The alternative approach (let us call it 'extensive demand creation') involves opening up new areas of consumer demand by persuading people to buy from private corporations things which they previously obtained in quite different ways: for example, from the state, from the local community or from within the household.

What is new about the information society is not so much that information becomes an increasingly important element in economic life; it has been doing so for centuries, probably throughout human history. The new element is the speed with which information is becoming a commodity, produced by firms and sold in the market-place. This reflects a movement by corporations, in the face of the threat of decelerating demand for consumer durables, to extend their area of activity into the relatively unexplored regions of the commercial production of knowledge.

Here are a few examples of the ways in which the corporate production of knowledge creates new demand. The use of computers in schools opens up a market for educational software. This means that knowledge which was once provided by teachers (who were usually employed directly by the state) is now increasingly purchased from private companies. With the growing use of home computers, a similar transformation will take place. Adults, for example, who wish to further their education, and who in the past would have taken courses funded by the state or provided on a 'craft' basis by private tutors, will now buy knowledge in the form of programs produced and sold by software houses.

The teletext and videotext services which are central to the next stage of 'informisation' will take this process one step further. Consider, for example, home banking and home shopping – that is, the use of home computer terminals to buy goods and handle one's bank account. Just as, in the earlier stages of industrialisation, home-made soap (for example) came to be replaced by manufactured soap bought from a shop, so these new services will replace home-made information with commercially produced information. Instead of using his or her own time and energy to go to the shops and check the products and prices on the shelves, the consumer will now buy this information from a corporation. The savings in time which this involves (one might almost call it 'buying time' rather than 'buying information') means that the consumer has more time for money-earning activities. For example, home shopping will make it easier for women who were full-time housewives to go out to work. So workers can earn the money to buy the new products, and the capitalist system can expand its influence into new areas of human life.

This type of thinking underlies the recurring emphasis of the information society reports on the 'diversification of consumers' demands' and the 'increasing importance of "information values" as against the previously dominant material values'. This emphasis, in fact, seems a curious one in the light of our growing historical knowledge of the large share of time which even the earliest societies devoted to the satisfaction of non-material (religious, cultural or other) needs.[36] Although the reports pay frequent lip-service to the notion of consumer sovereignty, it has gradually become clear that these new, diverse demands and information values will not necessarily occur spontaneously, but will need to be nurtured by the state and by corporations, who require them for their own survival. In the words of the Information Society Plan:

> At the time of the realisation of industrialised society through the industrial revolution, creation of demand for industrial goods depended only on purchasability. There was no problem on the human side. So long as the goods produced were needed, they satisfied the human desire to possess them.
>
> However, use of information will find its value only along with the improvement of human intellectual creativity. In this field, theoretical thinking, self-control, and development of new ability are required.
>
> Thus, 'the development [of a] computer mind in the people's mind' has been established as an immediate target of this plan.[37]

Indeed, as the novelist Shirley Hazzard has put it, 'invention is the mother of necessity'.[38]

III Towards technological independence

Lastly, the proponents of the information society could argue that the fulfilment of their plans represented a necessary adjustment to Japan's new position in the world economy. As the possibilities of importing technology from overseas diminished, the call of the information society reports for a whole-hearted national commitment to research and development – for 'technological nation-building' (*Gijutsu Rikkoku*) – received a sympathetic response.

Already in 1969 both the Economic Council and the Industrial Structure Council had proposed, as a central plank of their information society plans, promotion by the government of research and development in the computer hardware and software industries.[39] But, as the idea of an information society matured, the role of technological research came to be seen in much wider terms. The Industrial Structure Council's outline of industrial policies for the 1970s, for example, while calling for the promotion of 'knowledge-intensive industries', observed that one of the most important ways of achieving this objective would be the promotion of research by means of grants, tax concessions and the establishment of cooperative projects linking governmental and privately funded research:

> We think that, as the technological gap, [between Japan and western industrialised countries] disappears, it will become increasingly difficult to rely upon foreign countries for innovative technology. It must be stated that this problem will present a great challenge to our nation. Furthermore, since new technological advances are the essential element in opening the way to the rapidly changing economy and society of the next generation, our country must take up the challenge of leading the world into uncharted fields of research.[40]

IV The information society and the international economy

The same report also represents the knowledge-intensive industrial structure as a solution to worsening difficulties of Japan's international economic relations. As Japanese industry raised its technological level, it was argued, exports would become diverse. Textiles and electrical appliances (which had been such troublesome causes of trade friction with the west) would cease to play a dominant part in Japan's export structure. At the same time, with domestic industries becoming more competitive and more technologically independent, it would be easier for Japan to liberalise restrictions on imports of goods and capital.[41]

In retrospect, this view of 'informisation' as a means to harmonious relations among developed countries may seem an optimistic one, but this fact has not prevented it from being repeated in subsequent publications. The Industrial Structure Council's 1981 *Signposts to a Prosperous Information Society* states: 'Our country can help contribute to the world by providing a reliable supply of high-quality information, machinery and systems. Furthermore, our country is coming to be regarded as a valuable partner who possesses considerable bargaining power.'[42]

More importantly, it was believed that Japan, by becoming an information society, could resolve the growing dilemmas of relations with the Third World. Rather than protecting its basic industries from the growing competition of Third World exports, Japan would move forward towards new fields of activity into which the newly industrialised countries – with their paucity of independent research and technology – could not hope to follow. In this way, Japanese industry would remain constantly 'one step ahead'. This view was particularly cogently argued by the Industrial Structure Council, who couched their views in the characteristic Ricardian terminology of liberal development economics: 'The basic need is for every country to raise its industrial structure in line with its level of economic development and, by the promotion of industries in accordance with its own comparative advantage, to create a rational division of labour with countries at differing levels of development.'[43]

The fact that Japan's own earlier economic development had clearly run counter to its (conventionally defined) 'comparative advantage' was conveniently forgotten. In the information society, this argument ran, the nation's economy would be based upon its most abundant resource: knowledge. In this way international as well as national prosperity would be enhanced.

When the oil crisis came, it greatly strengthened the appeal of the information society concept. Soaring oil prices led the government to embark upon a programme of both short- and long-term energy-saving measures, and these, almost inevitably, coincided with many of the measures advocated by the prophets of the information society. On the one hand, information and knowledge-intensive industries were inherently less energy-consuming than traditional heavy industries. On the other, increased application of the new information technologies offered a promising avenue to the goal – repeatedly stressed by government and industry in the 1970s – of '*sho-enerugi-ka, sho-ryoku-ka*' (energy saving and labour saving). To give just one example, with the rapid computerisation of the Japanese iron and steel industry in the 1970s, pig-iron production *increased* by 2.2 per cent a year from 1977 to 1979, whereas the amount of fuel used in pig-iron production *fell* by 1.9 per cent a year.[44]

The political persuasiveness of the information society concept can best be understood by comparison with other policy proposals, such as the Tanaka Plan or the demands for a welfare state. Both of these alternative proposals attracted fierce criticism from sections of the establishment. The first was opposed because it threatened to aggravate inflation and spread, rather than control, environmental problems; the second, because it seemed likely to increase the budget deficit and divert capital from private industry. By contrast, the information society proposals were whole-heartedly condemned only by a radical fringe. For many people, particularly within business and the Liberal Democratic Party, they provided the prospect of a solution to all the country's most pressing economic problems.

Not only the concept of 'informisation' as a whole, but even quite specific aspects of 'informisation', could be endowed with almost magical problem-solving potential. As we have already seen, the research team engaged in work on the fifth-generation computer began their studies with an attempt to define the major problems which would face Japanese society in the 1990s, and to design a machine which would solve these problems as effectively as possible. The five major 'social bottlenecks' which they identified were:

1 the need for improvement in low-productivity areas (includ-ing office work, engineering design and education);
2 the internationalisation of the economy and the consequent need to maintain competitiveness and overcome resource shortages;
3 the need to adapt to structural changes in society, including the growing proportion of elderly people in the population and changes in the national work ethic;
4 the need to promote social efficiency and reduce communi-cation gaps; and
5 the provision of effective communications systems for individuals.[45]

These five fundamental bottlenecks were then subdivided into 30 more detailed problems, and a rather complex system was devised, through which it was demonstrated that a particular combination of information technologies could solve most of these problems at one fell swoop.

The interesting point about all this is that the research team never specifically considers the question, Problems (or bottlenecks) for whom? And yet the answer to this question is implicit in the very problems which they have selected for consideration. These are all, quite clearly, problems concerned with the maintenance of corporate profitability and growth, and not (for example) with issues of economic or social equity, at home or abroad.

Like the fifth-generation computer, the entire concept of an information society is at first sight a convergent solution to a knot of complex economic and social problems. On further examination, though, these problems can be reduced to a single issue: how to maintain the profitability of private enterprise in the circumstances of the late twentieth century. It is this problem, rather than some impersonal force of technological evolution, which has given rise to the image of an information society, and to business strategies and government policies designed to convert aspects of that image into reality.

Notes

1 Y. Kosai and Y. Ogino, *The Contemporary Japanese Economy*, London, Macmillan, 1984, pp. 2–3.

2 Andō Yoshio, *Kindai Nihon Keizaishi Yōran*, Tokyo, Tokyo Daigaku Shuppankai, 2nd edn, 1979, p. 10.

3 A. Glynn and R. Sutcliffe, *British Capitalism, Workers and the Profits Squeeze*, Harmondsworth, Penguin Books, 1972, p. 80.

4 L. B. Krause and S. Sekiguchi, 'Japan and the World Economy' in H. Patrick and H. Rosovsky (eds), *Asia's New Giant*, Washington, D.C., Brookings Institution, 1976, p. 399.

5 Kokumin Seikatsu Kenkyūjo, *Kokumin Seikatsu Tōkei Nempyō*, 1969, Tokyo, Shiseidō, 1969, p. 70.

6 Andō, *Kindai Nihon Keizaishi Yōran*, p. 188.

7 Ibid., p. 182.

8 Fujiwara Akira (ed.), *Minshū no Jidai e* (vol. 11 of *Nihon Minshū no Rekishi*), Tokyo, Sanshodō, 1976, p. 121.

9 Statistics Department, Bank of Japan, *Hundred-Year Statistics of the Japanese Economy*, Tokyo, Bank of Japan, 1966, pp. 13, 17.

10 Sōrifu Tōkei Kyoku, *Nihon no Tōkei – Shōwa 55-Nen*, Tokyo, Ōkuro-Shō Insatsu Kyoku, 1980, p. 19.

11 Statistics Department, Bank of Japan, *Hundred-Year Statistics*, p. 13.

12 See, for example M. Morishima, *Why Has Japan 'Succeeded'?*, Cambridge, Cambridge University Press, 1982; Lim Chong-Yat (ed.), *Learning from the Japanese Experience*, Singapore, Maruzen Asia, 1982.

13 E. Hobsbawm, *Industry and Empire*, Harmondsworth, Penguin, 1969, p. 187.

14 Kokumin Seikatsu Kenkyūjo, *Kokumin Seikatsu Tōkei Nempyō*, pp. 120–1.

15 H. C. Wallich and M. I. Wallich, 'Banking and Finance' in H. Patrick and H. Rosovsky, *Asia's New Giant*, p. 257.

16 R. Komiya, 'The Supply of Personal Savings' in R. Komiya (ed.),

Postwar Economic Growth in Japan, Berkeley and Los Angeles, University of California Press, 1966, pp. 157–81.

17 Andō, *Kindai Nihon Keizaishi Yōran*, p. 166.

18 S. Fujiwara, 'Foreign Trade, Investment and Industrial Investment in Postwar Japan' in T. Morris-Suzuki and T. Seiyama (eds), *Japanese Capitalism Since 1945: Critical Essays* (forthcoming).

19 T. Nakamura, *The Postwar Japanese Economy*, Tokyo, University of Tokyo Press, 1981, p. 212.

20 See, for example, *Rōdō Hakusho*, 1968, and *Keizai Hakusho*, 1968, both of which emphasise the need for a fundamental restructuring of Japanese industry.

21 Andō, *Kindai Nihon Keizaishi Yōran*, p. 188.

22 Robert E. Cole, 'Changing Labor Force Characteristics and their Impact on Japanese Industrial Relations' in L. Austin (ed.), *Japan: the Paradox of Progress*, New Haven and London, Yale University Press, 1967, p. 167.

23 Japan Institute of Labour, *Japanese Working Life Profile 1985*, Tokyo, Japan Institute of Labour, 1985, p. 17.

24 Kokumin Seikatsu Kenkyūjo, *Kokumin Seikatsu Tōkei Nempyō*, pp. 44–5.

25 Mutō Ichiyō (ed.), *Gakusei Undō*, Tokyo, Chikuma Shobō, 1969, p. 280.

26 N. Huddle and M. Reich, *Island of Dreams: Environmental Crisis in Japan*, New York and Tokyo, Autumn Press, 1975.

27 J. A. A. Stockwin, Japan: *Divided Politics in a Growth Economy*, London, Weidenfeld and Nicolson, 2nd edn, 1982, p. 112.

28 Ibid., p. 234.

29 Nakamura, *The Postwar Japanese Economy*, pp. 218–20, 238.

30 H. Kitamura, *Choices for the Japanese Economy*, London, Royal Institute of International Affairs, 1976, p. 180.

31 Computerisation Committee, Japan Computer Usage Development Institute, *The Plan for an Information Society: a National Goal Toward Year 2000*, Tokyo, Japan Computer Usage Development Institute, 1972, p. 15.

32 Sangyō Kōzō Shingikai Jōhō Sangyō Bukai, *Yutaka Naru Jōhōka Shakai e no Dōhyō*, Tokyo, Computer Age, 1982, p. 158; D. L. Slotnick and J. K. Slotnick, *Computers: Their Structure, Use and Influence*, Englewood Cliffs, N.J., Prentice-Hall, 1979, p. 2.

33 Keizai Shingikai Jōhō Kenkyū Inkai, *Nihon no Jōhōka Shakai – Sono Kadai to Bijon*, summarised in *Zaikei Shōhō*, No. 822, 3 Nov. 1969, 23. It should be noted that the Japanese definition of 'robot' includes non-programmable manual manipulators and fixed sequence robots, commonly excluded from US and other statistics.

34 *Yutaka Naru Jōhōka Shakai*, p. 158; Tsūsan Kikaku Chōsakai, *Nihon*

no Robotto, Tokyo, Tsūsan Kikaku Chōsakai, 1983, p. 210.
35 *Plan for an Information Society*, p. 10.
36 This point is convincingly argued in Jean-Pierre Dupuy, 'Myths of the Informational Society' in Kathleen Woodward (ed.), *The Myths of Information: Technology and Postindustrial Culture*, London, Routledge & Kegan Paul, 1980, p. 5.
37 *Plan for an Information Society*, pp. 15–16.
38 Shirley Hazzard, *The Transit of Venus*, London, Macmillan, 1980.
39 See *Nihon no Jōhōka Shakai*; Hiramatsu Morihiko, 'Sutāto Shita Jōhōka Seisaku', *Ekonomisuto*, 24 June 1969.
40 Sangyō Kōzō Shingikai (ed.), *70-Nendai no Tsūshō Sangyō Seisaku*, Tokyo, Sangyo Kozo Shingikai, 1971, p. 12.
41 Ibid., pp. 42–4.
42 *Yutaka Naru Jōhōka Shakai*, p. 141.
43 *70-Nendai no Tsūshō Sangyō Seisaku*, p. 43.
44 Tokita Yoshihisa, *Nihon Shihonshugi to Rōdōsha Kaikyū* (vol. 7 of *Konnichi no Nihon Shihonshugi*), Tokyo, Ōtsuki Shoten, 1982, pp. 42–3.
45 M. Toda and K. Sugiyama, 'Needs-oriented Structural Analysis for Fifth Generation Computer Systems' in H. Eto and K. Matsui (eds), *R & D Management Systems in Japanese Industry*, Amsterdam, New York and London, North Holland, 1984, p. 6.

5 Information Capitalism: an Alternative Analysis of the Information Society

History is full of instances where classes or interest groups, attempting merely to defend their positions in a changing economic environment, have become the catalysts of social transformation. So corporations in Japan and other advanced industrialised countries, by reacting to the economic challenges of the late 1960s and early 1970s, have brought about a technological transformation which has had profound implications for the social system. The outcome of this transformation is the structure which Masuda, Hayashi and others call 'information society', but which I should like here to analyse, in a slightly different way, by using the notion of 'information capitalism'.

The contrast between the two terms reflects an issue which is a recurring theme of this discussion: the issue of technological determinism. While the phrases 'industrial society', 'information society' and so on imply an indeterminate 'society' being structured by the dominant technology, 'information capitalism' suggest the interaction of a particular form of technology with a particular social and economic system; in this case, a system in which the ownership and control of the means of production confers on private individuals the power to appropriate the surplus wealth created by society. This social system constrains the range of alternatives for the development and application of technology just as much as technology defines the possible futures for the social system.

But 'information capitalism' also suggests a type of capitalism recognisably different from those which have existed in the past. In this sense, to use the term is to contradict the views, quite widespread among socialists, either that current technological changes involve *no* real qualitative change in the pattern of wealth creation and exploitation, or that they herald the final death-agony of the capitalist system.[1]

If we describe the system which is emerging in Japan and other advanced societies as 'information capitalism', what does this really mean about the ways in which the system works, the ways in which profits are generated and growth pursued? To try to explain this, I shall take a popular radical description of modern capitalism – the one outlined by Baran and Sweezy in their book *Monopoly Capital*,[2] and then show how information capitalism seems to me to differ from this description. Like all models abstracted from the real world by social scientists, this outline of information capitalism is not intended to be a full description of reality. The present-day economic system of Japan is of course an immensely complex combination of decaying and emerging elements. This sketch is intended only to pick out particularly important parts of the whole and indicate their relationship to one another. In later chapters I shall try to link the main features of this sketch to certain trends in contemporary Japanese society.

Monopoly Capitalism

Baran and Sweezy begin their analysis of monopoly capital with the concept of economic surplus.[3] In order for a capitalist economy to generate profits and to grow, it is necessary that, in any given period, everything used up in the processes of production should be replaced, and something additional should remain. This 'something additional' is the economic surplus which provides the source both of income for the property-owning classes and of new private investment (as well as of government spending, economic waste and so on).

According to Baran and Sweezy, the age of monopoly capitalism is one in which this economic surplus becomes progressively greater, and the problems of putting it to use become commensurately more serious.[4] The reasons for this trend, very briefly, are these. The modern industrial economy is dominated by large managerial firms, each of which is aware of the prices charged by its major competitors, and is able to adjust its own prices and output accordingly. In this oligopolistic situation there are strong economic pressures against raising prices, while lowering prices tends to lead to mutually destructive price-cutting wars. Large firms tend to hold their prices relatively steady, and compete by perpetually striving to reduce their costs of production. This is achieved mainly by labour-saving innovation, which makes it possible to reduce the wage bill and so increase the surplus left over at the end of the production process.[5] Because big corporations hold their prices constant while their costs of production fall, this ever-expanding surplus is not distributed evenly throughout society, but remains concentrated within the corporate sector, and much of *Monopoly Capital* is devoted to an analysis of the problems which large firms face in using this surplus without either undermining their own political power or triggering a crisis of under-consumption.

One point which needs to be made about this model of monopoly capitalism is its ambiguous approach to technological change. Technological innovation, as the main means by which costs are cut, clearly lies at the heart of the whole analysis. And yet in many sections of their book Baran and Sweezy appear curiously reluctant to recognise the innovative force of the large corporation. They specifically reject Schumpeter's visions of 'gales of creative destruction' created by 'competition from the new commodity, the new technology, the new source of supply, and the new type of organisation'.[6] Instead, they argue that the large corporation's desire to maintain market stability will restrain it from entering into fierce competition based on product innovation. The research and development programmes of large firms are therefore regarded as being, to a large extent, glorified sales promotion the result of which is not so much technological innovation as the creation of a 'profitable "product-mix"'.[7] This approach has been disputed by other radical analysts such as André Gorz, who suggests that in the post-war period product innovation became increasingly important as large firms sought to ward off the spectre of market saturation.[8] Baran and Sweezy's view of innovation, therefore, may even have been inappropriate to the society which they were analysing. As we shall see, it is certainly inappropriate to the analysis of information capitalism.

Monopoly Capital explicitly excludes detailed discussion of the labour process, and, as a result, its comments on class formation are also rather fragmentary. These points, however, were later taken up by other writers, most notably by Harry Braverman, whose book *Labour and Monopoly Capital* offers a clear and richly documented analysis of the labour process under monopoly capitalism. Braverman's central argument is this. In order to reduce costs, large corporations need not only to make labour more productive but also to maximise managerial control over the labour process. The result (exemplified in Taylorism) is an extreme form of the division of labour, where physical work is reduced to its most deskilled and degraded form, while the tasks of planning, control and decision making are removed from the workers and concentrated in the hands of an expanding managerial and technical hierarchy.[9] To support this hierarchy, a growing stratum of white-collar office workers is required, but here again cost-cutting pressures cause deskilling, and the office worker is reduced to a level little better (and sometimes worse) than that of the factory labourer.[10]

Braverman does not see this expanding mass of deskilled labour as containing much revolutionary potential. On the contrary, he implies that the almost irresistible dominance of monopoly capital is depriving workers of the power to influence their own lives. The new technical and professional strata, meanwhile, are in an ambivalent position – at once exploited and exploiting – and therefore unlikely to provide a catalyst for the overthrow of the system.[11] In this respect he differs from those who, like Serge Mallet,[12] have seen technicians as a 'new working class' possessing the power and motivation to effect radical social change.

Very briefly, then, the model of monopoly capital derived from Baran and Sweezy and Harry Braverman can be seen to consist of these main elements:

1. an economy dominated by large corporations whose competitive instincts are constrained by a powerful urge to mutual self-preservation;
2. an ever-increasing economic surplus channelled to non-productive uses (the sales effort, militarism and waste) and yet always threatening to engulf the system;
3. a managerial ruling class whose ownership of capital has been generalised (i.e. the class as a whole owns most of the capital as a whole, but individuals do not normally own the particular fragment of capital which they manage);
4. a large, deskilled and generally passive working class; and

    5 a stratum of technical and professional workers who, in Braverman's words, constitute a 'real middle class', that is, their economic position is in effect an intermediate one between the controllers and the controlled.

Automation and Information Capitalism

The most vital distinction between this model of monopoly capitalism and information capitalism lies in the labour process. In the pursuit of cost-cutting and automation, something crucially important has happened to labour itself.

In essence, all labour involves the purposeful application of human knowledge to the natural world. In its simplest form, this application occurred directly, without the intervention of tools or machinery. All knowledge was contained within the human community, and passed on directly from one generation to another. Little by little, however, knowledge came to be embodied and stored in other forms. There were two ways in which this occurred: firstly, through the development of tools and machinery. These not only contained 'congealed labour power' but also preserved and transmitted accumulating knowledge in such a way as to make the process of production easier (and, often, less skilled) for the human producer.

The second way in which knowledge was stored was in written form, and later through other visual and auditory media. These made it possible for productive information to be transmitted from one human being to another without face-to-face contact. Since information stored in this way could only be understood by human beings, however, it was necessary for people to absorb the knowledge (by reading, learning and so on) before it could be put to use. Whereas the storing of knowledge in machines tended to deskill labour, the storing of knowledge in books increased levels of learning. The mechanisation and deskilling of relatively routine tasks went hand in hand with a demand for increased levels of 'book learning' in the spheres of supervisory and technical work.

The central innovation which accompanied the development of computing, however, was that recorded instructions (software) could now be 'read' directly by the machine (hardware) without being interpreted by a human intermediary.

This innovation has proved to have enormously wide implications. It means, in the first place, that a single machine may be
made to perform a variety of tasks without alteration to its
mechanical structure. The wave of computer-based automation
which is currently occurring in Japan and elsewhere is, for
this reason, quite different in nature from earlier phases of
mechanisation which were based on knowledge embodied in the
structure of the machine.

Secondly, the information which is fed into the machine enters
it in the form of impulses which can be transmitted over long
distances. Even though a human worker is still required to enter
new instructions into the machine or to alter old ones, the worker
can now perform these tasks while physically far removed from
the machine itself. The development of new communications
networks will greatly increase the practical possibility of this
separation of worker from machine.

Ultimately, and most importantly, the creation of software
implies a revolutionary fission of labour itself. For any task which
involves logical sequences of thought or movement, it is now
conceptually possible to extract the knowledge of how to perform
the task from the mind of the human worker and transfer it directly
to the machine. In the past, Braverman could correctly observe
that

> labour, like all life processes and bodily functions is an
> inalienable property of the human individual. Muscle and
> brain cannot be separated from the person possessing
> them. . . . Thus, in the exchange [of labour for wage] the
> worker does not surrender to the capitalist his or her capacity
> to work. The worker retains it, and the capitalist can take
> advantage of the bargain only by setting the worker to work.[13]

But with the use of software in production the situation is
fundamentally altered. The worker for example, who programs
the playback robot by guiding its arm through a series of movements
(which it will then endlessly repeat) does in a very real sense
'surrender to the capitalist his or her capacity for work'. The
physical coming together of worker and machine is sundered,
and we are left with, on the one hand, machines which work
automatically, endlessly responding to the instructions provided
by workers who may be physically far removed from the production

site; and, on the other, the increasing channelling of living labour into the process of designing, composing and altering those instructions themselves.[14]

The Production of Information

The outcome of this fission is that the centre of economic gravity shifts from the production of goods to the production of innovation – that is, of new knowledge for the making of goods. This happens for two main reasons. Firstly, the process of auto-mation enormously increases the speed and reduces the cost with which goods can be produced. Given the existing physical restrictions on the size of the market, this would rapidly result in market saturation and stagnation if corporations did not devote a growing share of their resources to the continual alteration and upgrading of their products.[15] Secondly, as fewer and fewer workers are required in the production of goods themselves, so it becomes increasingly difficult for corporations to extract profits from the exploitation of their manufacturing workforce. Socialist analyses of capitalism have generally rested on the idea that this exploitation was the primary source of profit. It therefore seems to follow that, as the workforce shrinks, either profits will dwindle or the level of exploitation will have to rise to impossible levels. The inescapable conclusion, some writers believe, is that auto-mation will lead to the spontaneous collapse of capitalism.[16]

Perpetual innovation, however, offers a way out of this trap. For one thing, it means that, while the number of people producing material goods shrinks, the number of producers of knowledge grows. The commodities made by these workers (inventions, programs for automated equipment and so on), however intangible they may appear, can be bought and sold at a price. The corporation, therefore, can exploit the knowledge-producer's labour to create a profit in just the same way as it could exploit the labour of the industrial blue-collar worker. But the shift towards the production of innovation not only provides a means of continuing the traditional methods of exploitation. It also opens up a new method for the private appropriation of the economic surplus: one which has extremely far-reaching social and economic implications. In a moment, we shall examine the way in which this new source of profits works; but first it is necessary to illustrate and analyse the tendency for corporations to become producers of innovation.

This tendency underlies the frequent emphasis, in Japanese writings on the information society, upon the shift from large-scale, standardised production to small-scale, diversified production. Rather than concentrating on the cheapest possible production of a particular line of goods, the enterprise concentrates on the perpetual alteration of product specification and design, so that no item is ever allowed to become standardised. This is made possible by the new organisational structure suggested by MITI (see Figure 2.1, page 12), where computer-automated production is closely integrated with a hierarchy of computer-aided design, research and management centres.

Although fully computer-integrated enterprises of the type envisaged by MITI have barely begun to take shape in the real world, the tendency towards perpetual innovation is already evident in automating factories. Take, for example, Masuda Seisakusho, a subcontracting company making parts for Honda motorcycles. From 1980 the firm's Hamamatsu factory began to introduce robots in arc welding and later in metal pressing. The immediate effect of this was to reduce their workforce by 10 per cent and the cost of their products by about 30 per cent. With further automation, the firm calculated, the unit cost of their motorcycle parts could be cut by as much as 50 per cent.[17]

However, this is not the end of the story. As their future plans for 90 per cent automation of the factory advance, the company's activities will shift increasingly to software production. In the words of the factory manager: 'While the functions [of robots] improve, so the relative importance of the software section increases, and we must make preparations so as not to be left behind by this trend.'[18]

In response to these predictions, the company had already (by 1983) trained 13 of its shop-floor workers in software engineering. Falling costs of production, therefore, were going hand in hand with increasing emphasis on design and on the diversification of products.

The company has a future policy of strengthening small-scale, diversified production by means of robotisation. In this factory in particularly . . . preparations are being made in response to the growing variety of makes of motorcycles. The main reason given for this is that 'the need to adjust to product diversification' makes robotisation absolutely necessary, and since 'teaching' [the robot] is simple, if the factory has a positive attitude it can always be ready to meet the challenge of the increasingly multiform specification of parts.[19]

The interpretation implicit in this quotation is that the company was obliged to introduce robots in order to keep pace with rapidly changing consumer demand. But an alternative interpretation is possible: namely, that product diversification is the consequence, rather than the cause, of automation.

When parts for a new model of motorcycle are first developed, a good deal of design and programming is necessary. Possibilities therefore exist for extracting profit from the labour of the workers. Besides, the newly designed parts, when they first appear on the market, will probably be unique. Until competitors begin to produce similar parts, the company will enjoy a temporary monopoly, which will enable it to charge relatively high prices. Once automated production is in full swing, however, the situation changes. Designs and computer programs, like all forms of knowledge, can be used over and over again in the production process without ever being 'used up'. After the new product is launched, therefore, hardly any labour is required, as the parts pour out in an unending stream from the computer-controlled equipment. Competitors may also begin to emulate the design, and to produce their own versions at lower prices. The company loses its monopoly, and, incidentally, is left with the problem of how to employ its now redundant design and programming staff. All these pressures will force the company to continue the innovative process, perpetually putting employees to work to design new parts for different machines, to compose new programs for the manufacturing equipment, and so recreate its market, restore its monopoly position and maintain the possibility of extracting profit from labour.

This process is not just occurring in Masuda Seisakusho or in the motorcycle industry as a whole. It is reflected in the trend observed by Hayashi, when he suggested that the 'information costs' of products would rise relative to their material costs.[20] Many Japanese surveys since then have confirmed the tendency towards what they term the 'softening of the economy' – that is, the growing importance of 'soft' inputs such as research and design as against 'hard inputs' such as raw materials and direct manufacturing labour. Between 1968 and 1978, it is estimated that the percentage of workers in all enterprises engaged in indirect labour (management, clerical work, planning, design, programming and so on), as opposed to direct production, rose from 37 per cent to 52 per cent.[21] A study by MITI shows that the main areas of growth have been research and development, planning and information management.[22]

Knowledge and Exploitation

The discussion so far has been based on the assumption that the profitability of enterprises in information capitalism rests on the forms of accumulation emphasised by traditional radical theories: the exploitation of labour (further refined by the charging of monopoly prices). But it is crucial to recognise that the shift in emphasis from the production of goods to the production of innovation has opened up a quite different source of profit: the private expropriation of social knowledge.

There is, after all, one fundamental difference between the commodity production of innovation and the commodity production of physical objects. In the case of physical objects, various sorts of raw materials are used in production. As long as these materials are bought in a competitive market, they must be paid for at a price which approximates to their cost of production. So, when people seek the sources of exploitation in capitalism, they normally look for them, not in the methods by which raw materials are obtained, but in the labour process by which these materials are turned into finished products.

But in the production of knowledge the main raw material is . . . knowledge itself. In other words, new ideas are formed by combining existing ideas and data in ways which are (sometimes) undreamed-of or (far more often) merely superficially different. Whereas the knowledge which comes out of this commercial production process is the private property of the corporation, fenced around with monopoly barriers which endow it with market value, the knowledge which goes in as raw material is mostly social knowledge, produced and owned jointly by society as a whole. The process which uses social knowledge to create private knowledge can generate profits far larger than those which could be obtained from the simple exploitation by the corporation of its workforce.

To explain this more clearly, we might consider an example such as the projects sponsored by the Japanese government for the development of new materials for integrated circuit (IC) production (see page 37). These projects clearly involve fairly substantial investments in laboratory buildings and equipment, but ultimately the crucial element in their success is the knowledge which the research team can bring to their task. This knowledge can be envisaged as consisting of two levels. The lower level is the basic 'infrastructure' of general knowledge – the understanding of language, the rules of social behaviour and so forth – upon which more specialised scientific knowledge is constructed. This lower level of knowledge is mostly acquired outside the framework of economic exchange, through parental education, social intercourse and so on. The higher level of knowledge consists of scientific expertise itself: knowledge, perhaps, of chemistry or electronic engineering. This, too, is in theory freely available: most of it is contained in textbooks to which the reader can have free access in libraries. In practice, however, its very complexity means that only a privileged few can obtain this knowledge, normally through the state-financed but highly selective education system.

The secret of large enterprises (in this case, heavily backed by the government) is their ability to bring together a number of highly educated individuals whose knowledge, of limited use when dispersed, can when pooled produce very profitable results. The recruitment of these research workers may not even be an extremely expensive process for the corporations concerned. Scientists in Japan are reasonably well paid, but are often more interested in the quality of the working environment than in financial reward alone. The average yearly income of an ordinary research worker in 1982 was around US$17,000, far lower than that of a manager or doctor, and not much different from that of a bus driver. Researchers on prestigious projects like the next-generation IC projects can expect considerably higher incomes, but these are mere drops in the ocean when compared to the enormous monopoly profits which firms can expect to reap from the patenting and application of new IC technology.

Information economist Imai Kenichi observes that there is a perpetual tendency for 'private knowledge' to become 'public knowledge'. New ideas inspire imitation; patents and trade secrets cannot be maintained for ever. For this reason, information flows from the private control of large corporations into the ever-deepening pool of social knowledge, and so, Imai believes, the power of economic oligopoly is diluted.[23] But in this respect Imai's analysis is rather like the observation of a meteorologist who sees rain falling from clouds but does not see the process by which evaporation from the earth replenishes the clouds. Corporations use their power to draw from the pool of social knowledge the information needed to create innovation, and it is only when they have extracted monopoly profits from that innovation that they at last allow it to flow back into the realms of public knowledge. To put it another way, corporations make use of existing knowledge – which has use value but not exchange value – in inventive activity. This activity is supported (as K. J. Arrow puts it) 'by using the invention to create property rights'.[24] Property rights enable the corporation to fence off the new corner of knowledge from the public and to make a profit from its application, and it is only when profits have been obtained and the invention is obsolescent that it is returned to the domain of public use.

Information capitalism, therefore, not only exploits the labour of those directly employed by corporations, but also depends, more than any earlier form of economy, on the indirect exploitation of the labour of everyone involved in the maintenance, transmission and expansion of social knowledge: parents, teachers, journalists – in the end, everybody. The old society in which the microcosmic exploitation of the worker by her/his boss precisely mirrored the macrocosmic exploitation of the proletariat by the ruling classes is replaced by a society where the crucial struggle (in Alain Touraine's words) is that 'between the different kinds of apparatus and user – consumers or more simply the public – defined less by their specific attributes than by their resistance to domination by the apparatus'.[25]

More precisely, the economic system itself becomes a vast mechanism for converting the knowledge created by society into a source of corporate profits: profits which are then redistributed to the few on the basis of their financial stake in the corporate system.

Competition and Information Capitalism

The picture of competition which emerges from this analysis, then, is distinctly different from the picture suggested by Baran and Sweezy. Theirs is essentially an oligopolistic model, where a handful of giant firms, producing relatively standardised products, conspire either overtly or covertly to maintain prices at a particular level. In information capitalism, however, we have something much closer to the classical model of monopolistic competition, in which the corporation's ability to market a product slightly different from anything offered by its competition allows it temporarily to reap monopoly profits. If the product is successful, however, competitors will rapidly imitate it (or, more probably, produce their own slightly improved version). Prices and profits will fall, and the development of new products will be necessary to restore the profitability of the innovating corporation.

This perpetual leap-frogging of innovation, where firms incessantly strive to keep one step ahead of their competitors and so avoid the trap of falling prices, is vividly illustrated by the case of the microchip industry, which follows regular cycles of boom and crisis as new products come on to the market and old products lose their value.

From this it will be clear that Baran and Sweezy's concept of a rising economic surplus is invalid in the context of information capitalism. Here, the processes of research and development, design and marketing are not unnecessary excrescences which serve only to absorb the cancerous growth of monopoly profits, but are an absolutely vital source of profit itself.

On the other hand, this analysis offers no support for the theories of those, like Imai, who have argued that current technological change is *reducing* monopoly power and re-creating a competitive form of capitalism.[26] Imai reaches this conclusion by contrasting traditional heavy industries, where massive capital investment raised high barriers to entry, with the new 'information-intensive' industries, where capital costs may be lower and markets therefore more 'contestable'.[27] But this approach fails to recognise that, in the environment of perpetual innovation, the main barrier to entry arises from the large corporations' power to mobilise knowledge resources (in the form of research teams, patents, accumulated know-how, data collections and so on) which their small competitors cannot hope to emulate. The power of knowledge to protect monopoly is clearly illustrated by the case of the Japanese trading sector, where accumulated know-how rather than high capital costs have for many years ensured the continued dominance of the 'big six' trading companies.

The emergence of information capitalism, then, does not have an immediate or obvious tendency either to increase or to decrease the economic surplus, but instead sets in motion two counteracting forces. On the one hand, the automation of production, and the accompanying mechanisation of many administrative, research and design activities, lowers the costs of 'reproducing the system' – that is, of producing the goods consumed by the workforce and of replacing old machinery with new. From this point of view, the processes which Baran and Sweezy saw as inflating the economic surplus continue and are actually intensified. But at the same time the shift towards knowledge production has a quite different effect on the costs of production. The growth of a stratum of research and design workers requires the associated development of an expanding sphere of education and service activities. From the employer's viewpoint the cost of a scientific or technical worker is inevitably higher than that of an unskilled manual worker, for the scientific worker must not simply be fed and clothed but also provided with a steady flow of information through books, mass media and so forth, and offered a living environment conducive to mental effort. In macroeconomic terms, the self-replication of information capitalism involves not only the replacement of the physical factors of production (machinery and labour) but also the conservation and transmission from one generation to another of the complex structure of knowledge, technology and culture which makes perpetual innovation possible.

Summary

The main characteristics which separate information capitalism from Baran and Sweezy's model of monopoly capitalism, then, can be summed up like this:

1 In information capitalism, the progressive automation of manufacturing causes a shift in the focus of corporate

activity from the production of goods to the production of new information.

2 This results in a corporate structure where large firms, rather than colluding to maintain oligopoly prices, use their innovative activity to acquire temporary monopolies of particular areas of production.

3 In this situation, oligopoly no longer results in an ever-rising surplus. Rather, corporations are able to tap a new source of profit by their use of freely obtained social knowledge to create private knowledge.

4 Information capitalism forms a complex and apparently self-regulating system in which profit derived both from the direct exploitation of the corporate workforce and from the indirect exploitation of a mass of ancillary service workers is channelled through large firms into the hands of the managerial ruling class.

Whereas most writings on the information society present a picture of a harmonious system where social conflicts diminish and technological change brings equal benefits to all, this alternative analysis obviously implies the survival, in new forms, of old antagonisms between those at the top and those at the bottom of the economic structure. Whether the new technologies will affect the working lives of those at the bottom in the ways predicted by Braverman is a question which we shall need to explore in later chapters. At present it is sufficient to suggest that, although the new technologies bring many genuine social benefits, neither the benefits nor the costs are equally distributed throughout society.

Like older forms of capitalism, the new system is a paradoxical one. By linking profit to innovation, it gives new impetus to the eternal human desire to discover and create new knowledge, but at the same time, the content of this new knowledge is distorted precisely by the fact that it emerges from the pursuit of profit. Information capitalism not only exploits the mass of social knowledge but also alters its structure and influences the patterns of the development of knowledge. It possesses the potential to liberate human individuals from material want and physical drudgery, but incorporates them more firmly than ever into a pervasive, complex and exploitative social system whose workings are difficult to unravel and to challenge.

In spite of this, the system is not an all-powerful or an

indestructible one. In fact, in many ways it is very fragile. Its survival rests, not only on the ability of corporations to produce a never-ending stream of innovation, but also (most importantly) on the capacity of the market to absorb the never-ending stream of new products. This is made more difficult by the fact that automation is being applied to the production of information as well as to the production of material goods. The spectres of a shrinking workforce, unemployment and under-consumption are always present. Japan so far has avoided these evils, but even there (as we shall see in the next chapter) the problems are somewhat greater than they at first appear.

Notes

1 For example, E. Mandel, *Late Capitalism*, London, New Left Books, 1975; Tokita, Yoshihisa, *Gendai Shihonshugi to Rōdōsha Kaikyū*, Tokyo, Iwanami Shoten, 1982.
2 P. Baran and P. M. Sweezy, *Monopoly Capital*, Harmondsworth, Pelican Books, 1968.
3 Ibid., pp. 23–4.
4 Ibid., ch. 3.
5 Ibid., pp. 78–80.
6 J. Schumpeter, *Capitalism, Socialism and Democracy*, quoted in Baran and Sweezy, *Monopoly Capital*, p. 81.
7 Ibid., p. 134.
8 A. Gorz, 'Technology, Technicians and Class Struggle' in A. Gorz (ed.), *The Division of Labour*, Brighton, Harvester Press, 1978, pp. 163–4.
9 H. Braverman, *The Degradation of Work in the Twentieth Century Labour and Monopoly Capital*, New York and London, Monthly Review Press, 1974, Parts I and II.
10 Ibid., ch. 15.
11 Ibid., ch. 18.
12 S. Mallet, *La Nouvelle Classe Ouvrière*, Paris, Editions du Seuil, 1963.
13 Braverman, *Degradation of Work*, p. 54.
14 The preceding paragraphs are adapted from my earlier article, 'Robots and Capitalism', *New Left Review*, no. 147, 1984, 109–21.
15 Gorz, 'Technology, Technicians and Class Struggle', p. 164.
16 E.g. Mandel, *Late Capitalism*.
17 This description is derived from Seisan Kikaku Chōsakai (ed.),

Nihon no Robotto, Tokyo, Seisan Kikaku Chōsakai, 1983, pp. 113–18.
18 Quoted in ibid., p. 112.
19 Quoted in ibid., p. 112.
20 Hayashi Yūjiro, *Jōhōka Shakai*, Tokyo, Kōdansha, 1969, pp. 64–5.
21 Mirai Kōgaku Kenkyū-sho, *Kimmu Taiyō to Komyunikēshon ni Kansuru Shōraigata no Kenkyū*, Tokyo, Mirai Kogaku Kenkyū-sho, March 1983, p. 28.
22 Ibid., p. 29.
23 Imai Kenichi, *Jōhō Nettowaku Shakai*, Tokyo, Iwanami Shinsho, 1984, pp. 55, 142.
24 K. J. Arrow: 'Economic Welfare and the Allocation of Resources for Invention' in D. M. Lamberton (ed.), *Economics of Information and Knowledge*, Harmondsworth, Penguin Books, 1971, pp. 141–59 (quotation is from p. 149).
25 A. Touraine, *The Voice and the Eye* (trans. A. Duff), Cambridge, Cambridge University Press, 1981, p. 7.
26 Imai, *Jōhō Nettowaku Shakai*.
27 Ibid., pp. 137–42.

6 Employment and Unemployment in Japan's Information Society

The proponents of the information society argue that 'informisation' will not simply increase material abundance, but – most importantly – that it will raise the quality of human life. As we saw in Chapter 2, a central theme of the information society reports is the contrast between industrial society, where the emphasis was on the growing production of a growing number of goods, and information society, where non-material values such as creativity and self-fulfilment will be paramount.

It is obviously too early to make conclusive judgements about these claims. The concept of the information society is too new, and the policies designed to bring it to fruition are too young. What we can do, though – and what we urgently need to do – is to observe the transformations which are taking place at present within the social system, and to ask whether they are at least heading *in the directions* suggested by the theorists of the information society. In this way we can form a preliminary assessment of the information society concept, and develop appropriate responses to those who seek its realisation.

The chapter will focus particularly on the quantity of employment in information capitalism. Outside Japan the issue is one which has attracted intense interest: so much so, in fact, that discussions on the social impact of information technology often concentrate almost exclusively on the dangers of unemployment. This concern is certainly related to the fact that recent technological developments have coincided, in many western countries, with a period in which unemployment has reached exceptionally high levels. But it also reflects, more fundamentally, an underlying tension which seems to threaten the foundations of information capitalism.

As we saw in the last chapter, the system not only makes possible but also depends upon the production of a perpetual stream of new products. It therefore requires an affluent and expanding market willing to buy those products. At the same time, the quickening pace of automation – of mental as well as physical tasks – constantly reduces the size of the workforce needed to produce any given quantity of goods. The survival of the system depends upon a balancing of these two forces: upon the job-creating effects of new products continuously counteracting the job-destroying effects of automation. Otherwise, rising unemployment, as well as causing severe social problems, is liable to reduce the size of the market and undermine the foundations of the economy.

In Japan, in spite of the spread of computer-based automation, unemployment levels have remained low by international standards, and official attitudes to unemployment have generally been optimistic. The information society has been portrayed as a social order in which unemployment will generally be temporary and frictional, rather than structural and prolonged, and where new and more creative job opportunities will constantly be created. By looking at the background to and reasons for contemporary low unemployment in Japan, we can come to some conclusions on the accuracy of these predictions for the future.

Employment in Japan – the Background

The introduction of new technology does not have identical effects on employment in all societies. Instead, technology interacts with existing employment structures to create systems which vary, in small but significant ways, from country to country.

In Japan, the patterns of employment created by industrialisation had a number of special features, reflecting both the social structures of agrarian Japan and Japan's status as a relatively late and rapidly industrialising nation. The most prominent of these features was the phenomenon normally referred to as 'dualism': the coexistence of capital-intensive and highly productive industries alongside very labour-intensive, technologically unsophisticated agriculture, services and small-scale manufacturing. This form of dualism is not unique to Japan. It appears to a degree in many countries where industrial technology has been imported and where modern, capital-intensive techniques have been superimposed upon a basis of peasant smallholder agriculture.[1] Dualism in Japan, however, does seem to have been unusually strongly marked, and it has had some very interesting effects on the shape both of employment and of society as a whole.

Most importantly, it has meant that what might be called 'the classical working class' – the stratum of blue-collar manual workers employed in modern manufacturing – has always been relatively small in Japan. Although manufacturing output grew at a phenomenal rate – over 15 per cent a year from 1956 to 1971 – this growth was based on the importation of highly productive, capital-intensive technologies from overseas, and the rate of growth of *employment* in manufacturing was much slower: under 5 per cent per annum.[2] Blue-collar industrial workers in Japan have never amounted to more than a third of the total workforce. The peak was attained around the mid-1970s, and all indications are that the proportion is now declining. By comparison, at its peak in the early 1950s, the US blue-collar industrial workforce exceeded 41 per cent of all employees, while in Britain the figure for the early 1960s was just under 50 per cent.[3]

Not only was the blue-collar industrial workforce relatively small in Japan, but a quite significant section of that workforce was employed in tiny, (usually) family-owned workshops. In 1970 more than 16 per cent of manufacturing workers were in establishments with fewer than ten employees. The figures for Britain and the US at around the same date were just over 2 per cent.[4] The divisions between workers in large enterprises and those in small enterprises were deepened by the renowned Japanese 'lifetime employment' system. This system, which involves the assurance of continued employment, together with regular wage rises, is sometimes presented by writers, both within and outside Japan, as being an almost universal feature of employment in Japan. In fact, however, it has applied only to a select group of workers; essentially, to male skilled and semi-skilled workers in large enterprises. The system, in other words, created a kind of working-class elite, whose pay and employment conditions were rather different from those of the majority of industrial workers.[5]

Many writers, comparing Japan with older industrialised countries like Britain, have commented on Japan's apparent lack of a solid working-class ethos and identity. Often, this has been attributed to peculiarities of Japanese culture, such as the supposed 'group consciousness' and 'vertical structure' of Japanese society.[6] Clearly, though, the questions of class consciousness and class culture in Japan have to be seen against the background of the numerical weakness and rather recent development of the Japanese industrial proletariat.

Japan's dualistic development has also had a great impact on unemployment levels. The less technologically advanced sections of the economy, with their low productivity and flexible wages, served to absorb the surplus labour regularly disgorged by the modern manufacturing sector in times of recession, and so kept the numbers of wholly unemployed workers well below the levels familiar in many western industrialised countries. Traditionally, it was agriculture which played this cushioning role: redundant urban workers returned to their villages to work on the land; firms in financial difficulties failed to recruit the temporary or seasonal labour which, in better years, they would have hired from the rural areas.[7]

More recently, as the number of farm workers has dwindled (to around 10 per cent of the workforce at the beginning of the 1980s), as agricultural productivity has risen and as more and more people have adopted a fully urban way of life, the role of agriculture as a cushion against unemployment has diminished. But a similar function continues to be filled by other sections of the economy, particularly by the commercial sector.

It is rather surprising to observe, in an age when Japanese industry is renowned for its efficiency, that the overall productivity of labour in Japan is still only around two-thirds of the US level. This is mainly the result of very low productivity in the commercial and services sector, particularly in retail trade. A walk through almost any quarter of a Japanese town will confirm that retailing remains dominated by small, labour-intensive enterprises. Supermarkets were not widespread before 1970, and even in the 1980s little specialised stores, along with numerous cafés, restaurants and fast-food shops, continue to give a peculiar charm to the Japanese urban landscape.

These small service enterprises, often family-run and making use of relatively low-wage labour, continue to play a part in some ways similar to the traditional role of agriculture as the absorber of surplus labour. In 1980, sales workers constituted more than 25.1 per cent of Japan's non-agricultural workforce. The figures for the United Kingdom and West Germany were 12.8 per cent and 12.7 per cent respectively.[8]

Superficially, then, Japan's employment patterns already show a fleeting resemblance to the pattern predicted by Daniel Bell for the 'post-industrial society' and by Masuda Yoneji for the 'information society': the blue-collar manufacturing workforce is comparatively small; large numbers of people are employed in so-called tertiary activities such as sales and service work; and social conflict, although certainly not absent, does not often seem to fall into readily identifiable categories of class confrontation.

This similarity, though, can be explained in terms of the particularly uneven way in which the Japanese economy has developed, with capital-intensive and technologically sophisticated heavy industry existing side by side with, and interacting with, labour-intensive agriculture, commercial and service sectors. In this sense, these patterns are not so much auguries of an advance into post-industrialism as legacies of a traditional structure which is now undergoing rapid change.

Automation and 'Lifetime Employment'

The introduction of computer-controlled equipment has made it possible both for many manual tasks to be performed wholly by machines (automated) and for many types of intellectual work to be assisted by machines (mechanised). These processes have occurred at a time when most industrialised countries were experiencing rates of unemployment unprecedented since the world depression of the 1930s. So it is hardly surprising that the connection between computerisation and unemployment has become an issue of impassioned debate in the west.

But Japan, where the rate of computerisation and automation has been among the fastest in the world, continues to have a relatively low level of unemployment. Between 1977 and 1982 the number of numerically controlled machines in use in Japanese factories increased by about 76,000 and the number of industrial robots (as defined by Japan's Ministry of Trade and Industry) by about 90,000;[9] the number of computers in use in industry increased by an estimated 47,504 (1977–81);[10] and yet the official unemployment rate, between 1977 and 1982, rose only from 2.0

per cent to 2.4 per cent.[11] This naturally makes Japan a particularly interesting subject of study for anyone concerned with the relationship between contemporary technological change and unemployment. Have Japanese enterprises, or has the Japanese government, in some way discovered the secret of combining the benefits of rapid automation with the blessings of full employment?

As we have already seen, the Japanese government itself, in explaining Japan's continued low levels of unemployment, tends to point to two factors; on the one hand, Japan's unique 'lifetime employment' system, and, on the other, the demand-creating effects of technological change, which it sees as balancing or even outweighing the job-displacing effects. These factors have also been emphasised by writers outside Japan. Barry Jones, for example (while noting various other reasons for low unemployment in Japan), writes enthusiastically of Japanese companies' reluctance to dismiss their workers: a reluctance which has given rise to the phenomenon of the *madogiwa-zoku* (window gazers), employees who continue to be retained on the company's pay role although they have nothing left to do but sit at their desks and gaze out of the windows.[12]

Surveys of Japanese companies have shown that a major aim in introducing computer-controlled equipment is to reduce labour inputs and labour costs in the production process.[13] How have companies managed to reconcile this aim with the concept of lifetime employment? It seems fairly clear that factory automation by Japanese firms *has* commonly resulted in a decline in the number of shop-floor workers employed by these firms. The most comprehensive study of the effect of factory automation on employment is probably the investigation into the impact of microelectronics on manufacturing, conducted by the Labour Ministry in 1982. This study surveyed a large, nationwide sample of factories, and found that over half (59.3 per cent) had introduced equipment controlled by integrated circuits (ICs). A substantial number of these factories (38.5 per cent) had reduced their workforce as a result of introducing IC-controlled equipment; only 2.3 per cent had increased their number of workers.[14] Similar findings emerge from several regional studies of the impact of factory automation conducted in various Japanese prefectures.[15]

The effects of office automation are more ambiguous. Office automation has been accompanied by a very rapid increase in the volume and complexity of office work and, whereas factory automation (at least in the initial stages) has mostly been directed to reducing the costs and increasing the efficiency of existing types of production, office automation has, much more frequently, made entirely new types of administrative activity possible. There is no doubt that, despite the rapid progress of office automation, the total number of office workers in Japan has been growing rapidly in recent years.[16] The results of research on the direct impact of office automation in individual firms have been equivocal. Some regional studies have shown that automation commonly resulted in a decline in the number of office workers, but a Labour Ministry survey of the head offices of large Japanese firms showed that automation (between 1975 and 1981) had been accompanied by a slight increase in employment.[17]

One point, however, is certain. All the available studies emphasise that, where automation has led to reductions in the workforce, these have rarely been achieved by dismissing workers. The Labour Ministry's survey of firms using IC-controlled equipment (mentioned earlier) found that only 0.4 per cent of these firms had made workers redundant.[18] In most cases, the workforce had been cut by natural wastage or by moving workers to new jobs within the enterprise. Occasionally, where this was impossible, workers had been found positions in other, related firms.

It is fair to view the results of this study with a little scepticism. Firstly, of course, participation in the survey was voluntary, and one can imagine that managers of firms which *had* dismissed workers might have felt some reluctance in filling in the thick white questionnaire which arrived on their desks from the Ministry's researchers. Secondly, the survey only looked at enterprises with more than 100 workers. A regional study by the local government of Hiroshima Prefecture, conducted the following year, predictably showed that redundancies were more common in the case of smaller firms. Their survey of firms which had introduced numerically controlled (NC) machinery and robots showed that 24.2 per cent of smaller enterprises (with 30 to 299 workers) had subsequently reduced their workforce. Of these, 4.5 per cent had achieved the reduction by means of redundancies.[19]

Even allowing for sampling biases, however, these surveys would seem to suggest that it is relatively uncommon for Japanese workers to be made redundant as a direct result of automation. This impression is reinforced by the fact that media reports of large-scale dismissals of workers have been quite rare in recent years.

All of this leads the Labour Ministry to the rather complacent conclusion that

the labour saving efficiency of mechanical automation based on the introduction of I.C. controlled industrial equipment has not been associated with serious problems of redundancies. We consider that the reasons behind this fact are both the need for new technicians which accompanies the introduction [of new equipment], and the smooth maintenance and expansion of the activities of enterprises, resulting from improved quality and accuracy of productions, cost reductions and diversification. Furthermore, we believe that our country's industrial employment traditions and the practice of holding prior negotiations between labour and management has been of great significance in relation to the key issues of concern in the protection of employment. It is hoped that, in the future too, the introduction of micro-electronic equipment will not be associated with serious employment problems and that labour and employers will from the outset be able to make appropriate adjustments.[20]

The problem about this statement is that, from the point of view of society as a whole, it is not only redundancies which cause unemployment. The process of 'natural wastage' means that companies no longer replace the workers who retire from the firm. Moving workers to posts within the enterprise means that these posts will not be filled by new recruits from outside. In both cases, the number of jobs available to people seeking employment is reduced. The sad fact is that, although a commitment to the ideology of lifetime employment may restrain some firms from pruning their workforce to the rational minimum, no capitalist enterprise can afford to *hire* people just to sit at desks and look out of windows.

In other words, the lifetime employment system in large firms has probably shielded some Japanese workers from the fate, so common elsewhere, of finding oneself in middle age on the scrap-heap of redundancy. But at a macro-economic level, lifetime employment cannot create jobs and therefore cannot ultimately prevent automation from producing unemployment.

Demand Creation and Job Destruction

If lifetime employment is not the key to Japan's low unemployment levels, what of the other main factor emphasised in the information society reports: the demand-creating force of technological innovation?

It is obvious that the development of computer-related technologies has not only resulted in the automation of manual tasks, but has at the same time stimulated demand for a host of previously unimaginable products: from electronic games to CAT-scanners and from flexible manufacturing systems to programmable sewing machines. The wealth generated by these new industries in turn creates demand for other goods and services, and so the effects spread, like ripples in a pond, to a point where their limits are no longer clearly discernible.

It would be pleasing to be able to add up the number of jobs created in response to this expanding demand, and to weigh them against the number of jobs lost through automation, but in practice any accurate assessment of this kind is simply impossible. It is possible, though, to get some rough impression of the more direct job-creating effects of 'informisation'. One independent research body which has examined this issue has come up with estimates of the numbers of jobs created in the manufacture of the implements of automation themselves: computers, industrial robots, NC equipment and their components (see Table 6.1). They found that more than 93,000 new jobs were created in these industries between 1977 and 1982.[21] The growth of the software industry, which has accompanied the spread of automation and computerisation, has had a particularly great impact on employment: over 83,000 new jobs were created in computer software and related industries between 1975 and 1981.[22]

In a wider sense, the technologies of automation also give rise to new consumer products: among them electronically controlled gadgets, watches, games and home computers. There are no detailed figures of the employment created by each of these new products, but they undoubtedly account for an important share of the growing number of jobs in the electrical industry sector. (Employment in this sector grew by 12.8 per cent between 1980 and 1983, a growth rate much higher than the manufacturing industry average of 1.7 per cent.[23])

Table 6.1. *The Growth of Microelectronics-related Industries in Japan, 1976–82 (shipments are given in Y100 million)*

		1976	1977	1978	1979	1980	1981	1982
Integrated	Shipments	1,516	1,646	2,819	6,324	9,623	12,887	16,725
circuits	Employees	16,723	16,314	22,856	30,853	42,806	58,479	72,028
NC	Shipments	513	805	1,076	2,054	3,394	4,341	4,218
machinery	Employees	3,312	5,436	7,342	14,317	22,052	25,926	24,138
Industrial	Shipments	—	103	40	49	100	271	741
robots	Employees	—	542	430	417	992	2,153	4,328
Computers &	Shipments	7,616	9,101	11,002	13,525	15,863	17,290	21,389
associated hardware	Employees	58,654	61,413	60,690	64,619	69,189	68,090	76,955
Consumer electronic products	Shipments	23,254	23,305	22,163	23,056	29,522	36,867	34,046
Information service industry	Employees	(1975) 74,235	—	101,954	—	—	157,542	—

Source: Maikuro Erekutoronikusu no Koyō ni Oyobosu Eikyō ni Kansuru Chōsa Kenkyū Iinkai, *Maikuroerekutoronikusu no Koyō ni Oyobosu Eikyō ni Tsuite*, p. 26

On the negative side of the employment balance sheet, the General Research Institute for Employment and Trades (*Koyō Shokugyō Sōgō Kenkyū-Sho*) calculated that every NC machine introduced by Japanese industry displaced 0.85 workers, while the *Nikkei Mechanical* magazine's researchers estimated that the typical industrial robot in use in the early 1980s displaced 1.26 workers.[24] If these figures are anywhere near correct, the number of jobs lost in Japan because of the introduction of NC machinery and robots would have totalled around 180,000 between 1977 and 1982. It is, of course, important to remember, though, that the job-displacing effects of automation equipment increase dramatically as technology progresses. The flexible manufacturing systems now being introduced in some Japanese manufacturing enterprises may cut the factory workforce to a twentieth of its initial size.[25]

The direct effects of computer and microelectronics-controlled equipment – both in creating and in destroying work – are only the visible portion of a very large and slippery iceberg. The total impact of automation on the volume of employment in Japanese society is far more profound and complex than can be conveyed by the rough employment estimates given here. Despite their drawbacks, however, these figures do suggest that the spread of

NC equipment, robots, computers and so on has so far had considerable job-creating as well as job-displacing effects in Japan, and that the job-creating effects have gone some way towards offsetting the diminution of industrial employment caused by automation.

However, there is one particularly important aspect of this job-creating side of the picture which must not be overlooked. The expansion of production and of employment in the electronic equipment industry has been inseparably connected with Japan's success in winning a rapidly growing slice of the world market for industrial machinery.[26] This becomes apparent when we look at the export figures for the electronics industry. In 1971, only 15.1 per cent of Japan's output of electronic industrial equipment was exported, but by the first six months of 1983 this figure had risen to over 35 per cent (see Table 6.2). The figures for the electronics industry as a whole were even more striking. Between 1971 and the first half of 1983, the export dependence of the industry rose from 30 per cent to 50 per cent.[27]

The implications of this are clear: as automation technology advances and the labour-saving impact of computer-controlled equipment grows, Japan is likely to be able to maintain low levels of unemployment only if it continues to expand its share in the world market for industrial products, or if it restructures its domestic economy in such a way as to stimulate domestic demand radically. In the present political framework it is hard to imagine that the initiatives necessary for the second option will be forthcoming. At the same time, protectionist pressures overseas will

Table 6.2. *Exports of Electronic Products as a Percentage of Total Production, Jan. 1971 to March 1983*

	1971	1972	1973	1974	1975	1976	1977	1978	1979	1980	1981	1982	1983 (Jan.–March)
Consumer electronic equipment	48.3	48.4	45.8	51.9	58.6	70.7	67.8	62.6	64.7	69.8	71.0	72.2	68.5
Industrial electronic equipment	15.1	14.9	16.1	17.3	21.5	24.0	20.8	20.9	21.1	24.2	27.8	31.6	35.3
Electronic parts and components	19.5	21.4	23.3	31.8	34.9	36.3	39.9	41.6	48.0	49.5	47.4	51.4	49.9
Total	30.1	30.3	29.2	33.9	38.9	46.4	44.6	41.4	43.2	47.5	49.3	50.9	50.1

Source: Tsūshō Sangyō-Shō: Denshi Kōgyō Nenkan 1984, Tokyo, 1984

coming. At thè same time, protectionist pressures overseas will make the first option extremely difficult. Looking at the situation from this perspective, the prospects for employment levels in Japan seem insecure: even the Japanese government itself is predicting a steady rise in unemployment, from its 1984 official level of 2.7 per cent to around 5 per cent by the end of the century.[28]

Concealed Unemployment

As well as the factors emphasised by the Japanese government – the lifetime employment system and the job-creating effects of new technology – there are a couple of other possible reasons for Japan's low unemployment rate which need to be discussed. First of all, there is the possibility (commonly mentioned by overseas writers) that Japan's low unemployment is a statistical illusion.

Every country has its own peculiarities in the way in which it puts together its unemployment figures, and Japan is no exception in this respect. Japan's unemployment statistics are based on a monthly labour force survey (*Rōdōryoku Chōsa*) conducted by the Labour Ministry. This treats as 'unemployed' all people over the age of 15 who have no job and have been actively seeking work for at least a week. It is more restrictive than the similar surveys conducted in many European countries, in that it excludes those not actively seeking employment, as well as those who have been out of work for less than a week, but more inclusive than its British and French equivalents in that it treats school and college students who are seeking work as unemployed.[29]

There is one widespread misconception about Japanese unemployment figures (common both within Japan and abroad) which needs to be cleared up: that is, the belief that Japan's unemployment statistics include only those who have previously been employed, and therefore exclude school leavers who have not yet found a job.* Jones, repeating this misconception, and noting that the Japanese retirement age is usually 55 to 60, suggests that the

---

* This misconception presumably arises from a confusion between the way in which unemployment is calculated and the way in which unemployment benefits are administered. School leavers are not eligible for unemployment benefits, but are included in the official unemployment statistics.

that the 'real' unemployment figure may be as high as 10 per cent.[30]

In fact, the discrepancies between Japan's and other countries' methods of calculating unemployment are not great enough to conceal a problem of this magnitude. Studies which have attempted to recalculate Japanese unemployment using the American system of classification have produced relatively small upward revisions, of between 0.2 per cent and 1.2 per cent.[31]

All of this, however, is not to say that the Japanese figures conceal no problems. For one thing, as unemployment rises many people (particularly married women) who would like to work will give up hope of ever finding a job, cease actively to seek employment, and so disappear from the official unemployment figures. In this sense, the Japanese figures, particularly in times of increasing employment, certainly fail to reflect the full measure of the problem. But this is a problem shared by all countries (including the United States, Italy, Canada and Australia) which define the 'unemployed' as those purposefully seeking work.

The rather moderate rise in the aggregate Japanese unemployment figure (see Table 6.3) also fails to uncover the fact that, for some groups in the population, the rise in unemployment has been much more sudden and severe. As in other countries, it is the youngest and oldest groups of workers who have been most vulnerable to the pressures of unemployment. During the period of high economic growth of the late 1950s and 1960s, the youth

Table 6.3. *Unemployment Rates in Japan, 1965–81 (by Age-groups) (%)*

	Age-group	1965	1973	1981
Women	Under 20	1.6	1.8	4.2
	20–24	1.2	2.3	3.7
	25–54	1.2	1.0	2.0
	Over 54	0.0	1.0	1.4
	Total	1.1	1.3	2.2
Men	Under 20	1.5	3.8	6.8
	20–24	0.8	2.2	3.6
	25–54	0.5	1.1	1.7
	Over 54	0.9	1.8	3.6
	Total	0.7	1.4	2.3

Source: Rōdōryoku Chōsa (various years)

employers to hire young workers who could be trained in new skills; and the growing percentage of young people remaining in education through high school and college. As one might expect, however, the combination of automation and the lifetime employment system in large firms is now beginning to have a serious impact on the job openings for young workers, particularly for those school graduates who would, in earlier years, have expected to obtain secure and reasonably well-paid skilled manual jobs in large firms.

At the opposite end of the scale, there are the older workers who are having increasing difficulty adapting to new technologies and the changing structure of employment. In the past, it was common for male workers to retire from the job in which they had spent most of their working lives in their late fifties, and then to be re-employed in (supposedly) less strenuous and (almost inevitably) lower-paid work until around their mid-sixties. Technological change, however, is making it increasingly difficult for these workers to find new work after retirement, and is therefore adding to the financial pressures of the elderly in a society whose pension and welfare system still leaves much to be desired.

As far as the future of Japanese society is concerned, it is this older group of workers whose fate will be particularly important. Unemployment is affected, of course, not only by the number of jobs being created or destroyed, but also by the growth of the workforce. In the case of Japan, the overall growth rate of the workforce during the next 15 years is expected to be small – an average of 1.2 per cent a year from 1980 to 1999 and 0.5 per cent a year between 1970 and 2000 – but, although the number of workers in the 15–24 age-group is actually expected to *fall* (by about 1.0 per cent a year) in the 1990s, the number of workers aged 55 and over will probably rise quite rapidly (by about 1.9 per cent).[32]

The social problem of technology-induced unemployment, in so far as it emerges in Japan, will above all be a problem of elderly workers with small savings or inadequate pensions, who will find it harder and harder to adapt their skills to employment conditions in the brave new world of the information society.

The Changing Structure of Employment: a New Dualism

Lastly, the threat of unemployment in the information society may partly be deflected in a quite traditional way. As workers find themselves unable to enter industrial employment, they may increasingly compete for jobs in the diminishing area of employment unaffected by automation – particularly some parts of the commerce sector and the personal services (jobs like cooking, bartending, hair-dressing, cleaning and so on). Here enterprises are mostly small-scale, barriers to entry are low and labour is mostly non-unionised. As a result, these sectors can quite easily expand their workforces to absorb the unemployed, but this expansion will occur only at the cost of a relative decline in wages. In this way, the traditional dualistic gap between low-paid, unmechanised occupations and the relatively 'elite' group of employed required in highly mechanised sections of the economy is perpetuated.

There are two signs which suggest that this sequence of events is actually occurring in Japan. Firstly, the proportion of workers in very small firms (with fewer than 30 employees) is gradually increasing, while the proportion in large firms is declining (see Table 6.4). Secondly, and most importantly, there is the question of the gap between the wages paid by large firms and those paid by small firms. This gap, which is a sensitive indicator of shortages and surpluses of labour in Japan, narrowed rapidly during the 1960s, as competition for workers during the years of high growth forced small enterprises to raise the starting wages which they offered. The turning point came at the end of the sixties: since then, the wage gap between large and small firms has widened –

Table 6.4. *Employment by Size of Establishment (Non-agricultural), 1974–82 (in thousands)*

Size of Establishment	1974		1982	
1–9 employees	5,383	(16.17%)	7,701	(18.39%)
10–29 employees	4,721	(14.2%)	6,464	(15.4%)
30–99 employees	4,937	(14.8%)	6,382	(15.2%)
100–299 employees	3,475	(10.4%)	4,720	(11.2%)
300–499 employees	9,291	(27.9%)	5,119	(23.4%)

Source: Rōdō-Shō, *Rōdō Keizai no Bunseki 1983*, Statistical Appendix, p. 24

at first slowly, but then with increasing rapidity. In 1975, the average male worker in a firm with 5–29 employees earned 71.1 per cent of the average wage of a male worker in a very large firm (over 500 employees). By 1983, this ratio had fallen to 65.8 per cent. For women workers, the decline was even sharper: from 72.5 per cent in 1975 to 65.6 per cent in 1983 (see Table 6.5).

The secret of Japan's low unemployment levels, then, lies partly in what (for want of a better word) we can call 'positive' factors: the rapid growth of new industries, the relatively slow growth of population and the large number of young people staying on at school or college. But it also lies in two factors which cast something of a shadow over the future: firstly, it is related to the incursions which Japanese high-technology goods have made into world markets; and secondly, it is rooted in a system where unemployment is absorbed by the creation of labour-intensive, low-paid jobs, usually in small enterprises and outside the manufacturing sector. (It is interesting to observe that a somewhat similar 'dualistic' gap appears to be developing in other countries in the climate of rapid technological change.[33])

It can be said, of course, that being forced to find relatively low-paid employment in commerce and services is at least better than being wholly unemployed. On the other hand, though, evidence of the emergence of a 'new dualism' suggests that the information society reports' optimistic visions of a world where work would become increasingly intellectual and fulfilling, and where social divisions and conflicts would be diminished, need to be subjected to some critical scrutiny.

Notes

1 See A. Boltho, *Japan: an Economic Survey*, Oxford, Oxford University Press, 1975, pp. 27–9.
2 T. Nakamura, *The Postwar Japanese Economy*, Tokyo, Tokyo University Press, 1981, p. 156.
3 Sōrifu Tōkei Kyoku, *Nihon no Tōkei* (various years); N. W. Chamberlain and D. E. Cullen, *The Labour Sector*, New York, McGraw-Hill, 2nd edn, 1971, p. 25.
4 Boltho, *Japan: an Economic Survey*, p. 26.
5 See Y. Sugimoto, H. Shimada and S. Levine, *Industrial Relations in Japan*, Melbourne, Japanese Studies Centre, 1982, p. 6.

Table 6.5. *Wage Differentials by Size of Firm, 1970–83 (Average Wages in Firms with over 500 Workers = 100)*

Workers	Average for All Sectors			Construction			Manufacturing			Commerce			Services		
	1970	1975	1983	1970	1975	1983	1970	1975	1983	1970	1975	1983	1970	1975	1983
Men															
Over 500	100.0	100.0	100.0	100.0	100.0	100.0	100.0	100.0	100.0	100.0	100.0	100.0	100.0	100.0	100.0
100–499	88.1	89.5	89.2	84.1	82.3	77.6	88.0	88.0	87.8	66.0	75.5	76.6	93.6	91.8	92.7
30–99	80.3	84.1	79.8	75.2	74.6	61.3	78.2	79.0	75.9	61.9	66.7	60.3	85.4	91.0	84.7
5–29	69.7	71.2	65.8	65.3	67.4	54.4	68.7	70.6	68.0	52.9	58.6	52.4	95.4	70.2	73.8
Women															
Over 500	100.0	100.0	100.0	100.0	100.0	100.0	100.0	100.0	100.0	100.0	100.0	100.0	100.0	100.0	100.0
100–499	86.2	89.5	84.9	76.7	78.1	79.6	82.3	84.9	82.1	84.8	86.1	78.3	91.3	88.7	84.7
30–99	77.9	86.6	78.9	72.2	74.5	65.7	71.5	68.9	66.8	72.2	79.0	64.5	94.4	100.0	89.7
5–29	74.0	72.5	65.5	69.9	71.4	64.2	65.9	61.6	62.0	65.0	69.5	61.6	94.8	74.7	68.3

Source: Nihon Tōkei Nenkan (various years)

103

6 See, for example, J. Abegglen, *Management and Worker: the Japanese Solution*, Tokyo, Sophia University Press, 1973.

7 See K. Taira, 'The Inter-Sectoral Wage Differential in Japan 1881–1959', *Journal of Farm Economics*, xliv, 1962, 322–34.

8 Nihon Ginkō Chōsa Tōkei Kyoku, *Kokusai Hikaku Tōkei*, Tokyo, Nihon Ginkō, 1984, p. 136.

9 Tsūshō Sangyō-Shō, *Denshi Kōgyō Nenkan 1984*, Tokyo, Denpa Shinbun-Sha, 1984, pp. 494 and 514–16. These estimates omit imported equipment.

10 Ibid., p. 278.

11 *Nihon No Tōkei*, 1984, p. 26; Keizai Kikaku-Chō Chōsa Kyoku, *Keizai Yōran*, 1984, p. 178.

12 B. O. Jones, *Sleepers, Wake!*, Oxford and Melbourne, Oxford University Press, 1982, p. 130.

13 See Rōdō Daijin Kanbō Tōkei Jōhō-bu, *Gijutsu Kakushin to Rōdō ni Kansuru Chōsa Hōkuku*, Tokyo, March 1984, p. 32.

14 Ibid., pp. 19 and 29.

15 Hyōgo-Ken Rōdō Keizai Kenkyū Sho, *Sangyō-Yō Robotto no Dōnyū ni Tomonau Koyō e no Eikyō oyobi sono Taiō-Saku no Chōsa Kenkyū Hōkoku-Sho*, Kobe, March 1983; Ōita-Ken Shōkō Rōdō-bu Rōsei-ka: *M.E. Kika Dōnyū Jōkyō Chōsa Hōkoku-Sho*, Ōita, Sept. 1983; Hiroshima-Ken Shōkō Rōdō-bu, *M.E. Kika Dōnyū Jōkyō Chōsa Hōkoku-Sho*, Hiroshima, March 1984; an exception was Aichi-Ken Koyō Kaihatsu Kyōkai's *Koyō Kanri Jittai Chōsa Hōkoku: M.E. Kikai Dōnyū Jōkyō to Koyō e no Eikyō*, Nagoya 1983, whose survey of firms using ME equipment found that more firms reported increases than decreases in employment.

16 See *Nihon no Tōkei 1983*, p. 32.

17 Rōdō-Shō Shokugyō Antei-kyoku: *Shōwa 56-nen Shokugyō Betsu Rōdō Kyoku Jittai Chōsa Kekka Gaiyō: Dai-Kigyō Honsha ni Okeru Ofisu Ōtomēshon to Koyō no Jittai*, Tokyo, Aug. 1982, p. 9; see also Hiroshima-Ken Shōkō Rōdō-bu, *M.E. Kika Dōnyū Jōkyō Chōsa Hōkoku-Sho*, p. 29; Ōita-Ken Shōkō Rōdō-bu Rōsei-ka, *M.E. Kika Dōnyū Jōkyō Chōsa Hōkoku-Sho*, p. 23; Aichi-Ken Rōdō-bu, *OA Kika Dōnyū Jōkyō Chōsa Kekka Hōkoku-sho*, Nagoya, 1983, p. 9.

18 Rōdō Daijin Kanbō Tōkei Jōhō-bu, *Gijutsu Kakushin to Rōdō ni Kansuru Chōsa Hōkoku*, p. 32.

19 Hiroshima-Ken Shōkō Rōdō-bu, *M.E. Kika Dōnyū Jōkyō Chōsa Hōkoku-Sho*, p. 63.

20 Rōdō-Shō, *Shōwa 58-Nen Rōdō Keizai no Bunseki*, Tokyo, Rōdō-Shō, 1984, pp. 41–2.

21 Maikuroerekutoronikusu no Koyō ni Oyobosu Eikyō ni Kansuru Chōsa Kenkyū Iinkai, *Maikuroerekutoronikusu no Koyō ni Oyobosu*

Eikyō ni Tsuite, Tokyo, Koyō Shokugyō Sōgō Kenkū-Sho, April 1984, p. 25.

22   Ibid., loc. cit.

23   *Nihon no Tōkei*, 1984, p. 37.

24   Maikuroerekutoronikusu no Koyō ni Oyobosu Eikyō . . . , *Maikuroerekutoronikusu no Koyō ni Oyobosu Eikyō*, p. 29.

25   See Kamio Kazuya, 'Gijutsu Kakushin to Rōdō Mondai' in Nihon Keizai Chōsa Kyōgi-Kai (ed.), *Fakutorī Ōtomēshon no Shinten to Koyō*, Tokyo, Nihon Keizai Chōsa Kyōgi-Kai, 1984, p. 91.

26   See Maikuroerekutoronikusu no Koyō ni Oyobosu Eikyō . . . , *Maikuroerekutoronikusu* . . . , pp. 28–9.

27   *Denshi Kōgyō Nenkan 1984*, p. 51.

28   Iiboshi Kōichi, 'Koyō: Shin-Gijutsu to no Masatsu' in Namiki Nobuyoshi (ed.), *Gijutsu Kakushin to Sangyō Shakai*, Tokyo, Nihon Keizai Shimbunsha, 1983, p. 278.

29   Sasajima Yoshio, *Nichi-Bei-Ō no Koyō to Shitsugyō*, Tokyo, Tōyō Keizai Shinpōsha, 1984, pp. 146–7.

30   Jones, *Sleepers, Wake!*, p. 130.

31   Sasajima, *Nichi-Bei-Ō no Koyō to Shitsugyō*, p. 148. See also C. Sorrentino, 'Japan's Low Unemployment: an In-Depth Analysis', *Monthly Labour Review*, March 1984, pp. 18–27; K. Taira, 'The Labour Force Survey and Unemployment: a Philosophical Note', *Japanese Economic Studies*, Fall 1985, pp. 3–33; S. Nagayama, 'Is Japan's Unemployment Rate Too Low?' *Japanese Economic Studies*, Fall 1984, pp. 34–61.

32   See Iiboshi Kōichi, 'Koyō: Shin-Gijutsu to no Masatsu', p. 254.

33   Joan Smith, for example, notes a growing gap in the US between certain low-wage service industries (typically dominated by relatively small firms) and other industrial sectors. See Joan Smith, 'The Paradox of Women's Poverty: Wage-Earning Women and Economic Transformation' in Melvyn Dubovsky (ed.), *Technological Change and Workers' Movements*, Beverly Hills and London, Sage Publications, 1985, pp. 211–33.

7 'Informisation' at Work: the Quality of Work in the Information Society

The claim, by proponents of the information society, that '"informisation" will result in the blossoming of intellectual creativity' can be interpreted in two ways. In the first place, we could imagine a situation where the new technologies of the information society neither destroyed old jobs nor created new ones, but simply made the content of existing jobs more intellectual, creative and satisfying. It is this upgrading of the content of work which the information society theorists seem to have in mind when they suggest that 'With the construction of the information communications infrastructure and the diffusion of information equipments, people will spend considerably less time going from place to place, delivering documents and looking for reference material. At the same time, the amount of time used for intellectual activities is expected to increase.'[1]

Secondly, by contrast, we could imagine that information technologies had no impact on existing job specifications, but that they made work more creative by destroying existing routine manual jobs and replacing them with entirely new intellectual, exciting jobs. This change in the structure of employment is implied where the information society reports state that 'With the progress of FA (factory automation), dangerous operations or operations performed under unfavourable working conditions, such as welding and coating, continue to decrease, and simple operations in areas such as processing and assembling are also declining. . . . It is expected that this trend will become even stronger and that there will be an increasing amount of work such as research and development, supervisory management and decision-making, etc.'[2]

In practice, of course, the technological changes occurring in Japan are altering both the content of work and the structure of employment, and these two facets of change are closely intertwined with each other. For practical purposes, though, it is useful, when we attempt to answer the question 'Is work really becoming more creative and fulfilling under information capitalism?' to subdivide it into two questions: first, 'Is the quality of existing work improving?'; and second, 'Are the newly emerging jobs more creative than those which they replace?' I shall try to answer the first question in this chapter and the second in Chapter 8. A final assessment of the quality of employment in Japan's information society can, of course, only be obtained by combining the evidence in both chapters: the fact, for example, that assembly-line production jobs might be becoming more pleasant would hardly be very significant if we also found that assembly-line work was rapidly disappearing.

Automation and Alienation

The question of the impact of computer-based technologies on the quality of work has been the subject of long and impassioned debate both outside and within Japan. An early, optimistic view of the effects of computerisation was popularised in the 1960s by the American sociologist Robert Blauner. Blauner suggested that, while work in assembly-line industries such as the automobile industry was characterised by low levels of skill and high levels of boredom, jobs in the chemicals industry – at that time the most highly automated area of production in the US (and indeed the world) – involved greater responsibility and variety. According to Blauner, this reflected the fact that automation re-integrates the labour process which earlier forms of mechanisation had subdivided. As the worker moves from handling a single machine to supervising the operation of an automated system, 'his perspective shifts from his own individual task to a broader series of operations which includes the work of other employees. . . . His scope of operations also increases. Continuous-process technology thus reverses the historic trend towards the greater division of labor and specialisation.'[3]

From these observations, Blauner went on to suggest a general historical pattern – his famous 'inverted U-curve' – whereby deskilling and alienation increase in the earlier stages of mechanisation, reaching a peak in the assembly-line industries of the mid-twentieth century, but subsequently decline with the introduction of computer-based automation: 'with automated industry there is a countertrend, one that we can fortunately expect to become even more important in the future. . . . The alienation curve begins to decline from its previous height as employees in automated industries gain a new dignity from responsibility and a sense of individual function – thus the inverted U.'[4]

But this cheerful view of the future has not gone unchallenged. Braverman in particular has taken Blauner to task, arguing forcefully that new automation technologies represent a continuation and not a reversal of the historical trend by which work under capitalism has become more fragmented and dehumanised. Braverman (although he also discusses the chemicals industry) concentrates mainly upon the introduction of numerically controlled (NC) equipment in metal fabrication. 'Numerical control' refers to the process whereby the actions of a machine tool are programmed by computer, with the program either being transferred directly from computer to tool or stored on a tape which is then used to control the tool's operation. Braverman shows how the introduction of NC divides the work which was once performed by a single skilled machinist into three distinct parts. Firstly, there is the preparation of a program based on the specifications of the particular job to be performed. Secondly, the program must be transferred on to tape. And thirdly, the machine-tool operation must be started, supervised and stopped.[5]

> The unity of this process in the hands of the skilled machinist [writes Braverman] is perfectly feasible, and indeed has much to recommend it, since the knowledge of metal-cutting practices which is required for programming is already mastered by the machinist. . . . That this almost never happens is due, of course, to the opportunities the process offers for the destruction of craft and the cheapening of the resulting pieces of labor into which it is broken. . . .
> Numerical control is thus used to divide the process among *separate* operatives, each representing far less in terms of training, abilities, and hourly labor costs than does the competent machinist.[6]

According to Braverman, therefore, the promise, held out by automation, of liberation from drudgery and degradation is consistently thwarted by capitalism's desire to increase its control over the minds and bodies of its workers.

> An automatic system of machinery opens up the possibility of the true control over a highly productive factory by a relatively small corps of workers, providing these workers attain the level of mastery over the machinery offered by engineering knowledge, and providing they then share out among themselves the routines of the operation, from the most technically advanced to the most routine. . . . Yet this promise, which has been repeatedly held out with every technical advance since the industrial revolution, is frustrated by the capitalist effort to reconstitute and even deepen the division of labour in all of its worst aspects, despite the fact that this division of labour becomes more archaic with every passing day.[7]

Since the use of computer-based automation equipment in Japan today is so much more widespread than it was in the USA when Blauner and Braverman conducted their research,* it is interesting to review these conflicting views in the light of recent Japanese experience.

Factory Automation and Skill in Japan

On the face of it, the available evidence seems to lend support both to Blauner's optimism and to the rosy predictions of the information society reports. A comprehensive survey of the effects of automation conducted by the Labour Ministry in 1982 found that the main impact of new technology in manufacturing was to increase, rather than reduce, the variety of skills demanded of the worker. This was true (to varying degrees) of firms of all sizes and of all forms of automation. Overall, only 14 per cent of enterprises reported that automation reduced the level of skill required of

---

* Braverman's data is based on evidence from the late 1960s, at which time only 1% of machine tools in use in the USA were numerically controlled. By 1980, 47% of Japanese machinery producers were using NC equipment.[8]

their workforce, while 63 per cent reported that additional new skills were now required (see Table 7.1).

On closer examination, the implications of these figures become more complex. Much confusion in the debate over deskilling arises from the lack of a uniform definition of 'skill'. In the first place, the concept of skill has two distinct aspects: it may mean '*manual dexterity*', but in many cases it also implies the acquisition of the *factual knowledge* needed to perform particular tastes. Secondly, the notion of 'skill' is also socially constructed; that is to say that the labels 'skilled', 'semi-skilled' and 'unskilled' have emerged through a historical process by which certain groups of workers have succeeded in gaining recognition for their particular training and abilities. In this sense, levels of technical or 'objectively

Table 7.1. *Changes in Skills Required of the Workforce in Enterprises Using IC-controlled Equipment (Multiple Answer) (%)*

Size of enterprise	% of firms reporting change in skills	Previous skills are redundant and new skills required	New skills are required in addition to existing skills	A higher level of skill is required	A lower level of skill is required
All enterprises	67.5	(15.1)	(63.1)	(24.2)	(14.2)
Over 1,000 workers	72.2	(15.2)	(71.3)	(26.4)	(14.2)
300–999 workers	68.8	(14.2)	(63.2)	(24.6)	(13.4)
Fewer than 299 workers	65.5	(15.6)	(60.9)	(23.3)	(15.6)
Type of equipment used					
NC equipment	87.2	(16.3)	(73.4)	(20.2)	(10.2)
NC equipment only	85.7	(16.2)	(72.0)	(18.2)	(9.0)
NC + robots	91.0	(16.9)	(77.3)	(22.5)	(11.5)
Robots	75.8	(16.7)	(63.4)	(25.7)	(13.9)
Robots only	69.2	(17.9)	(57.4)	(24.5)	(13.9)
Simple robots	74.9	(15.3)	(63.5)	(26.1)	(14.6)
Simple robots only	67.8	(15.1)	(56.6)	(25.7)	(15.2)
Advanced robots	80.9	(20.3)	(65.2)	(25.3)	(12.3)
Advanced robots only	73.5	(22.3)	(59.6)	(22.6)	(10.5)
Other IC equipment	61.5	(13.5)	(62.3)	(25.4)	(16.2)
Other IC equipment only	55.5	(12.1)	(59.7)	(22.8)	(17.8)
Computer-controlled system	71.6	(16.1)	(62.6)	(28.1)	(13.6)
Computer-controlled system only	67.0	(16.0)	(58.8)	(25.9)	(13.8)

Figures in brackets = responses as % of all enterprises reporting a change in skills required.

Source: Rōdō Daijin Kanbō Tōkei Jōhō-bu, *Gijutsu Kakushin to Rōdō ni Kansuru Chōsa Hōkoku*, Tokyo, 1984, pp. 95–100

defined' skill.[9] Technological change clearly affects both the degree of dexterity and knowledge required to perform a given job and the social recognition of skill. In this chapter, however, I shall focus on examining the impact of information technologies on 'objectively defined' skill rather than upon the social definition of individuals as 'skilled' or 'unskilled'.

In general, the impact of factory automation in Japan has been neither a straightforward 'degradation' nor a straightforward 'upgrading' of work, but rather a twofold process. The importance of manual dexterity and work experience has been reduced, but at the same time, as many writers have observed, there has been a tendency for the scope of factory work to broaden, with workers being involved in a variety of tasks, including machine minding, maintenance, supervision and (sometimes) programming.[10] It is almost impossible to say whether the new (largely mental) skills required are of a higher level than the old, because they are qualitatively quite different. To compare them is like asking whether a shoemaker is more or less skilled than a railway clerk. The contrast is one of depth of knowledge in a single area as against breadth of knowledge of a number of tasks (each of which may be relatively simple in itself). The former involves high levels of manual skill while the latter mainly involves the memorisation of relevant information; or, to put it another way, the former mainly involves *procedural* knowledge (knowledge *how* to do something) while the latter involves a greater amount of *propositional* knowledge (knowledge of facts).

This can be illustrated with an example close to the heart of automation itself: the example of the microchip industry. In the early stages of integrated circuit production, many processes – such as dicing (the cutting of silicon wafers into individual chips) and wire-bonding (the attachment of gold wires linking the chip to its frame) – were performed manually, by workers using microscopes and very accurate cutting or bonding equipment. These tasks, involving intense concentration and a high level of manual dexterity, were normally performed by women workers.

Today, in most Japanese factories, these processes have been automated. The consequences have been both an enormous increase in the productivity of each worker and a radical transformation of the content of their work. In the dicing section of a microchip factory, for example, the workers – perhaps 10 to 15 of them if the factory is a large one – perform a variety of functions:

inserting new wafers in machines, using microscopes to check the position of the wafer in relation to the cutting blade, supervising the operation of several machines, making routine adjustments as needed, and finally collecting the cut chips for transfer to the next stage of manufacture. Like Blauner's chemical workers, but unlike the worker in the unautomated dicing shop, they are not tied to a single machine but move between machines and tasks, obtaining a fairly broad overview of their section of the production process.

A greater integration of tasks, including the repair of machinery, could almost certainly take place, but is stifled by the sexual division of labour. The workers in the dicing shop are still, almost invariably, women, while repair workers are men. In addition to the traditional prejudices against training women in machine repair, management is normally reluctant to spend money on higher levels of technical training for their female workers, because they benefit from the situation where women constitute a fluid labour force, retiring when they marry in their early twenties after about four years of work in the factory. In these circumstances, the levels of skill required for supervision and routine adjustment – involving as they do about one week's off-the-job training and a year's on-the-job training – are the most that management is willing to contemplate for women workers.

Yet even in this restrictive case, automation cannot simply be said to have caused 'deskilling'. Compared with earlier methods, automated dicing certainly requires less manual dexterity, but involves performance of a greater range of tasks and a wider comprehension of manufacturing processes. This pattern seems to be repeated in most (though not quite all) factories when automated equipment is introduced. We can confirm this by looking at a large-scale study of automation and skill conducted by a Japanese research group in 1982. Workers were presented with a list of tasks and asked to mark the ones which they performed in the course of their everyday work. The results for four occupations – machining, welding, electrical assembly and chemicals production – are shown in Table 7.2. In the machine, electrical and chemical industries, workers using automated equipment were more likely to give multiple answers, showing that their work involved a variety of different duties. Not surprisingly, the amount of 'hand-controlled' production work decreased, while supervisory and information processing tasks increased. (We might recall here the case of Masuda Seisakusho, described in Chapter 5, where the

Table 7.2. *The Content of Work of Skilled Operatives in Selected Occupations (Multiple Answer)*

Occupation	No. of workers	Direct production (%)		Supervision of automated equipment (%)	Information processing (%)	Repair/maintenance (%)	Supervision of others (%)	Other (%)	Not available (%)	No. of responses per worker
		Machine-controlled	Manually controlled							
Machinists (using NC equipment)	1,127	52.8	40.9	14.4	13.3	5.3	26.0	0.3	0.4	1.53
Machinists (not using NC equipment)	1,967	45.8	63.2	2.0	1.8	5.7	15.3	0.3	1.0	1.35
Welders (using robots)	84	28.6	45.5	6.3	8.1	2.4	39.3	—	—	1.30
Welders (not using robots)	671	19.6	71.8	0.9	5.3	4.8	24.1	—	4.3	1.31
Electrical assemblers (on automated lines)	816	26.6	28.5	8.9	15.1	12.8	49.4	5.3	0	1.47
Electrical assemblers (on unautomated lines)	2,252	13.7	57.7	1.7	11.7	6.4	31.7	10.3	2.6	1.36
Chemical workers (automated processes)	454	31.5	13.5	53.3	25.9	5.6	22.2	0.2	3.3	1.56
Chemical workers (unautomated processes)	631	32.4	33.6	8.9	12.8	4.7	33.9	1.7	5.5	1.36

Source: Koyō Sokushin Jigyōdan Shokugyō Kunren Kenkyū Sentā, *Mekatoronikusu Jidai no Jinzai Kaihatsu*, p. 160

introduction of robots led to workers being increasingly involved in programming.) Welding, however, was an interesting exception. Here automation did not lead to a greater variety of work, but only to a shift away from manual production towards machine production and supervision.

When, as in the case of welding, automation is not accompanied by a greater variety of tasks, it clearly leads to the degradation of work in the eyes of the worker. Welders using robots were less likely than their colleagues in non-automated plants to regard their work as important or to feel that it developed their skills. By contrast, in automated chemicals plants, where variety was greatest, levels of satisfaction were also relatively high, while in electrical assembly and particularly machining, the effects of automation from the workers' viewpoint appeared ambiguous (see Table 7.3).

The pattern just described, then, is at odds with Braverman's assertion that there is an inherent tendency for capitalism to dissect work into smaller and smaller particles. But it is worth considering whether the assertion itself is wrong, or whether Japanese capitalism is just an exception to the rule. It seems that in some other countries there has been rather more reluctance to integrate operations in the hands of a single worker. Bryn Jones, looking at five machine manufacturers in Britain, found that shop-floor workers were usually involved in the setting and supervision of numerically controlled equipment, but were rarely allowed to adjust the machine's program.[11] In order to enforce this division of labour, British firms were often obliged to make special arrangements which would block the access of factory workers to the tape-editing facilities commonly built into NC equipment. In one case, division was maintained by a sign attached to the editing controls which read, 'In no circumstances must this cabinet be unlocked'.[12] By contrast, over 40 per cent of Japanese firms claimed to entrust some programming to skilled operatives, though in most cases the tasks involved seem to have been minor alterations to programs rather than the overall composition of the software.[13]

The reasons for these differences between Japan and Britain are not entirely clear. The prevalence of craft, rather than company, unionism in Britain seems to play some role, but this is evidently reinforced by the social attitudes of management.[14] British managers appear to be as incapable of imagining that

Table 7.3 *Attitudes of Skilled Operatives to their Work (%)*

Occupation A – Agree D – Disagree N – Neither	'It suits my personality.'			'It develops skill.'			'It is important work.'			'It is simple work.'			'I feel used by the machine.'		
	A	D	N	A	D	N	A	D	N	A	D	N	A	D	N
Machinists (using NC equipment)	46.4	7.1	34.6	49.7	6.0	32.3	63.4	4.5	19.7	16.0	55.7	15.8	8.4	30.3	48.6
Machinists (not using NC equipment)	47.8	8.0	38.4	49.2	10.6	34.3	61.8	6.7	25.6	22.8	51.6	19.8	5.5	20.2	68.0
Welders (using robots)	31.8	11.1	46.4	45.4	8.4	35.5	57.5	2.4	26.9	24.3	43.7	21.3	13.5	36.2	39.6
Welders (not using robots)	48.4	8.0	36.2	50.0	10.3	32.3	65.2	4.6	21.9	25.4	47.9	19.2	3.1	20.6	68.1
Electrical assemblers (on automated lines)	46.0	11.0	32.8	52.3	12.2	25.3	73.0	4.7	12.1	16.5	55.7	17.6	8.7	25.0	55.7
Electrical assemblers (on unautomated lines)	45.5	8.3	35.8	45.1	10.9	33.4	61.0	8.2	19.4	19.8	51.1	18.2	1.6	10.1	75.1
Chemical workers (automated processes)	50.8	5.2	31.1	51.0	2.5	33.6	61.5	6.6	18.4	16.1	55.9	15.2	6.0	24.5	55.2
Chemical workers (unautomated processes)	37.7	12.9	44.8	40.8	14.7	38.6	55.1	11.4	26.8	29.1	52.3	13.5	6.2	17.2	69.6

Source: Koyō Sokushin Jigyōdan Shokugyō Sentā: Mekatoronikusu Jidai No Jinzai Kaihatsu, Tokyo, 1983, pp. 178–9

factory workers might be able to write programs as their Japanese counterparts are of believing that women workers can repair machines.

Braverman is almost certainly right when he says that automation offers the technological potential for a great reintegration of tasks, but that this potential is blocked by management's desire to promote social divisions (or sometimes simply by their inability to overcome traditional social prejudices). However, this blocking process does not go as far as Braverman believes. As he himself points out, there are sound financial reasons why management should wish to use the experience of their skilled workers in the supervision, maintenance and even programming of equipment. As the number of workers on the shop floor shrinks, it begins to make good sense for the company to encourage a certain diversification of the tasks performed by the few who remain. Shortages of specialist maintenance and programming skills may also encourage this trend. When managers balance these financial factors against the advantages, for example, of exploiting a cheap and fluid workforce, the result is normally a partial reintegration of tasks, within which factory work becomes broader and more varied in scope without the workers actually impinging on those higher-level technical or decision-making tasks which remain in the hands of the 'professional'.

Skill, Automation and White-Collar Work

Meanwhile, what is happening to the work of the technical and white-collar workers themselves? Left-wing writers in Japan have interpreted the evidence that we have just examined in two ways. Some have argued that, although a growing number of manual workers are now performing supervisory, maintenance and pro-gramming tasks, the new skills involved in these tasks are really no substitute for the old skills required of the experienced machinist. The production and editing of programs, for example, has become so simple that it can be learned without a high level of specialised knowledge. So, although automation may make factory jobs more varied, it also makes them less demanding in terms of expertise, and opens up a widening gap between the factory worker, whose technical knowledge is shallow and limited, and the highly skilled cohort of workers engaged in design, research and decision making.[15]

An alternative view, however, suggests that, while manual work is being 'upgraded', technical work is being 'deskilled'. The development of structured programming, for example, has made computer software production less creative and intellectually demanding, while the working conditions of computer programmers are little better (and sometimes worse) than those of factory workers. The result, it is said, will be the merging of the skilled manual workforce with technicians and clerical workers to form a large 'new class' of semi-technical workers.[16]

Here I shall distinguish among three groups within the workforce. Firstly, there are the manual workers who are engaged in the physical production of goods. Secondly, there are the managers, designers, researchers and so on. Their work is not only 'white collar' but also usually involves various elements which are not readily replicable by computers. These include the making of value judgements and, particularly in the case of research workers, the sorts of 'intuitive leaps' which are usually associated with human imagination and creativity. Whatever the future capabilities of artificial intelligence, the fact remains that neither of these tasks can at present be performed by a machine.

The third category of workers consists of those who support the activities of the managerial and technical group by performing work involving routine tasks of memory and logic: filing clerks, accounts clerks, typists and so on. Computer software workers are in fact divided between groups two and three. Those responsible for the planning and overall design of programs would fall into the former category; coders and key punchers into the latter. The progress of automation seems to be leading to a degree of convergence between groups one and three, while in some ways amplifying the divisions between these workers and the people in group two.

As far as the factory is concerned, we have seen how automation replaces the single craft skill with a variety of relatively simple mental skills. This brings factory work closer to the traditional model of office work, which has usually been characterised both by a relatively wide range of duties and by the use of memory rather than manual skills. The typical Japanese 'office lady', for example, is expected to perform filing, answer the telephone, deliver messages and, inevitably, serve tea to the boss.

But, while factory work becomes more like office work, I believe that automation is making routine office work more like factory work. This is a little difficult to document, because most of the major studies conducted in Japan have attempted to reach conclusions about the impact of office automation as a whole. This has involved lumping together the effects of many varieties of automation equipment (such as mainframe, mini and microcomputers, word-processors and facsimile machines) on many different types of employees (managers, research and design workers, clerks, secretaries and others). For example, the survey of office automation conducted by the Labour Ministry in 1983 covered *all* categories of employees in the head offices of some 6,000 companies.[17]

Its results, however, have some interesting features. Women were found to be more likely to use office automation equipment than men. The only exceptions were in the use of mainframe and personal computers, which were more often the preserve of men.[18]

(a) Workers answering that work had become more pleasant (31·5% of total): reasons given.

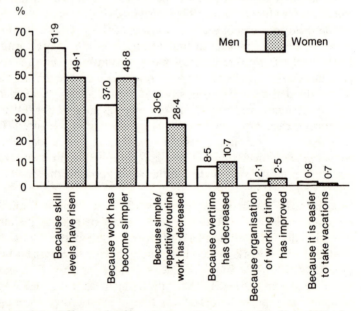

Figure 7.1. *Effects of Office Automation on the Quality of Work*

(b) Workers answering that work had become harder
(18·6% of total):   reasons given.

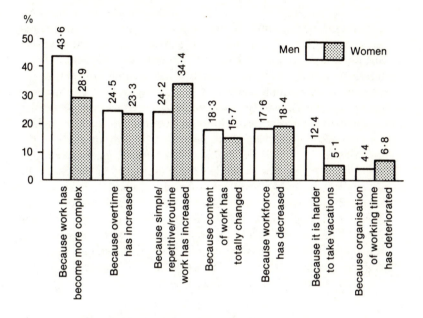

Source: M.E. – ka to Rōdō Kenkyu-kai Tokyo Rōdō–Shō,
1984, p.53 (unpublished report by Ministry of Labour)

When questioned about the impact of automation on the quality of their work, 32 per cent of all employees said that it had become 'more pleasant' (*raku ni natta*) and 19 per cent that it had become 'harder' (*kitsuku natta*), but within these answers again significant sex differences emerged. Most male workers felt that their work had become more enjoyable because the level of skill involved had increased, but women workers were almost equally divided between those who felt that their work had become more skilled and those who, on the contrary, replied that it was more pleasant precisely because it was now *simpler*. (One is inclined to believe that the authors of the questionnaire may have made deliberate use, in framing this question, of the ambiguity of the Japanese word '*raku*', which can mean either 'pleasant' or 'easy'.) Among those who felt that work had become harder, the division was even more distinct. For men, the main complaint was that the content of their jobs had become increasingly complex; for women, on the contrary, that 'simple, repetitive and routine work had increased' (see Figure 7.1).

The implications of this discussion are clear. Women in offices are predominantly employed as clerks or secretaries, while managerial and technical posts are mostly staffed by men. Male workers are far more likely than female workers to use computers in an interactive way, while the function of women in relation to computers is predominantly that of entering data.[19] The findings of the Labour Ministry's survey point to the conclusion that office automation provides mechanised support for the work of higher-ranking office employees, but alters the very core of many of the lower-status office jobs, making tasks more mechanised and routine. In other words, while factory automation increases the variety of the work performed, office automation narrows the scope of lower-status white-collar jobs, and ties the worker more closely to a single machine. This is not surprising, since the whole focus of the current revolution in information technology is upon the integration of many tasks into a single machine. Thus the computer communications network little by little takes over the functions of the pen, typewriter, telephone, telex, filing cabinet and so on.

Consequently, the most common effect of office automation on women workers in Japan is to transform them from general office workers into specialist keyboard operation (most often involved in word-processing).[20] A survey by the Electrical Workers Union (*Denki Rōren*), which confirms this trend, calls it the transformation of the 'Office Lady' (OL) into the 'Tekuno Lady' (TL).[21] This impact of office automation is even more pronounced in Japan than in other countries, because Japanese offices, before the advent of the word-processor, made relatively little use of typewriters and relied heavily on handwritten documents. (The Japanese-language typewriter was a monster which demanded great skill from its operator.) The introduction of the word-processor, therefore, has brought about, in less than a decade, a transformation of office work which in other countries has been occurring gradually over almost a century.

The way in which this transformation typically occurs is illustrated by the following example of an office worker in a subcontracting company making electrical components.

She entered the company in 1975. She was assigned to general office work, where her duties involved receiving telephone calls from customers and salesmen, making out sales bills and typing. But in 1977, her third year in the company, an online computer system with video display terminals (VDTs) was introduced, and she became an operator. An operator works mostly at a terminal, following the screen with her eyes and pressing keys with both hands. This work took up 70% of the working day, and sometimes continued for as long as six hours at a stretch.[22]

The more routine areas of computer software production have suffered in a similar way. The shift from the punched card system to the use of VDTs has meant that the pattern of work is determined by the machine rather than the programmer. Under the earlier system, because each stage of programming (the construction of flow charts, coding, editing and so on) was a self-contained one, the workers could divide their time among the tasks as they thought best. But with the VDT, as one programmer describes it: 'there are many pauses while you wait for the computer's response, but generally the waiting time is too short to allow you to get on with other tasks, so all you can do is wait. A work rhythm of "waiting-activity-waiting" is imposed by the system.'[23]

A detailed study of office automation in a single enterprise (NEC's Tamagawa plant) concluded that it had influenced women's work in the following ways:

1 All women workers, without distinction between general office workers and typists, became keyboard operators.

2 The number of women who spent all day operating word-processors and terminals increased.

3 As a result, general office workers began to perform work which gave rise to occupational health problems.

4 The number of people complaining of poor health because of chronic shoulder pains, tired eyes, nervous stress and ill health caused by air-conditioning systems increased.

5 In the case of women workers, when appointed to work on word-processors and terminals, they were simply given the operating manual and did not receive any training. This

policy of letting them learn as they performed their work was described as 'on-the-job training'.[24]

These cases force a reconsideration of the prediction of the information society reports that 'people will spend less time going from place to place, delivering documents and looking for reference material'. The people who traditionally performed these tasks were clerical and secretarial workers. When the storage and retrieval of documents is transferred on to a computer, the result is not to give these workers more time to perform 'intellectual activities' such as conducting scientific research or making decisions on company policy. Instead, the effect is to increase the productivity of their clerical work. The people whose intellectual activities benefit from this greater productivity are the managers and technicians whose needs the clerical workforce serves.

As in the case of factory work, it is misleading to describe the changes we have looked at either as 'deskilling' or as 'upgrading' the work process. The operation of computer terminals certainly involves new skills or knowledge whose acquisition, in the early stages, can sometimes be interesting and challenging, but these skills are wholly related to a single piece of equipment, and work therefore becomes less varied, more sedentary and more repetitive.

The examples cited here also touch on an aspect of automation which has probably aroused more concern among white-collar workers and unionists in Japan than any other: the issue of occupational health. While factory automation has undoubtedly reduced some forms of dangerous work, computerisation in the office has created new health hazards. A survey of VDT-users conducted by the national trade-union federation Sōhyō in 1984 found that more than 75 per cent suffered from eye-strain and 50 per cent from shoulder pains. In the case of women workers (who were more likely than men to spend prolonged periods at the terminal), the percentage complaining of eye-strain rose to just under 85 per cent.[25] The story of the office worker quoted on page 121 ends with her being moved to another job, at trade-union insistence, after suffering severe neck and shoulder problems.[26]

The Japanese trade-union movement has for some time been lobbying for restrictions on the periods of time which workers are allowed to spend at terminals. But at the same time (as we shall see in Chapter 8) companies are increasingly using part-time workers and agency staff to fill office jobs. This preference for part-timers will almost certainly increase if restrictions on terminal use are imposed, and the result will be, not greater variety in office work, but a greater number of workers performing monotonous work for a shorter number of hours (and for relatively low pay).

If the 'intellectual creativity' which the information society theorists promise us is to be found anywhere, it is surely in the higher-status technical, professional and managerial jobs. As far as these occupations are concerned, computerisation appears to bring systematisation but not necessarily deskilling. To illustrate this, we can take the example of the research department of any major enterprise. As competitive pressures for the production of new knowledge grow, so does the size of the research department, while computer-communications networks are increasingly introduced to enhance the productivity of the research workers.[27] Using these networks, researchers can readily communicate with other sections of the enterprise, and can tap data-bases which give them rapid access to existing knowledge in their area of research. This increases the time available for creative work, but simultaneously imposes certain restraints on the way in which research is carried out. In order for the enterprise to make the most efficient use of its computer-communications network, it is necessary for the researchers to provide regular reports of their findings, and to present these findings according to a specified format, which will make it easy for the report to be filed in the computer system.[28] All of this undermines the autonomy which has been regarded as the characteristic of the scientist. Computer systems, by improving communications between researchers within and outside the enterprise, make it easier to increase the division of labour in the production of scientific knowledge. This tendency is accentuated by the growing complexity of that knowledge, which forces researchers to concentrate their work in even narrower and more restricted fields. The scientific worker, therefore, becomes less and less an autonomous professional, and more and more a part of a knowledge-producing system whose total dimensions he or she is unlikely to comprehend.

As far as skill is concerned, however, there is little evidence of the degradation of managerial, planning or scientific work. On the contrary, the forces of competition demand higher and higher levels of knowledge from those in creative or decision-making occupations. This is reflected in the awareness of male office workers that their jobs are becoming more complex and more demanding (see Figure 7.1).

The essence of computerisation then, is that it makes possible the integration of a variety of control, memory and logic functions into the single machine. In the case of the factory, the tasks which are integrated by the computer are ones which were previously allotted to separate groups within the workforce. When automation puts these tasks together again, the individual workers find that the scope and variety of their work has increased. In the office, on the contrary, the various tasks subsumed in the computer were in the past commonly performed by a single individual – the secretary or clerical worker. For these workers, therefore, computerisation reduces variety and increases monotony. The overall effect is a convergence of factory and office work towards a single pattern of 'information transfer' or 'semi-skilled computer work', and a widening gap between the 'semi-skilled computer worker' and those in jobs whose creative and decision-making functions cannot yet be taken over by the machine.

It would be nice to be able to conclude that the growing similarities between the content of factory and lower-status white-collar work could provide the foundations for a stronger workers' movement linking both groups. This seems doubtful, however, because, although the nature of their work becomes more similar, a variety of organisational factors are weakening the potential for cooperation based on common work experiences. It is these factors that we shall consider in the following chapters.

Notes

1 Social Policy Bureau, Economic Planning Agency, *The Information Society and Human Life*, Tokyo, Economic Planning Agency, 1983, p. 33.
2 Ibid., p. 18.
3 R. Blauner, *Alienation and Freedom: the Factory Worker and His Industry*, Chicago, University of Chicago Press, 1964, p. 143.
4 Ibid., p. 182.
5 H. Braverman, *Labour and Monopoly Capital: the Degradation of Work in the Twentieth Century*, New York and London, Monthly Review Press, 1974, ch. 9.
6 Ibid., pp. 199–200. (Italics in original.)

7 Ibid., p. 230.
8 Ibid., p. 198; and 'Facts and Figures (2): NC Machines and the Machinery and Equipment Industry' in K. Ikehata *et al.*, *Industrial Robots: Their Increasing Use and Impact*, Tokyo, Foreign Press Center, 1982.
9 See, for example, Charles More, *Skill and the English Working Class, 1870–1914*, London, Croom Helm, 1980, pp. 15–18.
10 Itō Minoru, 'Mekatoronikusu-ka no Shinten to Shokuba Kōzō no Henka', *Nihon Rōdō Kyōkai Zasshi*, No. 294, Oct. 1983.
11 Bryn Jones, 'Destruction or Redistribution of Engineering Skills? the Case of Numerical Control' in Stephen Wood (ed.), *The Degradation of Work? Skill, Deskilling and the Labour Process*, London, Hutchinson, 1982, pp. 179–200.
12 Ibid., p. 195.
13 Koyō Sokushin Jigyōdan Shokugyō Kunren Kenkyū Sentā (ed.), *Mekatoronikusu Jidai no Jinzai Kaihatsu*, Tokyo, Ōkura-Shō, 1983, pp. 49–50.
14 Jones, 'Destruction or Redistribution of Engineering Skills? the Case of Numerical Control', p. 198.
15 Aomi Tsukasa, 'Ōtomēshon to Rōdō no Mirai', *Yūbutsuron Kenkyū*, No. 10, April 1984, 81–93.
16 Ōmori Nobuyuki and Hiroe Akira, 'Maikuroerekutoronikusu-ka no Shinten to Rōdō no Shitsu', *Tōkyō Gakugei Daigaku Kiyō*, Dec. 1984, 47–64.
17 This report, *Shōwa-58-nendo Gijutsu Kakushin to Rōdō ni Kansuru Chōsa*, is summarised in an unpublished report, *'M.E.-ka to Rōdō' Kenkyu-kai*, Tokyo, Rōdō-Sho, 1984.
18 Ibid., p. 24.
19 Sōhyō Maikon Chōsa Iinkai (ed.), *Mushibamareru Karada to Kokoro: VDT Rōdō to Kenkō Chōsa* (Interim Report), Tokyo, Sōhyō Maikon Chōsa Iinkai, 1984, p. 21.
20 See *'M.E.-ka to Rōdō' Kenkyū-kai*, p. 35.
21 See Shimoda Hirotsugi, *Tekuno Shindorōmu*, Tokyo, TBS Britanica, 1984, p. 38.
22 Kompyūtā to Josei Rōdōsha o Kangaeru Kai, 'OA Kakumei Ka no Josei Rōdōsha', *Keizai Hyōron*, 25 June 1983, 176–83. The quotation is from p. 177.
23 Nakamura Hiroshi, 'Sofutoueā – Shintō Suru Shisutemuka no Naka de' in ibid., pp. 152–3. The quotation is from p. 153.
24 Kompyūtā to Josei Rōdōsha o Kangaeru Kai (ed.), *ME Kakumei to Josei Rōdōsha*, Tokyo, Gendai Shokan, 1983, pp. 16–17.
25 Sōhyō Maikon Chōsa Iinkai, *Mushibamareru Karada to Kokoro: VDT Rōdō to Kenkō Chōsa*, pp. 102 and 109.
26 'OA Kakumei Ka no Josei Rōdōsha', p. 177.

27 See, for example, the description of the 'Research Information Processing System' in Tsukuba's 'science city', given in Katō Hideyuki, *Fujitsu no OA Senryaku*, Tokyo, Aoba Shuppan, 1982, pp. 216–28.
28 Kagaku Gijutsu-Chō (ed.), *Kigyō to Jōhō Katsudō*, Ōkura shō Insatsu Kyoku 1983, pp. 80–81.

8 More Intellectual Work? The Structure of Employment in the Information Society

One of the most widely accepted generalisations about the post-industrial or information society is that a growing share of its workforce will be employed not in farming or industry, but in the 'tertiary' sector. It is clearly true that tertiary employment has been expanding in many advanced economies of the second half of the twentieth century. But, as this trend has progressed, so it has become increasingly evident that the very idea of a tertiary sector containing everything other than farming, mining and manufacturing is too vague to be of much use in modern society. In response to this realisation, various writers have attempted to reclassify the employment structure in ways which would make better sense of contemporary occupational categories.

Perhaps the most influential of these redefinitions was the one proposed by Marc Porat in the first section of his nine-volume report, *The Information Economy* (published in 1977).[1] Porat suggested that, alongside the agricultural, industrial and service sectors, one could distinguish an 'information sector', which was concerned with the processing and provision of knowledge. While he recognised that *all* work involves the use of information in one form or another, he argued that the information sector could be seen as encompassing all workers whose incomes 'originate *primarily* in the manipulation of symbols and information'.[2] These include knowledge producers (such as researchers and scientists), knowledge distributors (for example, teachers and journalists), market search and coordination specialists (including managers and advertising agents), information processors (such as accounts clerks and bank tellers) and information machine workers (for instance, printers and computer operators). Workers who were mainly concerned with the distribution of goods, or with the provision of services other than information, were classified as being in the service sector.

Using this analysis, Porat was able to show that the proportion of the US workforce employed in the information sector had risen from about 15 per cent at the beginning of the twentieth century to almost 50 per cent by the 1970s.[3] Porat's analysis has been influential in Japan (where the first volume of *The Information Economy* was published in 1982)[4] and elsewhere has encouraged other writers to suggest further refinements to his four-sector scheme.[5]

The Information Sector in Japan

If we apply Porat's rather broad concept of an information sector to the contemporary Japanese economy, it seems clear that Japan is indeed rapidly becoming an information society (see Figure 8.1). Between 1977 and 1982, the percentage of the workforce employed in agriculture and industry fell, while the percentage employed in services rose only slightly. But by far the most rapid increase occurred in the information sector, which, in 1982, employed one in every three workers in Japan. Although this is lower than the comparable figure for the United States, it nevertheless makes the information sector the largest area of employment in Japan.

The problem is, of course, that Porat's idea of an 'information sector' is simply concerned with assessing the economic importance of the creation, manipulation and transmission of information. Porat is not trying to convey anything about the intellectual context of work itself, and his category therefore includes some jobs which could readily be classified as intellectual and creative (research and design, for example) and others (such as keypunching and newspaper delivery) to which those adjectives could only be applied with a considerable stretch of the imagination.

In fact, as soon as we attempt to assess the information society theorists' claims that the number of intellectually creative occupations will increase, it becomes evident that the notion of creativity is an extremely difficult and tenuous one, and that the creativity of a particular job may depend upon a whole range of

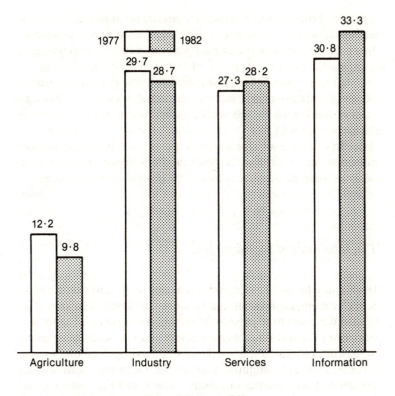

Source: Statistics Bureau, Prime Minister's Office,
Employment Status Survey, 1977 and 1982

Figure 8.1. *Changes in Japan's Employment Structure, 1977–82
(%) (View I)*

factors which are not necessarily evident from the job's written
specifications. While recognising these problems, though, the
adaptation of Porat's analysis can provide a somewhat clearer
indication of the changing role of intellectual work in a complex
society like that of Japan.

When we consider the production and distribution of material
goods, it is obvious that some people are mainly involved in the
making of goods, while others are mainly involved in their *transfer*
(that is, in the movement of goods from one place to another, or
in the transfer of goods from the ownership of one person to
another). In the case of information, the situation is more complex.

The production of information itself involves communication. (An idea which is not communicated to anyone does not constitute information in the normal meaning of the word.) Consequently, the production and the transfer of information cannot be wholly separated from each other. But it is, I believe, generally possible to distinguish jobs which involve a substantial degree of knowledge creation from jobs which are predominantly concerned with information transfer.

For the purposes of this analysis, we can say that 'information production' means combining existing data in new ways: as, for example, when an architect creates the design for a new building; a journalist compiles snippets of information, derived from various sources, into a news story; or a teacher takes data from various textbooks and combines them to make a lesson suitable for ten-year-olds. By contrast, 'information transfer' means the conveying of information from one person, place or medium to another, without altering its content. The distinction can be clearly seen when we compare the manager who dictates a letter (thus creating information, in however simple a form) with the secretary who takes down the letter in shorthand and then types it out (thus transferring the information from spoken to written form without adding to or subtracting from the message which it contains). An even more obvious example would be the contrast between the journalists who write the article in a newspaper, and the girls or boys who deliver the papers from door to door (and who also comprise part of Porat's information sector).

Using these definitions, we can then make an approximate division between those occupations where more than half of the working day is involved in information production, and those where more than half is devoted to information transfer. In the first category I have placed most managerial and technical occupations, though I recognise that in some cases this classification may be controversial; the more routine areas of technical work in the software industry, for example, involve a large element of information transfer, while medical technicians might be regarded as 'personal service workers' rather than 'information producers'. The second category involves employees in the communications industry (such as postal workers and telephonists), workers involved in the selling of insurance and financial services, and, most importantly, clerical and secretarial workers.

If we examine the Japanese workforce in the light of these

distinctions, and also separate jobs concerned with the transfer of goods from those involving the supply of intangible services, some interesting results emerge (see Figure 8.2). The number of jobs involving information transfer has traditionally been large in relation to the number involving information production. This reflects the fact that information (unlike material goods) only needs to be produced once. Once produced, it can then be repeatedly copied and transferred until it reaches every corner of its potential market. In the case of a newspaper, for example, a large number of people are required to print, package and distribute the paper, but a much smaller number to produce the information which it contains. So our Japanese 'information sector' turns out, on closer examination, to consist predominantly of jobs involved in information transfer, which account for about 20 per

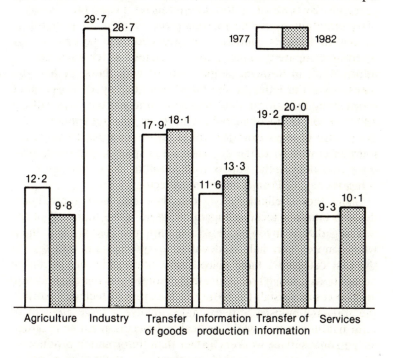

1977 ☐ ▨ 1982

Agriculture	Industry	Transfer of goods	Information production	Transfer of information	Services
12·2	29·7	17·9	11·6	19·2	9·3
9·8	28·7	18·1	13·3	20·0	10·1

Source: Statistics Bureau, Prime Minister's Office,
Employment Status Survey, 1977 and 1982

Figure 8.2. *Changes in Japan's Employment Structure, 1977–82 (%) (View II)*

cent of the whole workforce, while only about 13 per cent of workers in 1982 could be placed in the 'information-producing' category.

Employment in information production is growing more rapidly than employment in information transfer, presumably because the latter category of work has proved more susceptible to computer-based automation than the former. Future developments in technology, such as voice-operated processors and natural language computing, are likely to increase this tendency, making it easier for knowledge, once produced, to be instantly and automatically disseminated and reproduced. The Japan Economic Research Centre's predictions of future trends in the workforce suggest that employment in information-transfer occupations will begin to decline as a percentage of all employment towards the end of the century.[6] On the other hand, as we saw in the previous chapter, there is a tendency for automation to turn many manufacturing jobs into 'information-transfer' jobs – where the main tasks performed are the entering of programs, the reading of dials and so on. The trends recorded by the official employment statistics may therefore conceal the fact that a very substantial, and perhaps growing, percentage of the workforce are performing work which can best be described as 'routine information transfer'. In this sense, indeed, official statistics based on traditional sectoral divisions may come to tell us less and less about the real divisions of the content of work.

Knowledge-producing jobs, though some may be affected by computerisation (particularly by the spread of expert systems), are likely to continue to increase in both absolute and relative terms. But, even so, it is important to bear in mind that no more than 15–18 per cent of the Japanese workforce is likely to be engaged in these occupations by the year 2000.

This discussion gives a rather more sober perspective to the image of work in the information society. Potentially creative work, though expanding, will remain the preserve of the few. The mass of the paid workforce will continue to be employed in the production and distribution of goods, or the transfer of information, and, although technological change will lead to increasing convergence in the content of work in these sectors, the newly emerging patterns of work are likely to be as devoid of potential for personal self-expression as the old.

Besides the small information-producing sector, the only area of employment which shows much potential for growth in information capitalism is the 'intangible service' sector. This consists mainly of personal or office services: office cleaning and work in restaurants and bars accounts for much of the growth in the sector between 1977 and 1982. In a sense, however, the growth of personal service employment in Japan is an illusion. What is really happening is, not so much that service work is increasing, but rather that it is being transferred from the unpaid realm of the household to the realm of the paid workforce: a phenomenon widely discussed in Japan, and referred to as the 'externalisation' (*gaibu-ka*) or 'marketisation' (*shijōka*) of household services.[7] If we regard the unpaid providers of household services as 'workers', our picture of the workforce in the information society changes dramatically (see Figure 8.3). It is now clear that by far the largest percentage of adult working people in Japan are engaged in the provision of personal services, mostly within the household, but that this percentage is falling slightly, probably because the shift of service provision from the household to the commercial marketplace results in increases in productivity. Goods production, transfer of information and transfer of goods account for around 23 per cent, 16 per cent and 14 per cent of the workforce respectively, whereas information production accounts only for about 10 per cent.

Central and Peripheral Employment

This latter view of the Japanese workforce is important because it helps to bring into focus a very important change which is occurring in the structure of work: a change which has been less thoroughly analysed than the familiar shift from industrial to tertiary or information employment.

When we talk about 'work' in a modern industrial society, the word tends to convey certain implicit assumptions. Work, unless otherwise specified, means paid work, work performed for a wage. It also commonly means 'employment' in the sense of working for another person or organisation, typically a private enterprise. In addition, 'work' has come to be associated with a 'job' or 'trade', the lifelong occupation which defines the social status and even the personal self-image of the worker. We ask people, 'What do

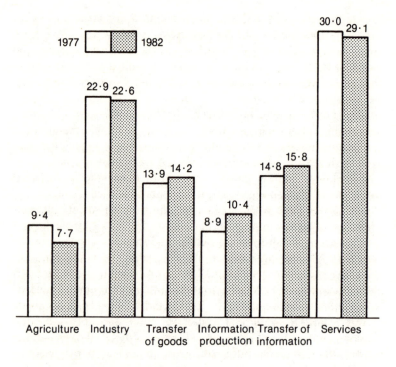

Source: Statistics Bureau, Prime Minister's Office,
Employment Status Survey, 1977 and 1982
and Nihon no Tōkei, 1983

Figure 8.3. *Changes in Japan's Employment Structure, 1977–82 (%) (View III)*

you do?' (meaning, 'What sort of paid work do you do?') and use the answer as a basis for making assumptions about the social life and interests of the person we are talking to. (According to anthropological mythology, Japanese workers normally respond to this question by saying, 'I work for X company', but I have never yet discovered anyone who has tested the truth of this particular piece of folklore.)

Regular paid employees can be seen as forming the core of the labour force in advanced industrial societies. They are the workers on whom the system directly depends for its profit-making and growth. But it also depends, indirectly but no less crucially, upon an 'outer circle' of other workers: self-employed people, those who perform unpaid work as parents and housewives, part-time and contract workers, and the unemployed.[8] This outer circle not only provides various goods and services vital to the survival of the inner circle, but also gives the labour market a flexibility which is essential to corporations when their demand for workers expands or contracts.

In the evolution from industrial capitalism to information capitalism, changes occur not only in the occupational structure but also in the relationship between the core and the periphery of the workforce. These changes seem to be similar in all countries where information capitalism is emerging, but in Japan, because of the speed of transformation, they are particularly clearly visible.

During the 1960s, the patterns of change in Japan's workforce were typical of an industrialising country (see Figure 8.4). The central core of employees expanded rapidly, while the outer periphery of self-employed, unpaid, part-time and unemployed workers contracted. This mainly reflected the movement of self- or family-employed small farmers, fishers and tradespeople into modern industrial employment. At the same time, a shift occurred in the composition of the periphery: men moved from self-employment into the core workforce; women moved from employment in the family enterprise (farm, shop and so on) to full-time housework.

Since 1970, however, and particularly since the mid 1970s, the pattern has altered. The central core of employees is no longer expanding rapidly. Indeed, between 1977 and 1982 it showed virtually no change at all. The main growth came in the percentage of unemployed and part-time workers. Meanwhile, the increase in the number of unpaid houseworkers has been reversed. These two phenomena are, in fact, connected. To put it in very simplified terms, during the period of rapid industrialisation, the corporate sector expanded by drawing the pool of (mostly male) self-employed agricultural workers into its full-time workforce. In the phase of 'informisation', it has expanded instead by absorbing the pool of (mostly female) unpaid houseworkers into part-time, temporary and contract employment.

Part-time Work

Why are increasing numbers of women going into part-time work,

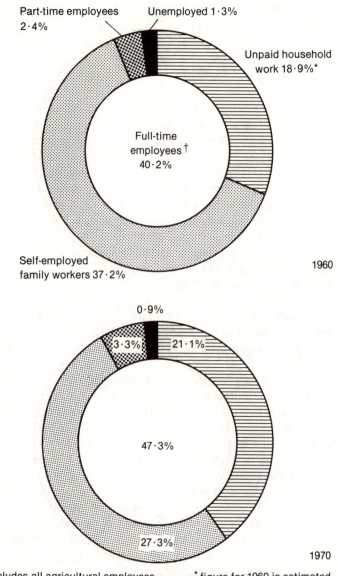

Part-time employees
2·4%

Unemployed 1·3%

Unpaid household
work 18·9%*

Full-time
employees †
40·2%

Self-employed
family workers 37·2%

1960

0·9%

3·3%

21·1%

47·3%

27·3%

1970

† includes all agricultural employees.   * figure for 1960 is estimated.

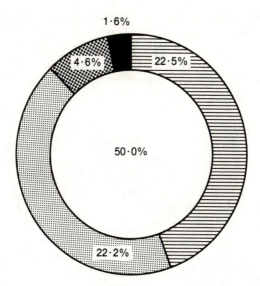

1977

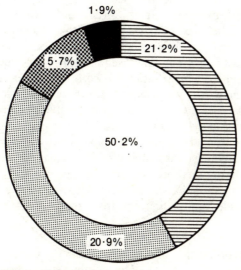

1982

Source: <u>Rōdōryoku Chōsa</u> (various years)

Figure 8.4. *Japan's Changing Employment Structure*

and what connection (if any) does this trend have with the technological changes which are the subject of this book? Many discussions of the issue place primary emphasis on supply factors; that is, on the motives which induce women to seek part-time paid employment. Takeuchi Hiroshi of the Long-Term Credit Bank of Japan, for example, writes:

> Women who have raised their children to a certain stage find that they have time to do something meaningful outside the home. By so doing they find something to live for. Naturally, they are eager to earn as much money as possible, but full-time employment is not consistent with the demands of housekeeping. They therefore have to accept part-time jobs that are generally lower-paying.[9]

Changing population patterns, it is often pointed out, mean that married women now commonly complete their childbearing at a relatively early age. At the same time, the desire for home ownership and for a good education for the children places heavy burdens on parents in their thirties and forties. Labour-saving devices are believed by some writers to have reduced the amount of time which must be devoted to housework.[10] The combination of these factors is frequently used to explain the growing tendency for married women to return to work once their children are at school. The particular propensity for these women to take up part-time work is usually attributed (as in the quotation from Takeuchi) to the fact that these women must combine paid employment with unpaid household duties. But some writers also associate part-time employment with alterations in Japanese cultural values. While working men are beginning to spend a greater amount of time with their families, women are seen as entering the workplace with attitudes quite different from those of their male fellow-employees:

> A large proportion of employed women today are married and work part time. . . . The women's obvious motive for working is to supplement the family budget, and they have little sense of the workplace as a quasi community. The family is clearly their primary group, and no conflict of loyalties arises because superiors and co-workers accept that the family is their priority. . . . The workplace attitudes of

young working women who are unmarried or have not yet had their first child are similar to those of married part-timers. Although these younger women have few or no family obligations, their private life comes first, and they work only to the extent that it does not conflict with their private concerns.[11]

There is no doubt that some 'supply side' considerations, such as changing patterns of childbearing and changing consumer expectations, are important. But a closer look at the realities of work in Japan raises doubts about the assumption that the growth of part-time employment is primarily a response to the desire of women for short working hours. Part-time work has, of course, been expanding in most industrialised countries during the past two decades. In fact, the proportion of part-time workers in Japan, although increasing rapidly, is still lower than in many of Japan's major trading partners. In 1983, 10.5 per cent of the total workforce and 21.1 per cent of women workers were employed on a part-time basis – that is, for less than 35 hours per week – (see Table 8.1). By comparison, 20.8 per cent of all workers in the

Table 8.1. *Trends in the Number of Part-Time Workers (Excluding Agriculture)*

Year	Both Sexes			Women		
	Total no. of employed (a)	Part-timers* (b)	$\frac{b}{a} \times 100$	Total no. of employed (a)	Part-timers* (b)	$\frac{b}{a} \times 100$
	(1,000)	(1,000)	(e)	(1,000)	(1,000)	(e)
1960	21,060	1,330	6.3	6,390	570	8.9
1965	27,170	1,780	6.6	8,510	820	9.6
1970	32,220	2,160	6.7	10,680	1,300	12.2
1975	35,560	3,530	9.9	11,370	1,980	17.4
1976	36,230	3,140	8.7	11,740	1,920	16.4
1977	36,820	3,210	8.7	12,210	2,030	16.6
1978	37,150	3,300	8.9	12,510	2,150	17.2
1979	37,930	3,660	9.6	12,800	2,360	18.4
1980	38,860	3,900	10.0	13,230	2,560	19.3
1981	39,510	3,950	10.0	13,590	2,660	19.6
1982	40,130	4,160	10.4	13,860	2,840	20.5
1983	41,190	4,330	10.5	14,510	3,060	21.1

* Working less than 35 hours per week
Source: Sōrifu Tōkei-Kyoku, *Rōdōryoku Chōsa* (various years)

United States and 15.4 per cent in Britain are part-timers.[12]

The main distinction between Japan and other industrialised countries, however, relates not to the prevalence of part-time work, but to the interpretation of the word 'part-time'. In most countries, the average working week of part-time employees is about half that of their full-time counterparts: 19.4 hours in the United States (as against 40.3 for full-timers); 16.1 (as against 40.1 in Australia. In Japan, by contrast, part-time employees work an average of 32.2 hours per week, or around 73 per cent of the average full-time working week.[13] In fact, a government survey found that 23.7 per cent of part-timers reported that there was *no* difference between their working hours and the hours of 'full-time' employees in the same workplace.[14] In the light of these statistics, it is not surprising that only 17.9 per cent of female and 10.9 per cent of male part-time workers claimed to have chosen their job because it offered short hours.[15]

Why, then, do people choose part-time rather than full-time employment? Certainly not for the money, since the statistics suggest that the hourly wages of part-timers amount only to around three-quarters of the hourly pay of full-timers.[16] In a typical company which I examined, full-time workers could expect to earn 1,120 yen per hour while part-time workers earn just over 500 yen for virtually identical work. The comments of workers in this company, however, suggested some interesting factors in the rise of part-time work. One married woman in her mid-thirties expressed a widely felt view when she said: 'Well, I would like to become a regular employee (*seishain*) because, you know, their bonuses and so on are quite different from ours. But when I think about it from the point of view of my age group, well, there are just such responsibilities that it is better to become a part-timer.'[17]

The point was elaborated by another married woman part-timer:

> If you have a family there are all kinds of conditions which make it difficult to become a regular employee, so it is easier to work part-time. For example, there are transfers. We are not transferred from one branch of the company to another, but regular employees are expected to accept transfers, so it is better for us to work like this. Full-timers can be transferred both within the Prefecture and to branches in other Prefectures and this would be very difficult if you have a family.

In other words, for these women it was not so much working hours as other expectations involved in regular employment (transfers, compulsory overtime, out-of-work activities and so on) which lead them to seek part-time work. But the repeated references to age and household responsibilities point to a further factor which is of great importance in the growth of part-time work. For many people who are attempting to return to the paid workforce in their thirties or forties, there is simply *no alternative* to part-time work.

This point was made to me most cogently by a group of women working part-time through the *haken* system (see the following section). Ms O., a married woman with two teenage children, who had worked on a part-time basis for seven years, was asked whether she would like to become a regular full-time employee. Her immediate response was, 'When I left school I was a regular employee for a while but once you have resigned from a job, you know, it is very difficult to be, as they say, re-employed'.

This view was echoed by Ms H., an unmarried woman in her late twenties, who had been obliged to leave a permanent position when she moved house to be near her elderly mother: 'In my case, I looked for all sorts of things, but once one has left a permanent job it is hard to find re-employment. I just have to earn my own living. The working hours really have nothing to do with it.'

In a sense, therefore, part-time work is a corollary of the 'lifetime employment' system. The ideology of the system is that, once one has joined an enterprise on leaving school or college, there is then a mutual obligation for the worker to stay with the firm and for the firm to provide employment for the worker. Although the fully fledged lifetime employment system has never embraced more than a fraction of the Japanese workforce, its philosophy has made employers reluctant to accept back into the fold women who have left the workforce during their childbearing years. For these women, re-employment has traditionally been made more difficult by the fact that Japanese enterprises relied very heavily upon the in-house training of their workers. As a result, there were relatively few opportunities for adults to acquire marketable skills outside the workplace.[18]

Recently, however, employers have become more and more willing, even eager, to re-employ married women – but only on a part-time basis. Some of the reasons for this eagerness lie in the consequences of contemporary technological change. A recent report by the Economic Planning Agency on the future of the labour market predicts that 'an increasing number of females will be employed as part-timers in proportion to the growing simplification of jobs because of the introduction of micro-electronics. In other words, workers will not be required to have "skills" due to the proliferation of factory automation or office automation.'[19]

In the banking sector, for example, the introduction of online computer systems has been accompanied both by a reduction in the workforce and by an increase in the proportion of part-timers. In 1984 almost 35 per cent of enterprises in the finance sector expected the percentage of part-timers to increase in the future.[20] One major bank was reported to have plans to fill up to 80 per cent of positions in its regional centres with part-time workers.[21]

However, it would seem that deskilling is not the only, or even the most important, reason for the growth of part-time work. Instead, other aspects of information capitalism seem to me to make part-time workers particularly desirable from the employer's point of view.

One particularly important aspect is the changing nature of skill. This relates to some comments which I made in previous chapters. In information capitalism, there tends to be both a convergence in the nature of work in factory and office, and a shift in importance from skill (know-*how*) to memorised information (know-*that*). At the same time, the pressures of competition demand perpetual innovation, resulting in rapid obsolescence of products and productive techniques. The effects of all this on the workforce are that, while fundamental *skills* (the pressing of keys, reading of data from screens and dials and so on) may remain fairly constant, the *knowledge* demanded of workers, and the ways in which skills are applied, are constantly changing. Workers may be expected to acquire knowledge and experience of equipment and production systems which, in ten or 20 years' time, will already be redundant. We have already seen examples of this in computer programming. The use of punched cards for entering and storing data in the computer gave rise to a boom in the number of card-punchers: a boom which rapidly subsided with the spread of online, real-time computer systems in the 1970s.

Life employment in Japan has always been based, not on inscrutable cultural traditions, but on the hard economic logic of skill formation. During rapid industrialisation, when manufacturing skills were in short supply, enterprises were obliged to train their own workforce. It was in order to prevent other enterprises from poaching these valuable trained workers that large enterprises, particularly in the 1920s, began to introduce the age-related wage scale designed to induce workers to stay with the company for life.[22] In the perpetually innovating economy of information capitalism, however, this logic is reversed. Firms continue to need workers with knowledge of tasks such as data entry, word-processing, or the operation of electronic cash registers, but they can confidently expect that changing technology will make this knowledge redundant within the 40-year working life-span of the average employee. When this happens, it would of course be possible to relocate and re-educate the worker (and this indeed often happens in the case of workers who are part of the lifetime employment system). But for the enterprise this option involves considerable difficulties. Workers in their late forties and fifties are notoriously slower to come to terms with new methods and new equipment, and those very close to retiring age may never repay the cost of their re-training.

The most desirable situation, therefore, is to have access to a flexible workforce: one which lacks a clear career structure, an expectation of steadily rising wages or a right to lifetime employment and the welfare and fringe benefits which that entails. Part-time workers fit the bill admirably. Not only are they cheaper to employ than full-timers, but also their conditions of employment involve no implicit or explicit protection from dismissal. A substantial number of part-timers (probably about 20 per cent) have no written contract,[23] and about 40 per cent have fixed-term (though usually renewable) contracts of up to one year.[24] Besides, the majority of people entering part-time work do so in their thirties, so their expected working life-span is relatively short and the level of natural wastage is high. (In 1983, 55 per cent of part-time workers were aged between 35 and 45.)[25] The advantages of this flexible workforce are succinctly expressed by Takeuchi, who, having outlined the reasons why he believes married women seek part-time work, goes on to state:

Part-time work is also advantageous to the company employer. Part-timers are mostly women with previous work experience. Thus they already know the ropes. Moreover, they are patient because they are accustomed to domestic chores.

The greatest merit of employing such housewives, however, is the lack of any need to pay them high wages. The company does not have to provide them with health insurance, pension or retirement allowances or other retirement benefits either. And most important, it can fire them in a recession.[26]

The *Haken* System

Technological change therefore tends to reduce the useful life-span of work-related knowledge to a length shorter than the normal working life of human beings. But at the same time it also reduces specific tasks to the point where they may occupy only half or a quarter of an individual's normal working week. This is the ultimate logic of automation: if you can increase the productivity of labour so much that a single worker can control a whole workshop, you can undoubtedly increase it so much that *less* than one worker is needed.

Cases of this type already exist. Trained workers, for example, are needed to perform data entry or word-processing, to write and adapt computer software and so on, but in many enterprises (particularly smaller ones) there is not enough work to occupy these employees full-time. Only a few hours of data entry, word-processing or similar work may be required each week, or, as in the case of software design, labour requirements may be very sporadic. When an enterprise installs a new computerised system, a great deal of labour is often needed to develop specialised software which meets the company's requirements. But once the system is operating smoothly, relatively little human invention is necessary until the system becomes obsolete, and the enterprise installs a new one.

In this situation, the enterprise has a choice between two alternative solutions. On the one hand, the problem could be overcome by increasing the variety of the individual worker's knowledge and responsibilities. It would not be beyond the capabilities of most managers or technicians to perform the more mundane tasks of office life. Word-processing, machine minding and similar duties could be shared out among the existing permanent workforce. This, however, would involve a radical alteration in the hierarchical structure of office and factory work. On the other hand, enterprises could approach the problem by developing a pool of specialist workers whose services are shared by several firms. Not surprisingly, it is this second solution which has proved the more popular choice.

In Japan, this is demonstrated by the rise of the *haken* system workers. *Haken*, approximately translated as 'despatch' or 'secondment', has no precise English equivalent. It is applied both to workers with employment agencies, and to workers who are formally employed by one enterprise but actually work in another. Broadly speaking, *haken*-system workers fall into three categories. Firstly, there are those (mostly women in their twenties and thirties) who work for secretarial agencies. Agencies of this sort, of course, have a fairly long history in the US and many European countries, but in Japan their rise has been closely associated with the progress of office automation. Secondly, there is a rather different type of worker who is also employed by an agency. Usually over 55 and male, these are workers who have retired from regular employment and are supplementing their pensions with jobs such as cleaners and caretakers. Lastly, there are the technicians: predominantly young, male and employed in the computer industries. These people seldom work for agencies, but are more often employed by a large computer manufacturer who allocates them on a short-term basis to client companies where they perform software design, maintenance and similar tasks.

Clearly, this phenomenon is not unique to Japan. Elsewhere, temporary employment agencies have also been expanding rapidly. (The US-based company Manpower, one of the largest of the agencies, employed over half a million workers world-wide by 1984.[27]) The startling increase in *haken*-system work, however, has aroused particular interest and concern in Japan, partly because it has necessitated changes in the labour laws. (These, from 1952 until 1985, had prohibited the procurement of labour by private employment agencies.) In spite of their uncertain legal position, however, the number of agencies in Japan expanded rapidly during the 1970s, and by 1979 it was estimated that around 15 per cent of enterprises were employing some *haken*-system workers. The percentage was highest among large firms – reaching 75.4 per cent in the case of enterprises of more than 5,000 workers – and was also particularly high in sectors such as finance, real estate, services and electricity, gas and water supply.[28]

The agency system suits the needs of corporations in a variety of ways. In the first place, it reduces costs, since companies can hire workers only for the precise length of time that they are needed, and can avoid the necessity of providing bonuses, insurance, fringe benefits and sick leave. Secondly, it offers great flexibility in the hiring and firing of workers, and also increases the power of management *vis-à-vis* the workforce (a point to which I shall return in Chapter 10). Last, but certainly not least, it is a method of externalising the costs of training workers in skills which may prove to be of transitory relevance to the company. As one study of the issue puts it, the *haken* system makes it possible 'to adapt to the circumstances of a growth in specialised occupations – information processing etc. – where existing employment practices such as age-related promotion and wage-rises are inappropriate (i.e. where the commissioning of workers from outside the company is more cost-effective than the internal development of personnel)'.[29]

Consider the example of the Y. Temporary Agency, a successful nationwide company with about 20,000 temporary workers on its books.[30] Although a small number of its employees are elderly people seeking post-retirement jobs, the great majority (over 80 per cent) are aged between 20 and 35. These workers, mostly women, are employed in areas such as general office work, key punching, word-processing, reception and product demonstration, and 70 per cent have relevant training (particularly typing, word-processing, telex operation and computer-related skills). The majority, however, have obtained these skills at their own expense, by attending one of the rapidly growing number of private colleges whose advertisements now adorn almost every suburban Japanese station, or by participating in a training course offered by the Y. Agency itself. (Most of these courses are fee-paying: in 1983 the cost of a crash course in word-processing was about Y34,000.[31]) Completion of a course makes workers eligible to register with the agency, and on registration they are able to indicate whether they wish to work regularly or only on an occasional basis. Agency staff may refuse jobs which they do not wish to take up, but, conversely, the Agency can and does avoid offering work to staff whom they consider 'unsuitable'.

From the point of view of the workers, the flexibility of hours offered by the *haken* system does not seem to be a significant attraction. One survey of some 5,000 *haken* workers found that only 3.2 per cent had chosen this type of work because they 'could work the days or hours that they wished'. The main reasons for joining the system were: for older workers, 'the possibility of being employed regardless of age'; for younger technical and office workers, 'the ability to develop one's skill and knowledge'; and for both categories (15.9 per cent of the whole sample), 'the absence of any other suitable employment'.[32]

People who become *haken* workers, in other words, generally do so because they need and desire some sort of training in order to obtain a reasonable wage in a competitive and education-conscious society, because they prefer office work and are attracted to the glamour of contact with new technologies. In return, they have to pay a considerable price. Some of the main dissatisfactions expressed by these workers concern the widespread lack of paid leave and the difficulty of developing good relationships with fellow employees.[33] Frequent transfers from one workplace to another can induce a sense of isolation which is rarely compensated for by contacts with agency colleagues. As Ms M., a young woman employed by one of the largest temporary agencies, and currently working in a bank, puts it:

It's very difficult to make friends with other agency staff
because we all come to the agency office alone. At Christmas,
we got together and some of us said, 'We ought to meet
regularly from time to time', but really it's very difficult to
do that. At the bank, well, there is one other woman of my
age, but most of the employees are older men. I do often
have tea with the woman who is the same age as me, but
time is too short. Even if I do make friends at the bank, it
will be difficult to keep contact with them after I have left.

Her work at the bank, which has lasted $1\frac{1}{2}$ months, is her longest single posting so far.

Conclusion

The spread of information capitalism seems, as the information society reports suggest, to be resulting in a gradual growth of knowledge-producing activities. But at the same time it is having quite a different and very significant effect on the shape of work.

Part-time and *haken*-system workers, although they remain a small percentage of the total Japanese workforce, are increasing rapidly in number, and, more importantly, illustrate a fundamental change in the character of work. In the future, I believe this change will influence the working lives not only of temporary and contract workers but also of those who are formally employed on a regular, full-time basis.

Increasingly, it is becoming common for workers to move, not only from firm to firm but also from occupation to occupation. Employers are coming to value not the full-time worker with a lifelong commitment to his or her trade, but the flexibility offered by workers whose involvement in the paid workforce is intermittent or marginal. This, inescapably, will alter the relationship between the worker and his or her employment. Occupation and workplace will become less significant as a source of social interaction and social identity. Working women are already accustomed to the situation in which employment does not imply a single continuous career but rather an interrupted sequence of jobs, often in unrelated enterprises and unrelated areas of work. As technological change increases the levels of automation and speeds the cycle of skill creation and obsolescence, this pattern of employment is likely to become common throughout the workforce.

This trend should not be seen in a purely negative light. It would be sheer romanticism to idealise the past in which the worker remained in a single trade or profession from school-leaving to retirement. Life employment offered stability and a sense of identity, but in return imposed the heavy hand of company control on the leisure, family and even cultural life of the worker. Part-time, contract and short-term employment may involve more free time and more horizontal mobility within the social system. At the same time, however, these forms of employment appear to be bringing with them greater social atomisation. It becomes harder for workers to know and to identify with their fellow employees, or to develop any real concern for employment conditions in their workplace. The danger is the emergence of a workforce whose labour is exploited, and yet whose individual members are isolated, apathetic and therefore more easily manipulated by their employers.

Notes

1   M. U. Porat, *The Information Economy: Definition and Measurement*, Publication 77.12(1), Washington D.C., U.S. Department of Commerce, 1977.
2   Ibid., p. 3.
3   Ibid., p. 121.
4   Translated by Komatsuzawa Seisuke, *Jōhō Keizai Nyūmon*, Tokyo, Computer Age Co., 1982.
5   For example, B. O. Jones, *Sleepers Wake! Technology and the Future of Work*, Melbourne, Oxford University Press, 1982, ch. 3.
6   Iiboshi Kōichirō, 'Koyō – Shin-Gijutsu to no Massatsu' in Namiki Nobuyoshi (ed.), *Gijutsu Kakushin to Sangyō Shakai*, Tokyo, Nihon Keizai Shimbunsha, 1983, p. 272.
7   See, for example, Yamaguchi Kikuo, 'Kakei no Sābisu-ka' in Nihon Nōritsu Kyōkai (ed.), *Sābisu Sangyō – Kore Kara no 10-Nen*, Tokyo, Nihon Nōritsu Kyōkai, 1983, pp. 76–104.
8   See data from the Institute of Manpower Studies (UK), reproduced in *The Economist*, 29 Sept. 1984, 71.
9   Takeuchi Hiroshi, 'Working Women in Business Corporations – the Management Viewpoint', *Japan Quarterly*, vol. 29, 1982, 322.
10 See Yamaguchi, 'Kakei no Sābisu-ka', pp. 102–3.
11 Okamoto Hideo, 'Corporations and Social Change', *Japan Echo*, vol. 12, no. 2, 1985, 65.
12 *Economist*, loc. cit.
13 Sangyō Rōdō Chōsa-jo, *Pātotaimā Hakusho*, Tokyo, 1984, p. 234.
14 Sōrifu Tokei Kyoku, *Rōdōryoku Chōsa Tokubetsu Chōsa*, Tokyo, March 1981.
15 Rōdō-shō, *Dai-Sanji Sangyō Koyō Jittai Chōsa*, Tokyo, 1979.
16 Sangyō Rōdō Chōsa-jo, *Pātotaimā Hakusho*, p. 236.
17 This and subsequent quoted statements are taken from personal interviews conducted in Japan, Jan.–March 1985.
18 G. R. Saxonhouse, 'Biotechnology in Japan: Industrial Policy and Factor Market Distortions', *Prometheus*, vol. 3, no. 2, Dec. 1985, 306.
19 Economic Planning Agency report, *Labour Market in Turmoil Facing the Year 2,000*, 1985, summarised in M. Kawashima, 'Japanese Labour Market in Growing Disarray', *Oriental Economist*, vol. 53, no. 897, July 1985, 24–5.
20 Sangyō Rōdō Chōsa-jo, *Pātotaimā Hakusho*, p. 191.
21 Shiga Hiroko, 'Ginkō-OA Gōrika-ka no Kamitsu Rōdō', *Keizai Hyōron*, 25 June 1983, 124.
22 S. B. Levine, 'Japanese Industrial Relations: an External View', in Y. Sugimoto, H. Shimada and S. B. Levine, *Industrial Relations in*

Japan, Melbourne, Papers of the Japanese Studies Centre, no. 4, 1982, pp. 46–7.

23 Unpublished study by the textile workers' union, Zensen Dōmei.
24 Sangyō Rōdō Chōsa-jo, *Pātotaimā Hakusho*, p. 195.
25 Ibid., p. 112.
26 Takeuchi, 'Working Women in Business Corporations', 322.
27 *Economist*, loc. cit.
28 Ōhara Institute for Social Research, Hōsei University (ed.), *Nihon Rōdō Nenkan*, 1985, Tokyo, Rōdō Jumpōsha, 1984, p. 47.
29 Ibid.
30 Details of the Y. Temporary Agency were obtained from company brochures and from interviews with company personnel conducted in Japan, March 1985.
31 'Shufa ga Sattō Zaitaku Wāpuro', *Yomiuri Shimbun*, 26 July 1985.
32 Ōhara Institute for Social Research, *Nihon Rōdō Nenkan*, p. 49.
33 Ibid., p. 51.

9 Mapping the Future: Information Technology, Centralisation and Decentralisation

Perhaps the most persuasive and alluring image conveyed by Utopian descriptions of the information society is the image of a revitalised regional community. In Japan, as elsewhere, industrialisation and urbanisation have weakened the close social bonds – the folk memories, the ceremonies, the mutual (if unequal) obligations – which held together the traditional village. A uniform education system and powerful, centralised mass media have diluted the cultural diversity in which regional identity and regional pride were rooted. Even among those who have few romantic illusions about the past, there is a sense that something has been lost in the anonymity, homogeneity and loneliness of modern urban life.

There is, therefore, a powerful appeal in the affirmation of the information society reports that 'it is important to use "informisation" to create regional communities so that people can live a convivial social life',[1] and in the assurance that information technology has the power to 'liberate us from many constraints on the location of industry, and so increase regional employment opportunity and make it possible for the population which is now concentrated in the urban areas to be dispersed to other regions'.[2]

The idea of the 'information revolution' as a means of recreating grass-roots regional communities is supported by two lines of reasoning. The first line emphasises contemporary technological change. The new media, as Hayashi Kōichirō points out, provide previously unimagined ways of overcoming geographical isolation. Already by the mid-1980s Japanese enterprises were making substantial use of facsimile services, through which documents of all types could be transmitted to their destinations at high speed. Data communications between enterprises and between regions were supported by nationwide circuit and packet-switching networks, and a 1984 survey of around 1,700 firms found that 32 per cent had computer networks linking various sections of the enterprise, and 20 per cent had networks linking them to other firms.[3] A teleconferencing service connecting Tokyo, Osaka, Kobe and Nagoya was initiated in 1984, making it possible for firms in those four cities to conduct meetings without time-consuming and expensive travel. (One major Kobe-based user estimated that the service saved their company Y11,240,000, or about US$56,000, per quarter.[4])

Households in many parts of Japan had access to teletext and videotex services, and although the Information Network System, which will eventually amalgamate these diverse forms of new media, was still in its experimental stages, it was expected to be in nationwide operation in a little over a decade. Meanwhile (as we saw in Chapter 3), other experiments in the creation of 'new media communities', such as the Hi-Ovis project, had given some glimpses of the potential impact of new information technologies on regional life.

One very important aspect of the new media is their interactive nature. Rather than merely conveying information from a central producer to passive consumers (as conventional radio and television do), they make possible a two-way communications flow. Consequently, proponents of the information society believe that they will not only bring regional communities closer together, but will also promote a more equitable flow of information between various regions and between various groups in society.[5]

But it is not only the new media which have been seen as a force for regional development. Many technologically sophisticated industries (including branches of biotechnology and of the microelectronics industry) produce goods which are relatively high in value and low in volume. These industries are therefore not greatly restricted in their choice of location by the costs of transport to major markets. This point is one of the ideas which support MITI's scheme for the creation of 'technopolises': eighteen new cities, distributed throughout the less developed areas of the country, which are to become local centres for the creation of high-technology industries[6] (see Figure 9.1). The technopolises, being developed with the support of central and local government funds,

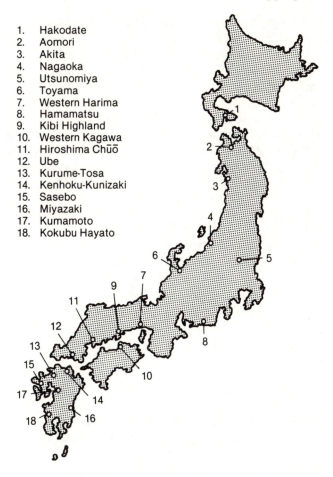

1. Hakodate
2. Aomori
3. Akita
4. Nagaoka
5. Utsunomiya
6. Toyama
7. Western Harima
8. Hamamatsu
9. Kibi Highland
10. Western Kagawa
11. Hiroshima Chūō
12. Ube
13. Kurume-Tosa
14. Kenhoku-Kunizaki
15. Sasebo
16. Miyazaki
17. Kumamoto
18. Kokubu Hayato

Source: Niyū Media Handobukku Tokyo, P.H.P. Kenkyūjo, 1986, p.130

Figure 9.1. *Site for 18 Proposed Technopolises*

are distinguished from other regional development initiatives (like the much-criticised New Industrial Cities of the 1960s) by their inclusion of research centres and housing schemes. MITI believes that, because of improved communications, the technopolises can create not only factory and routine clerical jobs, but also higher level managerial and research positions: 'Thanks to cheaper, efficient telecommunication services, it is now possible to set up a laboratory away from the main office without the R & D staff losing touch with the latest metropolitan market trends.'[7]

The second line of reasoning in favour of the idea of regional regeneration emphasises the social trends which will accompany the transition to an information society. Working hours, it is argued, will be reduced; opportunities for home-based work will expand; and, as a result, people will spend less time in their workplace and more in their local neighbourhood. The local community, therefore 'will assume greater importance as the place where people make contact with others and human relationships develop'.[8]

It is not only the neighbourhood, however, which is expected to become an increasingly important focus of social life. Technological and social changes, we are told, will also encourage the creation of a wide range of voluntary communities based upon shared hobbies, interests and social concerns, as well as upon local issues. Such communities, whether regional or interest-based, are seen as part of a general trend towards informal, autonomous social relationships and away from formal involvement in public and private enterprises.[9]

Information Society or Controlled Society?

Against these predictions of decentralisation, regionalism and voluntary community formation we can counterpose a quite different vision of the future: one which is becoming increasingly influential among anti-establishment groups in Japan. This is a vision not of 'information society' but of 'controlled society' [*Kanri Shakai*], where organisational power is increased and individual autonomy diminished.[10] The term 'controlled society' (like the term 'information society' itself) is used with a variety of differing emphases, and reflects the influence of diverse strands of thought, including those of Herbert Marcuse, Bertram Gross and George Orwell. But one important element in the concept of 'controlled society' is the idea that new technologies provide a frighteningly effective means for the accumulation of information by political, bureaucratic and managerial elites, and thus for the expansion of centralised power at the expense of regional and voluntary organisations and individuals.[11]

During the 1970s this concern was mainly focused upon the potential for accumulation and abuse of information by the political authorities, and resulted in a number of campaigns related to computer privacy (to be discussed in more detail in the following chapter). In the 1980s, however, there has been increasing awareness of the dangers of information gathering by large private enterprises. Two developments underlie this fear: firstly, the emergence of highly-automated, small-scale, diversified production systems makes it increasingly important for enterprises to acquire detailed data about the life-styles of potential customers; and secondly, computerisation creates the possibility of putting together large amounts of information from diverse sources into personal dossiers, whose subjects may be entirely unaware of their existence. It is pointed out, for example, that the home shopping service provided through the INS involves the registering of customers' orders in the computers of retail companies. Unless legislation is enacted to force companies to delete these records after use, it would be quite possible for a retailer involved in the INS home-shopping scheme to build up a complex profile of the consumption patterns of each customer, with or without the customer's knowledge and consent.[12]

The fear of information technology as a source of centralisation rather than regional revival is reflected in criticisms of MITI's technopolis projects. These are seen by some not as a way of spreading the fruits of the information society to all parts of the country, but as an opportunity for large enterprises, subsidised by local government funds, to extend their power into the regions at the expense of existing, locally based firms. The consequence would be more uniformity rather than less, and a growth, rather than a withering away, of centralised economic and political control. As one critic puts it:

the local economy will be made to collaborate in the creation of an environment for the shifting of capital into the 19 prefectures to promote technological development under the technopolis scheme. In this way, we have reached a point where it is inevitable that there will be a reverse flow of 'regional wealth' into the hands of capital.[13]

Changing Patterns of Control: a Model

There are various factors which make it difficult to decide on the merits of these contrasting points of view. For one thing, the information networks of the new media are still in their infancy, and their full impact upon the Japanese economic and political structure will take years, if not decades, to become apparent. For another, the terms in which the issues themselves are discussed are often broad and ill-defined, so that ideas which should be kept distinct readily melt into one another. In discussions of the information society, for example, there is often a sequence of implicit assumptions which runs something like this: the new media will improve communications with remote regions; regional development will therefore occur; development will mean greater regional and economic power; decentralisation of power will mean that individuals, as well as regional bodies, will have greater autonomy.[14] But closer examination of this argument raises doubts about the logical links between its various parts.

In order to explore some dimensions of the centralisation/decentralisation debate, I shall sketch a very rough model which may help to clarify some of the issues involved. This model rests upon two quite simple ideas. The first is that it is necessary to distinguish between *spatial* decentralisation and *organisational* decentralisation; and the second is that contemporary economic and technological changes are setting up counterposing forces which are resulting in the spatial centralisation of some types of activity and the decentralisation of others.

In the past, there has often been a close correlation between organisational centralisation (namely, a high level of control by the leadership over political, economic, cultural or other institutions) and spatial centralisation (the clustering of the organs of political and economic control in major metropolitan areas). For example, the rapid growth of seventeenth- and eighteenth-century Edo (Tokyo) was both a consequence and a symbol of the emergence of a centralised political regime. By contrast, countries which operate under a decentralised, federal system (such as Switzerland) have often been characterised by a relatively evenly distributed pattern of urban development. High levels of economic concentration have also been associated with the spatial concentration of economic activity and of population in capital cities. Yazaki, for example, traces a connection between the rise of the great pre-war financial conglomerates (the *zaibatsu*) and the expansion of Tokyo in the first decades of the twentieth century.[15] In general, he observes that an important factor in metropolitan growth is the form and degree the exercise of power takes in a society. In Japan's history this was evident in the ability of court officials in the ancient state and of the military leaders in the feudal order to acquire command over a large proportion of agricultural production. Similarly, the unprecedented expansion of the modern Japanese city was based upon the bureaucracy's taxing authority and the financiers' accumulative powers with respect to both industrial and agricultural productivity.[16]

Communications technology, however, affects the relationship between spatial and organisational centralisation. For example, when information can be conveyed very quickly, cheaply and reliably from place to place, it may be possible for various different administrative functions within an organisation to be located in different places without any loss of central organisational control. Figure 9.2 illustrates this point: in company A all the high-level functions of planning, financial control, personnel management, research and so on take place within a single headquarters; in company B they are divided into separate sections located in different places. But if communications networks allow information to flow between sections as effectively in company B as it does in company A, organisational centralisation will be equally great in both cases.

There is a further feature of information technology which separates spatial from organisational centralisation. With the development of computers and computer-controlled equipment, it becomes possible to encode the formal rules for the performance of particular tasks into the computer program. In a number of enterprises, for example, managers use project-planning software packages to help them organise major undertakings, from construction projects to the launching of new products or the publication of books. Managers feed into the computer the starting and intended completion date of the project, the relationship between the various tasks involved and the time that each task is expected to take. The computer will then provide a work schedule for the project, showing who should be performing which task on which day, and indicating to managers the parts of the project which should receive their maximum attention at various stages of completion. Data about the progress of the project are constantly entered into the computer, allowing planned and actual perform-

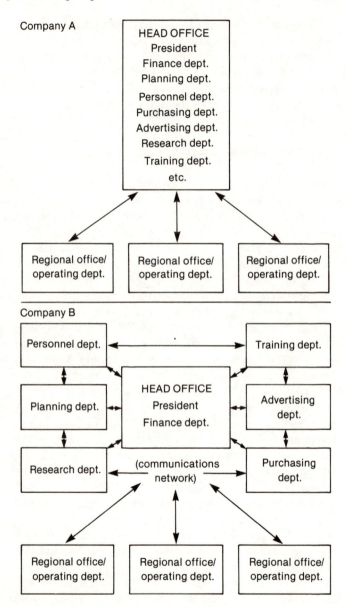

Figure 9.2. *The Spatial Arrangement of Managerial Functions: Two Models*

ance to be measured against each other.[17] These programs clearly
embody various fundamental principles of efficient profit-making:
that projects should be completed in the minimum possible period
of time; that they should consume the minimum possible amount
of human and material resources and so on. Although most have
a degree of flexibility (data, for example, can be altered to allow
for unforeseen delays), they still provide parameters which help
to prevent personal interests or the fallibility of individuals from
interfering with the efficient completion of the project.

As the enterprise develops an integrated computer network, the
rules of the organisation can be more widely and more uniformly
applied to all its parts. Increasingly accurate and detailed information on the performance of each section flows into and throughout the network. This means not only that senior management can
easily identify and discipline delinquent members of the firm, but
also that any areas of inefficiency quickly become apparent to
people at all levels of the organisation; and, since inefficiency in
one section usually means more work for those in other sections,
peer pressure is soon brought to bear on those who fail to abide
by the organisational rules. The result is what US scholars Rob
Kling and Suzanne Iacono call a shift from traditional 'managerial
control' to 'institutional control'.[18] Instead of management's objectives being achieved by means of constant supervision from above,
they are written into the enterprise's information system.

> The various work groups and departments depend upon each
> other to maintain and use the system accurately. They must
> cooperate to develop standard procedures that facilitate their
> interdependent use of the information system. . . . Every
> user in the organisation must abide by the standardisation
> arrangements, regardless of rank or role.[19]

Because of the spread of 'institutional control', with its encoded
rules, its standardised procedures and its ability to expose deviance,
direct personal supervision of many manual, clerical and lower
level managerial tasks becomes unnecessary. This again allows the
location of these tasks to be decentralised away from the watchful
eye of senior management, without any loss of centralised control
within the organisation.

Information technology, therefore, creates scope for large,
centrally controlled organisations, such as industrial corporations,

to become more spatially dispersed. Various specialised or lower-level managerial functions, which previously took place either within the company headquarters or in places to which senior management had ready personal access, can now be devolved to more distant locations without affecting the power of the organisation's leaders to implement their policies and attain their objectives.

But although information technology in general promotes spatial decentralisation, there are other aspects of the emergence of information capitalism which encourage spatial centralisation. These aspects are related not so much to the internal structure of enterprises as to inter-enterprise relationships. As a number of writers on the subject have pointed out, the new communications media are not effective in conveying all types of information. Studies of teleconferencing systems suggest that their users find them relatively satisfactory for communications which are unemotional, precise and fit into clearly defined formats: 'giving or receiving information', 'asking questions', 'exchanging opinions', 'decision making', 'giving or receiving orders'. They are considered less satisfactory where the information involved is less precise and clearly defined: for 'problem solving', 'generating ideas', 'persuasion' and 'bargaining'; and least satisfactory for communications with a high emotional content: 'getting others on one's side in an argument', 'resolving disagreements', 'maintaining friendly relations', 'resolving conflicts', 'getting to know someone'.[20] The tendency of teleconferencing to impose formality on meetings is also revealed by the fact that meetings held through teleconferencing systems tended to be shorter than those held face to face, and to involve less irrelevant chat.[21] Another important factor seems to be security: users are often reluctant to conduct very sensitive or private discussions through electronic media.[22]

All these findings imply that the new media will be of much more use in some situations than others. We might expect them to be most useful in relatively routine and regulated situations, such as the conveying of information or orders within the organisational hierarchy, or the conducting of formal meetings to arrive at specific decisions. On the other hand, they are less likely to be useful in those areas where informal, personal relationships are important. One of the most important of these areas involves the relationship between rival firms. Officially, of course, business competitors are distinct organisations which are most anxious to keep their affairs secret from one another. But in actual practice there are always informal, personal networks which allow certain trickles of information to flow between one company and another, helping each to make informed assessments of its rival's likely moves and to react accordingly. Similarly, personal relationships enable business leaders to gain an impression of the thinking of prominent political figures, and of the likely directions of future policies, as well as providing informal channels through which they may try to influence those policies. In these relationships, face-to-face contact will be preferred both because of the sensitivity of the information exchanged and because the relationships themselves depend upon emotional elements such as friendship and trust. According to one study, 83.8 per cent of Japanese firms expected teleconferencing to reduce travel to official meetings, but only 12.6 per cent expected it to be of use in negotiations with government ministries.[23]

Another important type of informal communication exchange occurs in the development of new ideas. Anyone engaged in research will be aware of the enormous importance not only of the formal exchanges of opinion with fellow-researchers which may be conducted through publications, the presentation of conference papers and so on, but also of the free-flowing mutual pursuit of ideas which occurs in informal conversations. The essence of these conversations is that they should not be subject to time constraints or specific agendas, and they are therefore often best conducted over a cup of coffee or a glass of beer. As we have seen, new media services such as teleconferencing, for all their convenience, seem to impose social constraints which inhibit the healthy growth of these relationships. A study of a rather different new media service, the US Electronic Information Exchange System, through which scientists can exchange written data or documents and ask questions of one another, showed that the scientists used the system in preference to mail or telephone service, but that it was not used as a substitute for face-to-face meetings with fellow-researchers.[24]

The main areas where I would expect face-to-face contact to remain important, therefore, are the areas of long-term corporate policy-making, where good intelligence is needed on the plans of rival corporations and on future developments in the economic and political environment; and frontier technological research, where easy, informal access to leading experts in related fields is vital. In a world in which successful innovation is the fountainhead of corporate profits, these areas will assume increasing importance, and will demand more and more abundant and reliable information. There will therefore be greater, rather than less, pressure for these policy-making, planning and research functions to be centralised in places where face-to-face contact between top management, politicians, scientists and other experts can readily occur. This centralisation of high-level planning and research tasks, however, may well be *specialised centralisation*; by which I mean that, rather than all of these tasks being concentrated in a single metropolitan area, there may be an emergence of several specialised metropolitan centres, one bringing together corporate planning activities, another financial activities, another scientific research and so forth.

From these considerations, I have produced the model of information capitalism sketched in Figure 9.3. This suggests a process of specialised centralisation of corporate policy-making and advanced research activities, but a dispersal of production and lower-level managerial and technical functions. None of this, however, implies any real increase in regional autonomy or any real loss of centralised power within political and economic organisations. Instead, these forms of spatial decentralisation are possible precisely because they no longer interfere with organisational centralisation.

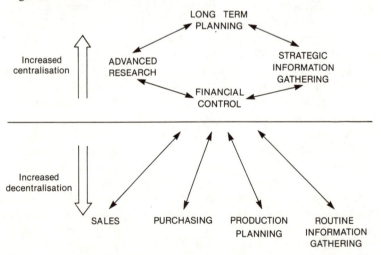

Figure 9.3. *Spatial Centralisation/Decentralisation of the Enterprise in Information Capitalism*

Information, Regional Development and the Power of the Metropolis

How does this model fit contemporary developments in Japan? The process of Japanese industrialisation has produced a rather uneven structure, with economic activity heavily concentrated in the 'Tōkaidō Belt', the line linking Tokyo and Osaka and running roughly along the Pacific coast of Japan. This pattern of development resulted not only in a comparatively wide gap in per capita incomes between the richest and poorest regions of the country[25] but also in a clustering of information-producing and decision-making activities in the Tōkaidō Belt, and particularly in the Tokyo metropolitan area. Some interesting indications of this are provided by the statistics in Table 9.1. The Kantō area (including Tokyo), with about 30 per cent of the Japanese population, produces some 88 per cent of the country's industrial and economic journals, 78 per cent of software sales and 66 per cent of registered patents. Tokyo predictably also has a much higher density of managers and professional people than more remote areas. In 1982, managers accounted for over 6 per cent of the workforce in the Tokyo metropolitan area, but around 3 per cent of the

Table 9.1. *Indicators of Information Production (per million population)*

	Patents issued (no.)	Designs registered (no.)	Daily newspapers (pages)	Industrial/ economic journals (no. of titles)	Journals published by experimental research bodies (no. of titles)	Sales of computer software (million yen)
Total Japan	1,920	475	718	32.1	17.4	3,072
Hokkaido	96	82	1,457	6.0	15.8	479
Tohoku	120	88	751	3.0	19.4	236
Hokuriku	244	431	1,165	2.2	21.7	666
Kanto	3,928	734	480	87.6	22.2	7,432
Tokai	946	426	682	5.1	13.3	889
Kinki	2,708	767	762	12.0	10.4	2,434
Chugoku	530	142	486	3.3	17.7	765
Shikoku	434	167	883	2.6	21.7	167
Kyūshū	136	130	917	2.0	14.1	254
(Period)	(1983)	(1983)	(Oct. '83)	(Apr. '84)	(1983)	(1983)

Source: Kyūshū Keizai Chōsa Kyōkai, *Jōhōka to Chiiki Keiza* Fukuoka, Kyūshū Keizai Chōsa Kyōkai, 1984, pp. 41 and 304

workforce in four prefectures which were chosen as representative of the remoter regions of Japan (see Table 9.2).

But the shift from heavy industrialisation towards high-technology industries has been accompanied by the development of new centres of production far from the traditional manufacturing heartland. The best-known example is probably the emergence of 'Silicon Island', the establishment of the southern island of Kyūshū as a major centre for the production of integrated circuits (IC's). By the early 1980s, Kyūshū's integrated circuit industry employed almost 18,000 people and produced about 35 per cent of Japan's IC's.[26] More recently, a number of major electronics companies have established plants along the highway system of the north-eastern regions of Tōhoku and Hokuriku, an area which has acquired the nickname of 'Silicon Road'. The rise of new industries in the less developed regions of Japan has resulted in a narrowing of the income gap between the richer metropolitan areas and the poorer outlying areas of the country (see Figure 9.4). There have also been changes in the occupational structure of outlying regions: Table 9.2 suggests that the percentage of professional and technical

Table 9.2. *Percentage of Managers and Officials/Professional and Technical Workers in Workforce (percentages)*

	Managers and Officials	
	1977	*1982*
Tokyo Met.	5.7 (100)	6.2 (109)
Aomori Prefecture	2.5 (100)	3.1 (124)
Niigata Prefecture	3.3 (100)	3.5 (106)
Kagoshima Prefecture	2.3 (100)	3.5 (152)
Kumamoto Prefecture	5.7 (100)	6.2 (109)

	Professional and Technical Workers	
	1977	*1982*
Tokyo Met.	10.3 (100)	11.9 (116)
Aomori Prefecture	6.7 (100)	8.3 (124)
Niigata Prefecture	6.6 (100)	7.8 (118)
Kagoshima Prefecture	6.9 (100)	8.5 (123)
Kumamoto Prefecture	7.7 (100)	9.1 (118)

Source: Sorifu Tokei-Kyoku, *Shugyō Kōzō Kihon Chōsa* (various years)

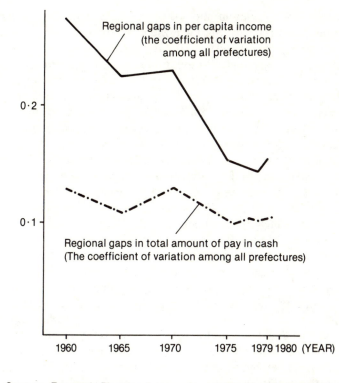

Source: Economic Planning Agency, <u>Annual Report on National Life</u> <u>1982</u>, Tokyo, Economic Planning Agency, 1982, p.78

Figure 9.4. *Trends in the Regional Gap in Per Capita Incomes,* *1960–80*

workers in these areas is increasing more rapidly than in the metropolitan area; the data on managerial workers, however, are more equivocal, with some areas appearing to be catching up with metropolitan Tokyo while others lag behind. (Interestingly, the figures for Kumamoto Prefecture, a focus for the development of the IC industry in the 1970s, show a slight fall in the percentage of managers in the workforce.)

However, the rise of new industries in the regions has not diminished the magnetic force which attracts high-level decision-making activities towards the capital. Economic growth in Kyūshū, for example, has led to the emergence of a number of highly successful locally based firms operating in areas of new technology such as robot production and software engineering. Once these firms reach a certain size, though, there is a tendency for them to transfer their headquarters to Tokyo. Reasons commonly given for this transfer are that information on technological trends and on national or overseas markets is easier to obtain in the capital.[27]

The continued significance of the capital as a centre for research and planning activities is confirmed by a survey of companies conducted in 1984 by the Japan Economic Research Council (*Nihon Keizai Chōsa Kyōgikai*).[28] This showed that the chief advantages of having a headquarters in Tokyo were perceived to be the availability of information about competitors and about the business world in general, access to government organisations, and convenience for handling sales and purchases. The main disadvantages included the high costs of office space and the need for employees to spend long periods of time commuting to work. In the future, the attractions of the capital are expected to increase rather than diminish, but the relative significance of the various centripetal forces is expected to alter in rather interesting ways (see Figure 9.5). A clear majority of firms foresee an increase in the importance of Tokyo as a centre for obtaining technological information and for monitoring the activities of competitors – precisely the sorts of informal intelligence-gathering activities which our model singled out as likely to become more centralised. Fewer firms emphasise the future importance of Tokyo as a location for routine corporate tasks (the control of operating departments, recruitment of staff, financial transactions). On the other hand, there is also relatively little emphasis on the future significance of contacts with government. This is one of those areas where informal information exchange is important, and therefore where centripetal forces might be expected to be great. However, the responses of enterprises to this factor are probably affected by the widespread perception that direct government intervention in industry is declining and will continue to do so in the future.

While the *advantages* of the capital for corporate control are expected to increase, some of the *disadvantages* – particularly problems concerning the availability and cost of office space – are also expected to grow more serious. Unfortunately, the Economic Research Council's questionnaire did not ask respondents to assess whether the overall benefits would outweigh the disadvantages. However, a survey conducted by the Tokyo metropolitan government showed that companies expected the importance of the

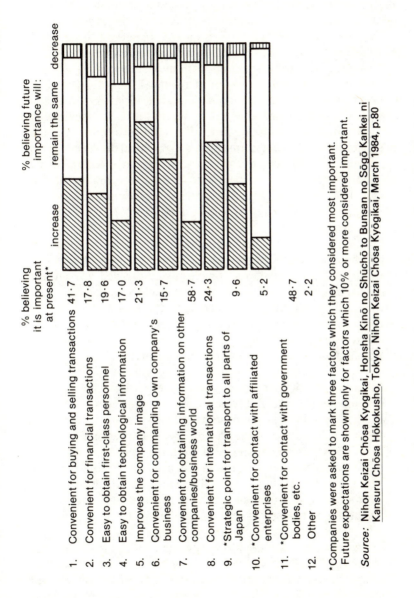

Figure 9.5. *Advantages of Tokyo as a Location for Corporate Head Offices*

% believing future importance will:

increase — remain the same — decrease

% believing it is important at present*

No.	Factor	%
1.	Convenient for buying and selling transactions	41·7
2.	Convenient for financial transactions	17·8
3.	Easy to obtain first-class personnel	19·6
4.	Easy to obtain technological information	17·0
5.	Improves the company image	21·3
6.	Convenient for commanding own company's business	15·7
7.	Convenient for obtaining information on other companies/business world	58·7
8.	Convenient for international transactions	24·3
9.	*Strategic point for transport to all parts of Japan	9·6
10.	*Convenient for contact with affiliated enterprises	5·2
11.	*Convenient for contact with government bodies, etc.	48·7
12.	Other	2·2

*Companies were asked to mark three factors which they considered most important.
Future expectations are shown only for factors which 10% or more considered important.

Source: **Nihon Keizai Chōsa Kyogikai, Honsha Kinō no Shūchō to Bunsan no Sōgō Kankei ni Kansuru Chōsa Hōkokusho, Tokyo, Nihon Keizai Chōsa Kyōgikai, March 1984, p.80**

Tokyo headquarters, particularly in the gathering of information on the international economy and on domestic competitors, to increase rapidly as new communications technologies proliferate.[29]

Information technologies clearly have an impact on the physical structure of the firm, making it possible for some vital managerial or technical tasks to be removed from the headquarters. Around 40 per cent of the firms surveyed by the Economic Research Council anticipated that the new communications media would make it easier for companies' computer and research facilities to be transferred away from the head office. But separation from the head office does not necessarily imply geographical decentralisation to remote regions. On the contrary, particularly where highly advanced, innovative research is concerned, the importance of informal information gathering provides powerful pressure for location near to the research facilities of other enterprises or public institutions.

It is ironical, in fact, that while MITI's technopolis scheme is supported by a belief in the future decentralisation of scientific research, MITI is at the same time actively involved in a project for the centralisation of frontier scientific and technological development. This project is the creation of the new science city of Tsukuba, about 50 kilometres north of central Tokyo. MITI has selected Tsukuba as the focus for its 'next-generation technology' research, and, in the words of one commentator:

Perhaps more than any other government project, the development by MITI of basic technologies for new generation industries demonstrates the advantages of the agglomerative effect of the science city. The location of nine of the 16 research institutes or laboratories operated by the AIST [MITI's Agency for International Science and Technology] at Tsukuba has facilitated the coordination of advanced research in areas such as data processing, energy resources, biotechnology and the new materials.[30]

The increasing separation of research and development facilities from the head office and the clustering of advanced research in Tsukuba seems to me to exemplify the tendency towards specialised centralisation which I suggested in the previous section. But, although specialised centralisation occurs in higher-level planning and development, some lower-level managerial functions are being devolved from the metropolitan headquarters to regional branches. This is occurring not so much by the hiving-off of specialised sections as by shifts in the boundaries of power between the head office and the various operating departments. The companies surveyed by the Economic Research Centre reported an expansion of head-office power in some areas during the past ten years, but a reduction in others. The areas in which the devolution of power to plant-level managers was greatest were sales planning and production planning. Thirty-one per cent of firms reported an increased devolution of power in sales planning, and 26 per cent in production planning. By contrast, the percentages of firms reporting that head-office authority over these areas had expanded were 15 per cent and 13 per cent respectively. On the other hand, the financial power of the head office appears to be growing. Eighteen per cent of firms stated that the role of the headquarters in corporate financing had increased, and only 5 per cent that it had decreased.[31] These figures fit in with the idea that, as computerisation progresses and institutional control is strengthened, relatively routine managerial activities can more easily be entrusted to staff lower down the corporate hierarchy. The devolution of sales and production planning power is probably also connected with the increasing use of small-scale, diversified production techniques, which make centralisation of these tasks less efficient.

All in all, the evidence provides some important support for the model outlined in the previous section. It is interesting, too, that a similar conclusion has been reached in researches by the Japanese government's Regional Planning Agency [*Kokudochō*]. In a study published in 1983, the Agency predicted that technological change would encourage the dispersal of lower-level managerial tasks to regional cities, but would intensify the centralisation of top-level strategic planning in the metropolitan area.[32]

Spatial versus Organisational Decentralisation: the Example of Computer Outwork

The second theme which recurs in descriptions of a decentralised information society is that not of regional economic revival but of a shift in the focus of human life from the factory or office to the home. Like the vision of renewed regionalism, the image of a revitalised home life seems to reflect a profound hope that the new technologies, while enhancing the material benefits of industrialisation, may restore the human relationships which industrial development weakened or destroyed. The declining social and economic cohesion of the family is lamented not only by the right wing in Japan but also by some left-wing writers who believe that this decline leaves individuals increasingly vulnerable to control by government, business and social institutions.[33] In these circumstances, it is possible to argue that the new media, by reducing working hours and increasing the range of activities (entertainment, education, shopping, banking) which can be performed from home, will help to create a society in which the autonomy of households, and of their individual members, will be increased.

An important element in this argument is the potential which the new media create for home-based employment [*zaitaku kimmu*]. Alvin Toffler's idea of the 'electronic cottage',[34] where computer networks will provide the basis for small-scale household-based work rather than factory or office employment, has been influential in Japan. A popular presentation of the information society concept by the business journal *Nikkei Sangyō Shimbun* describes how the agricultural household, with its cooperative economic activity, dissolved before the forces of industrialisation. First, the husband's work and the children's education were removed from the sphere of the household. Then, with higher levels of education, growing numbers of women too sought paid employment. This last trend is seen as likely to continue in the information age:

> but the form which it will take will be clearly different from
> that of industrial society. The futurologist A. Toffler, in his
> book *The Third Wave* has depicted the new form of the
> household, centred upon home-based employment, as the
> electronic cottage. It is predicted that family ties will be
> reinforced by the family's shared labour in the household.[35]

Evidence of the possible fulfilment of this prophecy in contemporary Japan is offered in the form of a report on a computer programmer who works from her home in a city to the north-east of Tokyo. The programmer, a 41-year-old woman with three children aged six, three and two, composes software for educational games. She works for a small software company, 14 of whose 22 employees are home-based. Because of the nature of her work, she is able to use her children's comments and criticisms as a basis for improving the design of the games. As the report's authors say:

> It is not yet possible to decide how this way of working will
> affect the bonds between parent and child or the nature of
> the family. But, by giving women who wish to participate in
> society and yet are tied to the family a chance to take part
> in society, it will certainly have an effect on the household:
> both on the relations between parent and child and on those
> between husband and wife.[36]

The *Nikkei Sangyō Shimbun*'s study, like most reports on the new home-based work in Japan, does not suggest that 'electronic cottages' will become the dominant form of household structure. A survey by the Japanese subsidiary of the US electronics company DEC, it is noted, found that more than 60 per cent of respondents felt that they would still wish to work outside the home even if opportunities for home-based work were available.[37] The new media, however, with their potential for home-based work, shopping, banking and education are expected both to strengthen some forms of family relationships and to offer a greater freedom of choice between a variety of possible household structures.[38]

The Social Policy Bureau's report on the *Information Society and Human Life* makes a similar point. Although it anticipates a decrease in the number of three-generation households (which still constitute around 20 per cent of all Japanese households) and a decline in the importance of some traditional functions such as housework, it sees the information society as offering greater freedom and variety in family formation and portrays the home as becoming an 'intellectual information centre' and a focus for voluntary community formation.[39]

The spread of the new media in Japan, as in other technologically advanced countries, is clearly resulting in a gradual emergence of new forms of home-based work: 'telecommuting', as it is sometimes called, or (perhaps more accurately) 'computer outwork'.[40] The main constraint on the growth of these new forms of employment appears to be a continued hesitation by some companies to entrust work to employees who operate outside the range of personal supervision. There is, however, no shortage of potential labour supply. A secretarial agency in Osaka which advertised jobs for 60 home-based word-processor operators received 4,500 applications from prospective employees, virtually all of them married women with family commitments.[41]

But the idea that computer outwork has the potential to re-create the bonds of cooperative family labour is a very questionable one. The case of the programmer of educational games, offered in the *Nikkei Sangyō Shimbun*'s study, is quite exceptional. Most home-based computer workers are engaged in routine key-punching or word-processing – jobs where the participation of small children is not likely to improve efficiency. Studies in the United States of women who combine child care with computer outwork have found that they suffer considerable psychological stress.[42] The growth of computer outwork also creates problems of monitoring occupational health hazards. One hopeful new recruit to a home-based word-processing scheme was reported as calculating that, at a rate of Y600 (about US$3) per A4-sized page, seven hours' work a day and 21 days' work per month would earn her a monthly income of Y220,000 (US$1,100).[43] But studies of office work suggest that a 36-hour week of continuous word-processing would be likely to have disastrous effects on mental and physical health.

An even more fundamental problem concerns the assumption that the spatial dispersal of work to the household will result in an increase in freedom for the employee. Instead, it seems to me that, as in the case of the regional dispersal of certain managerial tasks, new technologies make spatial decentralisation possible without weakening the organisational power of central management over the worker. In this context it is interesting to compare contemporary computer outwork with the traditional putting-out system of the early industrial age. Some historians have observed that the putting-out system gave way to factory production not only because the latter was more technologically efficient but also because it provided greater scope for managerial control of the workforce.[44] Under the putting-out system, uniform production standards were hard to maintain, output varied in quality and there were opportunities for workers to appropriate materials for their own use.

One of the features of computer networks, however, is the

potential which they provide for standardisation and control to be maintained without direct supervision of workers. Home-based word-processing in Japan, for example, typically works like this: a written manuscript is sent by facsimile to the worker's home. The worker types the document into a word-processing terminal, loaned free of charge by the employer. The document is printed out, checked and corrected in the home, and then automatically transmitted via telephone lines and a modem from the home terminal to the company headquarters, where it is examined and either accepted or returned to the worker for further correction.[45] The nature of the word-processing equipment makes it impossible that there will be any variation in the standards of the finished product: lines are always the same length, characters always the same size. An inexperienced operator may complete a task more slowly than her experienced colleagues, but, since payment is on a piecework basis, this is only a minor problem for management. The situation is quite different, for example, from that of the old home-based weaving industries, where unsupervised workers might produce yarn of differing thicknesses or cloth of variable quality.

Computerised equipment can also incorporate a variety of other control mechanisms. Many word-processors automatically monitor the length of time taken to complete a document and the number of key strokes made. Given the anxiety of corporations to maintain adequate control over home-based workers and the abundant potential supply of labour, it is likely that these forms of automatic monitoring will be demanded by employers and accepted by employees as computer outwork schemes expand.

Lastly, there is clearly little scope in computer outwork for workers to purloin materials for their personal use. The principal raw material which they handle is information, to be transformed from one medium to another, and since the outwork system is most unlikely to be used where secret or valuable information is concerned, there is little risk of the worker trespassing on the property rights of the firm.

For these reasons the development of computer outwork appears to represent not the liberation of the worker from the corporate work-place but the extension of corporate power into the home. It can be seen, therefore, as part of that rather significant transformation which is occurring with the emergence of information capitalism: the commercialisation of the areas of human life which until now have remained outside the sphere of the exchange economy. On the one hand, the shift of service work from the household to the market and the development of the new media are substituting purchased commodities for services (cooking, shopping, self-education, entertainment) which were once produced within the home. On the other, the development of these services leaves many people (particularly married women) with more time to devote to paid work, and computer outwork provides a particularly effective means by which their labour can be tapped. Using this system, corporations not only acquire an abundant and flexible new workforce but are also able to externalise many of their costs of production: the costs of training workers, providing an office, heating and lighting and so on. So the indirect exploitation of women's unpaid labour in the household is likely to be replaced by the direct exploitation of women's paid labour through home-based work.

The entry of the corporation into the household in the form of computer outwork also represents the logical extreme of the process of atomisation which we discussed earlier in the context of part-time and contract work. The home-based computer worker confronts only the machine: the single link which ties her or him to the corporate system. There is little contact even with immediate superior, and usually none with fellow-employees. Therefore there is no means by which the worker can obtain support in conflicts with management. In this sense, computer outwork greatly increases the power of central control and weakens the power of the individual *vis-à-vis* the organisation.

The assumption which is made in documents like *The Information Society and Human Life* is that people will compensate for the loss of work-based human relationships by using the new media to build community activities centred on the home, but in this respect the lessons of history are not encouraging. An absence of work-based social contact is hardly a new phenomenon. It is a problem which has faced women in advanced industrial societies for many decades. But the development of residential suburbs, far from city centres, where many women spent a large part of their lives, gave rise less to a blossoming of local community activities than to the social isolation of the housewife, with the concomitant problems of loneliness, boredom and frustration. Even the information technologies of the past have done little to overcome these problems. After all, the humble telephone, for all its limitations, might in theory be used to link together voluntary groups of individuals who share a common interest. In practice, however, it is mostly used to overcome the barriers of distance between individuals whose relationship with one another has already been established through family, school or work.

This is not to say that the new media have no potential to improve the quality of family or community life, but merely to suggest that social relationships are not simply determined by technological possibility, but are fenced around by a mass of cultural traditions and proprieties. Shared work (whether paid or unpaid) has always been a crucial source of shared social existence, and as long as new technologies are used to divide and isolate workers from one another, the result is likely to be a process of social atomisation which will far outweigh the community-creating effects of the use of these technologies for leisure activities.

Notes

1　Tsūshō Sangyō-Shō Kikai Jōhō Sangyō Kyoku (ed.), *Yutaka Naru Jōhōka Shakai e no Dōhyō* (Sangyō Kōzō Shingikai Jōhō Sangyō Bukai Tōshin), Tokyo, *Computer Age*, 1982, 67.

2　Hayashi Kōichirō, *Informyunikēshon no Jidai*, Tokyo, Chūkō Shinsho, 1984, p. 101.

3　Tsūshō Sangyō-Shō Sangyō Seisaku Kyoku (ed.), *Kigyō Jōhō Nettowāku*, Tokyo, *Computer Age*, 1985, 18.

4　Kyūshū Keizai Chōsa Kyōkai, *Jōhōka to Chiiki Keizai*, Fukuoka, Kyūshū Keizai Chōsa Kyōkai, 1984, p. 13.

5　See *Yutaka Naru Jōhōka Shakai*, p. 67; Iio Kaname, 'Jōhōka Shakai e no Shiten', *E.S.P.*, July 1984, 36–40.

6　'Technopolises', *Now in Japan*, no. 34, 1983, 2–9.

7　Ibid., 6.

8　*The Information Society and Human Life: the Outlook for the People's Lives in the Information Society* (Report of the General Policy Committee of the Social Policy Council), Tokyo, Social Policy Bureau, Economic Planning Agency of the Japanese Government, 1983, p. 56.

9　Ibid., p. 62.

10　See, for example, Kurihara Akira, *Kanri Shakai to Minshū Risei*, Tokyo, Shinyosha, 1975; R. Hidaka, *The Price of Affluence: Dilemmas of Contemporary Japan*, Sydney and Harmondsworth, Penguin Books, 1985; 'Jiyū no Saikentō: Nihongata Kanri Shakai o Megutte' (series of articles), *Sekai*, no. 470, Jan. 1985, 31–163.

11 E.g. Hosaka Masayasu, 'Anata wa Hadaka ni Sarete Iru', *Sekai*,
    no. 470, Jan. 1985, 59–69; Kikuchi Hitoshi, 'Kurejitto Kādo no
    Kyōi', *Bungei Shunjū*, vol. 64, no. 1, 1986, 314–24.

12 Hosaka, 'Anatalwa Hadaka ni Sarete Iru', 68–9.

13 Kumamoto-ken Sōhyō Tekunoporisu Taisaku Iinkai, *Kumamoto
    Tekunoporisu Kōzō to Rōdō Undō*, no. 1, Jan. 1985, 5.

14 Iio, 'Jōhōka to Chiiki Keizai', Imai Kenichi: *Johō Nettowāku Shakai*,
    Tokyo, Iwanami Shoten, 1984.

15 T. Yazaki, *Social Change and the City in Japan*, Tokyo, Japan
    Publications Inc., 1968, ch. 9.

16 Ibid., p. 490.

17 D. H. Freeman, 'PC Software Helps Projects Run Smoothly', *High
    Technology*, vol. 5, no. 5, May 1985, 73–5.

18 R. Kling and S. Iacono, 'Computing as an Occasion for Social
    Control', *Journal of Social Issues*, vol. 40, no. 3, 1984 77–96.

19 Ibid., 82.

20 J. Short, E. Williams and B. Christie, *The Social Psychology of
    Telecommunications*, London, John Wiley and Sons, 1976, pp. 149–
    51.

21 Ibid., p. 142.

22 Ibid., pp. 154–5.

23 Nihon Keizai Chōsa Kyōgikai, *Honsha Kinō no Shūchū to Bunsan
    no Sōgō Kankei ni Kansuru Chōsa Hōkokusho*, Tokyo, Nihon
    Keizai Chōsa Kyōgikai, March 1984, 82.

24 S. R. Hiltz, 'Impact of a Computerised Conferencing System upon
    Use of Other Communication Modes' in M. B. Williams (ed.),
    Pathways to the Information Society, Proceedings of the Sixth
    International Conference on Computer Communication, London,
    7–10 Sept. 1982, Amsterdam, North-Holland Publishing Co., 1982,
    pp. 577–82.

25 A. Boltho, *Japan: an Economic Survey 1953–73*, London, Oxford
    University Press, 1975, p. 25.

26 Kyūshū Economic Research Centre, *The Present Kyushu Economy
    and its Outlook*, Fukuoka, Kyūshū Economic Research Centre,
    1983, p. 15.

27 *Jōhōka to Chiiki Keizai*, pp. 22–3.

28 Nihon Keizai Chōsa Kyōgikai, *Honsha Kinō no Shūchū to Bunsan
    no Sōgō Kankei . . .*

29 Tōkyō-to Kikaku Hōdō Shitsu, *Tōkyō no Keizaiteki Chūsū Kinō no
    Jittai: Kigyo Honsha 'Ankēto Chōsa' ni Miru*, Tokyo, Tōkyō-to
    Kikaku Hōdo Shitsu, Feb. 1984.

30 G. Gregory, 'Science City: the Future Starts Here', *Far Eastern
    Economic Review*, 28 March 1985, 47.

31 Nihon Keizai Chōsa Kyōgikai, *Honsha Kinō no Shūchū to Bunsan
    no Sōgō Kankei . . .*, p. 102.

32 Kokudo-Chō Kikaku Chōsei Kyoku, *Chūsū Kanri Kinō Tō Kōji Toshi Kinō no Chiikiteki Tenkai to Toshi no Kōikiteki Kinō Renkan ni Kansuru Chōsa*, Tokyo, Kokudo-Chō, March 1983.

33 Takabatake Michitoshi and Kurihara Akira, 'Nihongata Kanri Shakai no Kōzō: Ika ni Norikoerareru ka', *Sekai*, no. 470, Jan. 1985, 42–3.

34 A. Toffler, *The Third Wave*, New York, Morrow, 1980.

35 Nikkei Sangyō Shimbun (ed.), *Kōdo Jōhōka Shakai*, Tokyo, Nihon Keizai Shimbunsha, 1984, p. 185.

36 Ibid., p. 186.

37 Ibid.

38 Ibid., pp. 185–6.

39 *Information Society and Human Life*, pp. 56–8.

40 Bettina Berch, 'The Resurrection of Out-Work', *Monthly Review*, vol. 37, no. 6, Nov. 1985, 37–46.

41 *Mainichi Shimbun*, 1 Oct. 1983.

42 M. H. Olson and S. B. Primps, 'Working at Home with Computers: Work and Nonwork Issues', *Journal of Social Issues*, vol. 30, no. 3, 1984, 97–112.

43 *Mainichi Shimbun*, 12 June 1983.

44 Stephen A. Marglin, 'What Do Bosses Do? The Origins and Functions of Hierarchy in Capitalist Production' in A. Gorz (ed.), *The Division of Labour*, Brighton, Harvester Press, 1978, pp. 13–54.

45 *Nikkei Sangyō Shimbun*, 9 June 1983.

10 Organised Labour and Information Capitalism

We have come a long way from the dream of computopia presented in Chapter 2. Information capitalism in Japan, as we have seen, has brought some benefits; for example, a broadening of the scope of certain types of factory work and a gradual increase in the number of information producers. But it has also generated new social problems. Unemployment has increased (particularly among the youngest and oldest groups of workers); trade friction has intensified; the wage gap between large and small firms has widened; some types of office work have become more routine and monotonous; insecure temporary and *haken*-system jobs have grown in number; the workforce appears to be becoming increasingly atomised. But perhaps the most alarming feature of the new economic and social order is the declining effectiveness of the very organisations which exist to articulate and confront these problems.

In industrial society the dissatisfactions of workers have traditionally been expressed through the trade-union movement. But trade unions have not only been divided and uncertain in their approach to the problems of the information society; their very foundations seem to be being eroded by contemporary social change. In Japan, trade-union membership fell from 34.4 per cent of the workforce in 1975 to 29.1 per cent in 1984, and a similar trend is occurring in several other advanced industrialised countries.[1]

If the popular wisdom about Japanese unionism were correct, this decline would not be a very important one. For the image presented in volume after volume on Japanese society is of a labour movement which is almost entirely submissive to the wishes of management and the 'interests of the company'.

the typical Japanese labor union represents the workers of only one company and, as a routine matter, adjusts its wage, bonus and overtime demands to the prosperity of that particular company at contract time. . . . [T]he fundamental explanation for the close cooperation between unions and management lies in a strongly perceived identity of interest between the two. In many Japanese companies, the union's leadership is treated almost as an arm of management. . . .

Far more than American or European workers, Japanese workers take it for granted that just as an individual must sometimes sacrifice to ensure national survival, so he must sometimes sacrifice to ensure corporate survival.[2]

But the fact is that, although there are surely individual unions and workers who conform to the picture painted by Robert Christopher, the image as a whole is a vast over-simplification. In this chapter, by examining union reactions to the introduction of new technologies and to the growth of part-time work, I shall try to show that the Japanese labour movement has not been passive or indifferent in the face of the social problems of 'informisation'. But at the same time it will become clear that there are many fundamental issues which the Japanese union system has so far failed to consider or resolve.

Unionism in Japan

In recent years, western studies on technological change have devoted increasing attention to the structure of Japanese labour relations. The idea repeatedly expressed is that Japanese society, by means of its unique industrial relations, has found a way of overcoming the instinctive hostility of workers towards new technologies. This point, for example, is argued at some length in a report on microelectronics by the British Policy Studies Institute (PSI). Japanese unions, according to the PSI,

are not backward in promoting what they, and many members of Japanese society, see as their legitimate industrial (not political) concerns. On the other hand, their attitude is pragmatic and co-operative, based on a practical recognition

of the necessity of introducing new technology in order to
maintain the company's competitive edge.[3]

This approach is seen as being exemplified by Japan's 'first ever'
agreement on new technology and employment, signed by the
Nissan Motor Company and the All Nissan Motor Workers' Union
in 1984. Among other things, the agreement recognises the duty
of management to consult with the union on the introduction of
new technologies; ensures the protection of union members from
lay-offs or dismissals as a result of technological change; and
commits the company to 'try to secure, in every way possible', the
health and safety of workers involved in the use of new equipment.[4]
In the US, too, the Nissan agreement has been seen as something
of a model for emulation. The Office of Technology Assessment
describes the document as 'important and unique'.[5]
The PSI report recognises that there is some variation between
Japanese enterprises, and presents the Nissan agreement as reflecting the effective negotiating abilities of the Union's President,
Shioji Ichirō. 'The Nissan Union', it says, 'is known for its strong
stance.'[6] Ultimately, however, the Nissan approach is viewed as
epitomising the pragmatic and conciliatory nature of Japanese
unionism.

It is an exaggeration to put this type of compromise down to
'loyalty', 'harmony' and other stereotyped notions so popular
among some Japanese and non-Japanese; but the recognition
of both management and unions that they are on the same
side, and that if the company goes down they go down with
it, can fairly be described as a triumph of good sense, good
communication and sound policy making.[7]

Out of this discussion, three main features seem to emerge.
Firstly, Japanese unions are seen as conforming, with some
variation, to a single pattern. Secondly, this pattern is presented
as one of compromise (rather than confrontation) within the
framework of a set of goals shared with management. And thirdly,
Japanese unions are said to be interested in strictly economic,
rather than political, objectives. The problem with this description
of Japanese unionism is, I believe, that it takes one particular type
of union – the private enterprise, large company union – and
misleadingly projects it as typical of the whole labour movement.

Furthermore, it implies that the views and interests of these company unions are identical with the views and interests of the workers which they claim to represent. A closer analysis will suggest, on the contrary, that in dealing with technological change, Japanese unions and workforces have been bedevilled by ideological fragmentation.

It is impossible, in the space of this chapter, to delve far into the rather complex history and structure of Japanese unions, but a few quick comments are necessary. Most of Japan's trade unions are indeed 'company' unions; that is to say, instead of representing workers in a particular occupation (such as welders or boilermakers) Japanese unions commonly represent all workers within a particular organisation up to and including lower-level management. But company unions form only the lowest of three major tiers in the union system. Many company unions are affiliated to industry-wide union federations, such as the Textile Workers' Federation (*Zensen Dōmei*) or the Electrical Machinery Workers' Federation (*Denki Rōren*). These in turn are commonly affiliated to nationwide union federations, of which there are four, the two largest being the General Council of Labour Unions (*Sōhyō*) and the Japanese Confederation of Labour (*Dōmei*).[8] Since 1982, a single umbrella organisation for private sector unions – the All Japan Private-Sector Labour Union Council – has been in existence, but ideological divisions between the four federations persist.

In simplified terms, *Dōmei*, to which 17.5 per cent of union members are affiliated, represents the right wing of the labour movement. It draws its support mostly from private industry, and particularly from the company unions of large private enterprises. *Dōmei*'s philosophy is essentially one of working within the system, promoting the expansion of the economy and increases in productivity in the belief that these will ensure the future welfare of the workforce. *Sōhyō*, the largest national federation in membership terms, claims to represent about 36 per cent of the Japanese workforce. *Sōhyō*'s support comes mainly from the public-sector federations such as the Teachers' Federation (*Nikkyōso*) and National Railway Workers' Union (*Kokurō*). *Sōhyō* represents a more militant tradition in Japanese unionism, although its affiliated unions are ideologically divided between those associated with the Japanese Communist Party and the larger number associated with various factions of the Socialist Party. It is also worth mentioning that a few unions, like the National Union of General Workers (*Zenkoku Ippan*), are not organised on an enterprise basis, but are open to the individual membership of workers from many firms. These structural divisions help to explain why the union response to new technology has been less uniform, less harmonious and more political than the popular image suggests.

Japanese Unions and Technological Change

In a time of rapid technological change, there are three alternative positions which workers' organisations can logically adopt. The first is the 'Luddite' position of total opposition to the introduction of new technology; the second is a willingness to accept new technology under certain specified conditions; and the third is an attitude of unqualified acceptance.

Luddite attitudes are commonly believed to be foreign to the Japanese workforce. Overseas observers commonly quote Nissan Union Leader Shioji's assertion that Japanese automobile workers treat the factory robots as partners: 'They talk to their robots, pat them on the arm and even give them affectionate nicknames.'[9]

Various sociological and historical explanations have been put forward for this amicable attitude to innovation. Japanese workers are said, like their American counterparts, to have such a positive attitude to change[10] that an official of the OECD's Directorate of Science, Technology and Industry (a European) feels able to speak of

a difference between European attitudes and those of people in the United States and Japan. The latter are eager to utilise the new developments because they recognise their wealth-creating potential and they are not concerned with the larger consequences for society and individual freedom. People in Europe, on the other hand, are more concerned with potential societal problems and start by asking questions.[11]

According to Robert Christopher:

Japanese sociologists and psychologists like to attribute their countrymen's receptivity to robots to the influence of

Buddhism – which, unlike Christianity, does not place man at the center of the universe and, in fact, makes no particular distinction between the animate and inanimate. As a result of this outlook, the theory goes, Japanese do not instinctively feel threatened by machines with human attributes as Westerners do.[12]

Whatever the influence of Buddhism, however, outright hostility to new technology in Japan has been more common than might be imagined. In 1977, for example, the government's Social Security Agency announced a plan to transfer social security records on to a nationwide online computer system. The response of the 1,200,000-member Local Government Workers' Federation (*Jichirō*), which represents social security workers, was prompt and straightforward. Computerisation, it claimed, was not only a threat to its members' jobs but was also likely to impinge upon the privacy and human rights of citizens. The Federation therefore pursued a line of 'total opposition to computerisation'.[13] Although strike action was not used, the campaign was conducted with considerable energy, using various methods peculiar to Japanese industrial conflict. Mass meetings were demanded between representatives of the Social Security Agency and hostile unionists; an education campaign was launched to inform workers of the dangers of computerisation; the Agency was inundated with reports, compiled by every social security office throughout the country, expressing opposition to the computerisation scheme; a campaign of sending telegrams of protest to the government was launched and so on.[14]

There were several reasons for *Jichirō*'s relatively militant stance on new technology. In the first place, *Jichirō* is not only affiliated to *Sōhyō* but is also associated with a left-wing faction of the Socialist Party.[15] Moreover, as public-sector employees, *Jichirō* unionists were in some ways in a stronger position than their private-sector counterparts. The argument, so often put forward by management, that 'we will go out of business if new technology is not accepted' could hardly be effective in this case. Lastly, the problem of privacy associated with the computerisation of social security records was one which evoked genuine and widespread concern, and gave the *Jichirō* struggle a public appeal that it would surely have lacked if it had merely been an issue of union members' jobs.

On the other hand, *Jichirō*'s situation had certain weaknesses. Government employees in Japan are legally prohibited from striking (although this law is in practice sometimes flouted). Besides, *Jichirō*'s members were already under threat on other fronts from plans to cut government spending and reduce public-sector employment.

Jichirō's campaign of 'total opposition' lasted two years, and ended in compromise. The joint memorandum drawn up by the Agency and *Jichirō*, which pre-dated the Nissan agreement by five years, allowed for computerisation under conditions which included the following:

> There will be no dismissal of regular employees as a result of online computerisation.
>
> Online computerisation will not be allowed to cause occupational health hazards; the necessary arrangements will be devised to protect employees' health.
>
> Secure means will be devised to protect the privacy of citizens under online computerisation.[16]

Though *Jichirō*'s offensive against computerised social security was a partial failure, other anti-computer campaigns have ended in victory for the 'Luddites'. One such success was the movement, involving trade unions, academics and local citizens' groups, against the creation of an online computer registration system for the Tokyo area. In Japan, records of birth, marriage, residence and death are kept by local government offices. In 1975 a plan was put forward to incorporate registers for the 23 wards of Tokyo into an online computer system. Proponents of the scheme argued that it would speed and streamline the present cumbersome registration system; opponents saw it as the thin end of a dangerous wedge, which would eventually offer government agencies access to secret and comprehensive computerised files on all their citizens.[17]

Attempts to initiate the scheme in various wards were blocked by vigorous and often unorthodox means, as illustrated by the case of Ōta ward. This outlying district of city, with almost 700,000 inhabitants, was designated as one of the first areas for computerisation. Plans for the introduction of the new system were discussed with the relevant local union leaders, who expressed willingness to accept the scheme provided various guarantees on employment and privacy were given. But the computerisation plan met with unexpectedly fierce opposition both from sections of the public and from younger members of the ward employees' union. These younger radicals forced the leadership to submit the issue to a members' ballot. Although the anti-computerisation faction failed to win an absolute majority, the vote was close enough to persuade the local authorities to postpone online computeris-ation.[18] Trade-union opposition was also a major factor behind the abandonment in the 1970s of proposals to issue each person in Japan with an identification number (similar to the US Social Security number) for use in computerised files.[19]

Whereas the Social Security Agency/*Jichirō* agreement was the result of the union's shift from total opposition to conditional acceptance of new technology, the 1984 Nissan agreement can be seen as the reverse: a movement by the Nissan Union from unconditional to conditional acceptance. A survey of events within the Nissan workforce during the 1970s also suggests that it was not quite as it has been depicted, a simple triumph of harmonious industrial relations.

There can be no questioning the power of the Nissan Union, nor that of its then leader, Shioji Ichirō ('Emperor Shioji', as the press has nicknamed him). The question is whether the union leadership exercises its power in the interests of the workforce, or whether, like the traditional American labour boss, it operates the union as a personal fief. One academic who has made detailed and critical studies of industrial relations in the automobile industry describes the situation like this:

The Nissan Automobile Company is probably, of all Japanese enterprises, the one which is most subject to disputes, both large and small. However, . . . the great majority seem to be, not so much simple 'labour–management disputes' as 'labour–labour disputes'. In more concrete terms, the typical case is one in which the Nissan Union, backed by the Company, is on one side, and groups or individuals opposed to the Union are on the other. . . .

The Nissan Union is relatively independent of the Company in terms of its structure, and does sometimes undertake the organised mobilisation of its members. . . . (But) since absolutely no criticism of the union executive is permitted, and those who persist with their own opinions are subject to repeated violence, ordinary members are wholly alienated

from the Union. In this sense, the Nissan Union can be said
to be a large permanent faction within the Company.[20]

In order to understand the role of the union in relation to
technological change in Nissan, it is important to recognise that
throughout the 1970s, when robotisation was occurring on a
massive scale, the union had a considerable input into the company's policy-making processes. This input occurred through a
system of management councils [*keiei kyōgikai*], whose apex, the
Central Management Council [*Chūō Keiei Kyōgikai*], consisted of
equal numbers of management and union representatives, and
played a central role in the formulation of overall company policy.[21]

In the second half of the 1970s, assailed by problems of slower
world economic growth and rising protectionism, Nissan began a
major drive to increase productivity. One aspect of this drive was
automation: in 1976 the company announced a plan for the
introduction of 74 Kawasaki-Unimate 1000 robots, more than
doubling the number of robots in use and almost entirely automating its automobile-body production. At the same time, it revealed
an intention to reduce its workforce by 3,600 within a year. The
second aspect of the policy centred on increasing the effort and
efficiency of the existing workforce, and here a vital element was
the P3 campaign, designed to win employees' total cooperation
with the target of a 30 per cent productivity increase by 1979.[22]

The P3 campaign, announced and implemented jointly by
management and the union, aimed at:

> raising the level of our workers' welfare and our citizens'
> welfare through the sound development of industrial
> enterprise. The three P's mean:
> *Participation* – The participation of workers and the co-
> operation of labour and management
> *Productivity* – The raising of productivity in each section and
> as a whole
> *Progress* – As a result, the progress of the company and the
> progress of humanity (workers and citizens) will go hand-in-
> hand.[23]

Union participation in the P3 movement included the organisation of activities such as compulsory meetings (outside working
hours), where workers were exhorted by union officials to increase

their dedication to the company and the quality of their work.[24] In this sense the Nissan Union was not merely passively accepting the view, common among the right wing of the labour movement, that increased productivity and profits are necessary to maintain members' jobs. It was very actively participating in the company's plan to raise productivity by technological innovation and the 'education' of the workforce.

This approach, however, was not to go unchallenged. One indication of opposition among the workforce was the 'Azuma incident' which began at Nissan Diesel's Kawaguchi plant in 1981.[25] The starting point for the incident was the claim for a 10 per cent wage rise which the union put forward during that year's annual wage round. The company had recently stopped overtime at the Kawaguchi plant, resulting in an effective cut of up to 15 per cent in the take-home pay of workers. Because of this, a union member by the name of Azuma criticised the wage claim as being inadequate. Azuma was immediately singled out by pro-leadership unionists who threatened him, attempted to force his resignation and, when he refused, beat him up. The result was a serious split within the union branch. Azuma and his supporters publicised his case in the press, and, at the next union election, he and a fellow-opponent of the existing system stood for places on the executive, basing their campaign, among other things, on opposition to the P3 ideology. It was the first time in the history of the union that there had been a contested election, and the union refused the anti-leadership candidates the right to present their election platform to workers on the shop-floor until threats of legal action forced them to back down. The anti-leadership candidates failed to gain election, but won sufficient sympathy both within and outside the workforce to encourage them to continue their campaign.

During the 1982 wage negotiation, the anti-leadership faction at Kawaguchi put forward their own independent demands to the company. Significantly, these included the following statements:

> Mechanised and robotised work is unpleasant. We demand the creation of a better workplace. . . .
> We oppose robotisation.[26]

There were other signs, too, of problems related to automation. The motor-vehicle industry makes extensive use of welding robots, which, as we saw in Chapter 7, were more likely to evoke dissatisfaction among workers than other forms of automated equipment. Opinion surveys at Nissan's Murayama factory, where robots were introduced on a large scale in the 1970s, revealed interesting changes in the work environment. While the number of workers expressing 'satisfaction with their work' rose somewhat, and the number suffering physical stress remained roughly constant, the percentage who reported psychological stress rose from 80.8 per cent to 98.0 per cent.[27]

All of these factors help to explain the changing approach of the union leadership in the 1980s. By 1981, Union President Shioji's faith in the happy relationship between worker and robot seemed to have given way to a more critical perspective. At the tenth Annual Congress of the Automobile Workers' Federation (*Jidōsha Sōren*), of which he was concurrently leader, he stated:

> The automobile industry has one quarter of the robots in use
> in Japanese industry, and yet I can remember no instance
> of any anti-rationalisation movement directed at the
> introduction of these robots. However, I wonder whether it
> will be possible to continue the same situation in the
> future. . . . I think that it will be necessary to alter our basic
> response to the policies of robotisation which have so far
> been taken in industry.[28]

This statement, and the 1984 Nissan agreement which followed it, can be taken as a recognition by the union leadership that their control of the workforce could be undermined if they persisted with a policy of 'unconditional acceptance' of new technology. This threat was all the more real because declining recruitment of new workers and the shrinking workforce in the automobile industry was already narrowing their power-base.

By the early 1980s there seemed to be a clear convergence amongst Japan's major union federations towards a policy of 'conditional acceptance' of new technology. But this convergence was not so much a pragmatic consensus as an uneasy narrowing of the gap between two contrasting approaches. On the one hand, the right-wing unions which had always favoured the introduction of more productive equipment were beginning to become sensitive to the employment, health and safety problems associated with new technology. On the other, the left-wing unions, although still deeply suspicious of robotisation and computerisation, were being forced to come to reluctant terms with the apparently inescapable force of technological progress.

At this point we can observe that the union movement in Japan, and in other countries, has found itself in an inherently untenable position in relation to technological change. For the union's sphere of activity is the work-place – the place where goods and services are produced. It is only when new technologies are ready to be introduced into the work-place that unions are offered consultation: a 'choice' between acceptance or rejection. But in a very real sense, by the time this stage has been reached, the choice has already been made. In a competitive environment it is, in the long run, impossible for an enterprise to operate using technology which is less productive than that of its competitors. Not until workers' organisations begin to be involved in the choice of the technologies *which are to be developed* will they effectively be able to escape the Morton's fork of Luddism on the one hand, or a reluctant surrender to the inexorable march of technology on the other.

Japanese Unions and the Peripheral Workforce

The weakening power of the trade unions, however, is not only a result of their difficult position in relation to the introduction of technological innovations. More importantly, technological innovation itself is eroding the social foundations of unionism. As we have already seen, the share of the workforce employed in blue-collar skilled and semi-skilled occupations, which formed the backbone of the post-war labour movement, is declining. The introduction of computerised equipment has not only reduced the demand for labour in many traditional industrial occupations, but has also changed the environment in which these jobs are performed: as we move towards the workerless factory, a small and increasingly isolated handful of individuals supervises a growing number of machines. These workers, besides, tend to be more and more marginal to the operation of the machines (more and more 'used by the machine'). They perform supervisory or maintenance functions, or are necessary to alter and adjust the machine's program. They are, however, rarely able to bring operations to a total and instant halt by withdrawing their labour, and in this sense their bargaining power against management is weakened.

Although unemployment has only increased gradually in Japan, redundancies have commonly been avoided by moving workers within the firm – often from the factory floor to office, sales, security and other departments. These transfers break up the continuity of occupation which provides the basis for the development of human relationships and workers' consciousness in the workplace.

Most importantly, technological change has been accompanied by a growth of 'peripheral employment', particularly in part-time and contract work. The new occupations created by computerisation (software production, data entry, word-processsing and so on) are especially characterised by these forms of transient or unstable employment. Part-time and contract workers are less likely than full-timers to develop the long-term sense of involvement which gives employees the incentive to strive for the improvement of their working conditions. At the same time, their bargaining power in relation to management is exceptionally weak. In the case of workers employed through the agency system, management does not even have to go to the trouble of sacking uncooperative workers: all they have to do is cease to offer them new placements. These changes, which I have described as the growth of social atomisation, are represented in their most extreme form in the appearance of 'computer outwork', where the machine forms the only connection between the employees and the enterprise for which they work.

Social atomisation, together with the growing powerlessness of the individual to comprehend the complexities of society and technology, tends to result in apathy, inertia and lack of faith in one's own ability to influence the course of events. This is most vividly and alarmingly illustrated by the public-opinion surveys conducted, at five-yearly intervals, by the Japanese broadcasting authority (NHK). Respondents were asked, 'What would you do if you became seriously dissatisfied with working conditions at a newly established company where you were employed?', and given a choice of responses: to wait and see without taking direct action, to appeal to the authorities for a solution, or to call others together and work with them in an active way to solve the problem. Between 1973 and 1983 the percentage choosing an active solution fell from 32 per cent to 25 per cent, while the percentage adopting a 'wait-and-see' approach rose from 38 per cent to 48 per cent.[29]

Japanese trade-union organisers are well aware of these problems, and are particularly conscious of the need to develop new methods of organisation and representation for part-time and contract workers. But there is no consensus about the best means of achieving this aim. Various attempts by individual unions and by union federations to deal with the 'part-time question' show only too clearly how intractable a problem it is.

There are essentially two ways of approaching the organisation of peripheral workers in Japan. Either existing company-based unions could be expanded to incorporate part-time as well as full-time employees, or quite new sorts of structure could be devised specifically to deal with the problems of part-timers. In recent years, both approaches have been tried with varying degrees of success and failure.

In August 1984 the Japanese press heralded the formation of a part-time workers' union in the Izumiya Company, a large supermarket chain based in western Japan. According to one report:

> This is the nation's first trade union organised by part-timers themselves. In the future, it is planned that it will unite with the Izumiya Workers' Union (the full time employees' organisation) . . . and it should be observed as a test case for the organisation of part-time workers.[30]

The formation of the Izumiya part-timers' union was in fact part of a trend within the retail sector for existing company unions to extend their boundaries to include part-time workers. In several other large department stores or supermarket chains, unions have begun to recruit some part-time workers into their membership. The Izumiya method of organisation is a slightly unusual one, but its development is worth studying because it highlights several important debates and dilemmas in the unionisation of the peripheral workforce.

During the early 1970s a number of large supermarket chains in Japan experienced phenomenal growth. In order to keep down costs in a period of tight labour supply, many began to recruit part-time workers on a large scale, and most continued this practice in the mid-1970s in response to falling profit margins and accelerating technological change. Among these companies was Izumiya:

> From about 1972, there was a rapid shift to part-time employment in Izumiya. The background to this trend was as follows:
>
> 1 As a result of improving working conditions for full-time employees (widespread pay-rises etc.), management sought to increase productivity by the use of lower-cost labour power.
> 2 As the standardisation and systemisation of shop work progressed, the part-time system came to be well-suited for work where full-timers were no longer necessary.
> 3 The demand of business for new school leavers was stronger than before, and such workers were therefore difficult to recruit. These circumstances held back the establishment of branches by large stores, and necessitated the creation of a large scale, reliable supply of labour-power.[31]

By the mid-1970s, over half the workforce in many chain-stores was part-time, and therefore non-unionised. Izumiya, by 1975, had around 3,600 regular employees, most of whom were union members, but these were easily out-numbered by some 7,000 temporary and part-time workers.[32] Since the great majority of those part-timers worked in the same sales areas doing virtually the same work as full-time employees, there was a strong logical case for including them in the union. (In this respect, the retail sector is rather different from manufacturing, where part-timers are more often employed in separate sections, and where few initiatives for unionisation have so far emerged.)

The first step taken by the union was an attempt to secure the upgrading of long-serving part-time workers to the status of 'fixed-contract regular employees', who would be eligible for various benefits, including union membership. This scheme, however, broke down in the worsening economic climate of the mid-1970s, and in 1978 the union began instead to encourage part-timers to form their own workers' organisation.

The outcome was the Izumiya Part-timers' Liaison Council (*Pāto-Taimā Rengō Kyōgikai*) organised along company union lines, with officials elected from the ranks of the part-time workers themselves, but given a strong guiding hand by the executive of the full-time workers' union. The brief history of the Part-timers' Liaison Council suggests a great deal about the problems of organising the newly emerging peripheral workforce – problems which are often casually explained in terms of the lack of political consciousness among 'housewives'. Yet housewives have shown themselves to be highly conscious and articulate in participating in anti-pollution and similar movements, and the apparent weakness of 'working-class solidarity' among part-time women workers can more credibly be attributed to the structures of a society which is still dominated by the principle of the male bread-winner (or, in this case, rice-winner). Part-time women workers, for example, are mostly aware that they are relatively poorly paid, and earn less than their full-time counterparts. But they are hesitant to press for wage rises because these might take them over the tax-threshold below which they are regarded as 'non-wage-earners'. If they pass this threshold (which stood around Y900,000 or about US$4,500 in 1985), they not only have to pay income tax but also push their husband's income into a higher tax bracket. Many husbands, particularly those employed in large firms, also receive allowances from the company on top of their basic wage if they are supporting a family. Once the wife becomes a taxpayer, the husband must make the admission (embarrassing to the more traditional-minded) that he is no longer the sole supporter of the family, and his allowance is cut.

Part-time workers in Japan, like women workers in many countries, bear the double burden of paid work and unpaid housework: all the part-timers I interviewed had sole responsibility for housework. As a result, it is extremely difficult for most to find the time for union activities outside working hours, and few are able or willing to take on the time-consuming tasks of union organisation. This is particularly true if (as in the case of the Izumiya Part-timers' Liaison Council) the union is not recognised by the company: all meetings must then be conducted outside work and union dues have to be collected individually rather than being automatically deducted from pay. All in all, the study of women part-time workers shows how neatly diverse structures of social oppression can be made to mesh together to the benefit of corporate profits.

Although the Liaison Council was successful in providing a forum for the complaints of its members (on everything from the lack of recreation facilities to the cold temperatures in the food sales areas during winter), attempts to gain management recognition came up against firm resistance. The company's official line was that those who worked short hours or were employed on limited-term contract could not be relied upon to be 'responsible' unionists: 'There is no way in which we can recognise the Liaison Council in its present form, in which all part-timers with their multitude of different employment arrangements are allowed to participate.'[33]

The eventual outcome, negotiated by the full-time workers' union, was a compromise. The Part-timers' Liaison Council was replaced by a new body – the Part-timers' Council (*Pāto-Taimā Kyōgikai*) – which received official recognition from the company management and so became a sort of loosely affiliated section of the Izumiya Workers' Union. In return, the union agreed that the new body should include only those part-time workers who worked more than five hours a day, five days a week, and had more than one year's continuous service to the firm. Some 1,800 of the original 3,800 members of the Part-timers' Liaison Council found themselves suddenly deprived of membership, compensated only by the assurance from the union that its negotiations would be carried out on behalf of all part-timers, and not only on behalf of those who were union members.

Officials of the Izumiya Workers' Union appreciate the paradoxes of the situation, and some recognise the ultimate need for organisations which will go beyond the traditional union structures. However, they take the view that gradual progress, little by little incorporating part-timers while maintaining the confidence of management, is the only way to proceed. Critics of this approach (of whom there are plenty within the Japanese union movement) argue that incorporating an elite group of part-timers into the existing company union structure merely perpetuates and legitimises discriminatory employment practices, while diverting any militancy which might emerge from the part-time workers themselves. But the approach of the Izumiya unionists was summed up by one official, who said:

> In the future I feel that there will be a limit to the capabilities of traditional Japanese-style company unions based on the workplace. The high-tech problem and the introduction of microelectronics are all part of this limit. For example, there is a lot of talk now about people working from home, but

how can we organise these home-based workers? The
Japanese labour movement hasn't touched that yet. And
then, the more the 'softening of the economy' progresses,
the more there will be problems of those specialist areas
where workers are employed on the *haken* system. Those
workers' employment relations really don't take place in the
company which employs them, but in the companies to which
they are sent out on contract. I think that there will be a
limit to what Japanese-style unions can do for those sorts of
people. In a sense, this part-time organisation is just
something like an intermediate point between the traditional
union system and that future state. But unless we develop
the present system on the basis of present-day realities we'll
never be able to progress to the structures of the future.[34]

Other Japanese unionists believe that it *is* possible to take a
more direct approach to the creation of these future structures,
by going outside the traditional institutions of labour–management
relations. But their efforts, too, have come up against difficulties
similar to those experienced by the Izumiya unionists.

Regional associations of unions have, in several areas of Japan,
taken an innovative approach to the problem of peripheral employment by setting up 'part-timers' hot-lines' (*Pāto 110-ban*). These
provide non-unionised part-time and contract workers with the
opportunity to seek advice from union organisers on work-related
problems. Where necessary, the organisers will take up complaints
of unfair dismissal or poor working conditions with company
management. In the large industrial city of Fukuoka, for example,
a part-timers' hot-line was established in 1982 by the regional
union federation (*Fukuoka Chiku Rōdō Kumiai Kyōgikai*).[35] The
system was advertised through newspaper and radio commercials,
and by distributing leaflets in the large housing projects where
many part-time workers live. These leaflets included a model
written contract for part-time work. (As we have seen, many part-
timers have only verbal employment contracts.) During its first
year of operation the hot-line received over 570 calls, but the level
then sank to around 100–200 per year, partly perhaps because the
effects of initial publicity were wearing off. The issue on which
callers most frequently seek help is unfair dismissal (more than 20
per cent of all calls relate to this problem). In the majority of
cases, workers are not seeking reinstatement, but rather the

payment of back pay or of wages in lieu of notice. The hot-line organisers give advice to callers on their legal rights, negotiate on their behalf with company management, and, in the small number of cases where no settlement can be reached, lodge complaints with the Ministry of Labour. They also handle a substantial number of calls on tax problems, late payment or non-payment of wages and lack of insurance cover.[36]

The chief advantage of the hot-line system is that it provides a means of protecting the basic rights of all workers, even those (like agency system and home-based workers) who are most difficult to unionise. It remains, however, at best a partial solution: one which prevents some of the more extreme forms of exploitation, but which does little to enable part-time workers to create their own organisations or to exert their own control over working conditions. Although the hot-line advisers sometimes suggest to callers that they should seek the support of their fellow-workers and approach management as a group to resolve specific grievances, this course of action often proves a difficult one for the vulnerable, isolated and politically inexperienced peripheral worker to take. The gap between making a telephone call (often anonymously) to a comfortably distant 'union expert' and becoming actively and visibly involved in a conflict with a very powerful managerial system is a wide one to cross.

Similar cautious steps towards resolving some of the more obvious problems of the peripheral workforce have been taken by the few Japanese unions which operate outside the company union framework. The *Sōhyō*-affiliated chemical workers union *Gōka Rōren* has created what it terms a 'Total Community Union', which is essentially a friendly society with branches organised on a regional basis and open to all workers, including part-time and contract employees. The Total Community Union runs various pension and loan schemes for members as well as offering advice and assistance on work-related problems, but does not involve itself directly in industrial action.[37] Other fully fledged and relatively militant non-company unions, such as the 123,000-member National Union of General Workers (*Zenkoku Ippan*), are also open to membership from part-time workers, but, since membership is on an individual basis, joining the union involves a rather determined and sometimes risky personal initiative – one that relatively few part-time workers have so far been willing or able to take.[38] Despite the growing proportion of workers employed on a part-time basis or in small firms, membership in the General Workers' Union has been falling, in line with overall union membership. Recently, the union has attempted to expand recruitment of part-timers by establishing a Tokyo-based pension scheme for part-time and contract workers.[39]

In essence, the problem of organising peripheral workers revolves around the inherently weak position of these workers in relation to management. Possessed of simple and often transient skills, lacking a strong involvement in a work-based community and, in many cases, caught in the double oppression of male-dominated and management-dominated society, this section of the workforce lacks the characteristics which favoured the development of unionism among the traditional blue-collar industrial workforce. For married women workers, even the exploitative nature of their very low pay may be obscured by the fact that the family's *total* income is reasonably adequate.

Without a stronger social basis for mobilisation among peripheral workers themselves, and a stronger network of support in the wider community, attempts at radical unionisation are liable to founder, and part-time and contract workers are likely to be left with a choice of company unionism for the few (as in the Izumiya model) or much more limited forms of protection for the many (as in the case of the part-timers' hot-line or Total Community Union). The constructive development of these innovative forms of organisation is also hampered by ideological divisions which restrict the scope for cooperation between the *Dōmei*-oriented company unions and the *Sōhyō*-oriented organisers of the hot-lines and other non-company structures.

Conclusions

These comments are not intended to belittle the considerable efforts of the Japanese union movement to confront the problems of information capitalism. But they do point to the limitations of work-based mobilisation.

The idea of 'organised labour' as the main opponent to the power of the bosses rests on two important notions. One is the notion that the workers' occupation is a relatively fixed and constant thing, and that workers can therefore be organised either on the basis of their trade (craft unions) or the basis of the enterprise which employs them (company unions). The second notion is the idea of exploitation as occurring within the workplace, through the payment of wages which do not represent the full value of labour. The function of the craft or company union then comes to be the redressing of this exploitation by mobilising workers to demand a just return for their labour.

But the analysis of information capitalism given in Chapter 5 suggests that a quite different form of exploitation – the private appropriation of social knowledge – is growing more and more important. This form of exploitation is not embodied in the wage contract between worker and boss, but in a sense permeates the whole of society. At the same time, the consequences of this new type of exploitation include the increasing transience of skill and occupation, and the growth of a new category of peripheral employment.

These facts suggest the need not simply for workers' organisations which transcend the boundaries of the traditional Japanese company union, but also for forms of mobilisation which transcend the limits of the workplace. It is no accident that Japanese unions have been most successful in influencing the adoption of new technologies in cases (like that of the citizen's identification number) where they have combined with forces outside the union movement itself.

Organisations are needed which can link the need for workers to control new industrial technology with the need of citizens to control new social technology. Resistance to the subordination of women in the peripheral workforce needs to be linked to resistance to their subordination to the family and the wider society. The problems of the social division and private control of knowledge need to be confronted simultaneously within the enterprise, the educational and the political system. The linking of these work and non-work issues raises great – but, I believe, not insuperable – difficulties. Some small sparks of hope, and some very preliminary suggestions as to how those sparks could be fanned, will be discussed in the concluding chapter.

Notes

1   Ōhara Institute for Social Research, Hōsei University, *Nihon Rōdō*

Nenkan 1985 (Labour Year Book of Japan 1985), Tokyo, Rōdō Junpōsha 1985, p. 185; and *Yomiuri Shimbun*, 30 Dec. 1984.

2   Robert Christopher, *The Japanese Mind: the Goliath Explained*, New York, Linden Press/Simon & Schuster, 1983, pp. 248–9.

3   J. Northcott, M. Fogarty and M. Trevor, *Chips and Jobs: Acceptance of New Technology at Work*, London, Policy Studies Institute, 1985, p. 128.

4   Ibid., pp. 118–19.

5   Office of Technology Assessment & Congress of the United States: *Computerised Manufacturing Automation: Employment, Education and the Workplace*, Washington, US Government Printing Office, 1984, p. 210.

6   Northcott, Fogarty and Trevor, *Chips and Jobs*, p. 120.

7   Ibid., p. 128.

8   Tadashi Hanami, *Labour Relations in Japan Today*, Tokyo, New York & San Francisco, Kodansha International, 1981, pp. 92–3; Ohara Institute for Social Research, *Nihon Rōdō Nenkan 1985*, ch. 1.

9   Quoted in Christopher, *The Japanese Mind*, p. 292.

10   Northcott, Fogarty and Trevor, *Chips and Jobs*, p. 106.

11   Hans Gassman, in M. McLean (ed.), *Mechatronics: Developments in Japan and Europe*, London, Francis Pinter, 1983, p. 127.

12   Christopher, *The Japanese Mind*, p. 292.

13   Rōdō Undō Kenkyū-jo, *Kompyūta Gōrika to Rōdō Undō*, Tokyo, San-Ichi Shobo, 1980, p. 126.

14   Ibid., p. 135.

15   *Jichirō* is associated with the Shakai-shugi Kyōkai-ha wing of the party. Ibid., p. 40.

16   Ibid., p. 127.

17   Kompyūta Gōrika Kenkyūkai, *Han-Kompyūta no Tatakai*, Tokyo, San-Ichi Shobo, 2nd edn, 1981, p. 130.

18   Ibid., pp. 151–9.

19   Ibid., pp. 124–44; Rōdō Undō Kenkyū-jo, *Kompyūta Gōrika to Rōdō Undō*, pp. 37–8.

20   Saga Ichirō, *Kigyō to Rōdō Kumiai: Nissan Jidōsha Rōshi-Ron*, Tokyo, Tabata Shuppan, 1984, pp. 199–200.

21   Ibid., pp. 130–2.

22   Ibid., pp. 135 and 236.

23   Kamata Satoshi, *Robotto Jidai no Genba: Kyokugen no Gōrika Kōjō*, Tokyo, San-Ichi Shobo, 1982, p. 60.

24   Ibid., p. 135.

25   Details of the 'Azuma incident' are based on ibid., pp. 43–66.

26   Ibid., pp. 64–5.

27   Saga, *Kigyō to Rōdō Kumiai*, pp. 248–9.

28 Ibid., p. 230.
29 T. Akiyama and Y. Muramatsu, 'Japanese Value Orientations (III): Changes over the Decade 1973–1983', *Studies of Broadcasting*, no. 21, March 1985, 146–7.
30 *Nihon Keizai Shimbun*, 20 July 1984.
31 Izumiya Pātotaimā Renraku Kyōgikai, *Kaiin Handobukku*, 1979, p. 7.
32 This outline of the process of unionisation in Izumiya is based on Izumiya Pātotaimā Renraku Kyōgikai, *Kaiin Handobukku* 1979 and 1982, and on an interview with a leading official of the Izumiya Workers' Union, March 1985.
33 Quoted in *Nihon Keizai Shimbun*, 20 July 1984, and *Yomiuri Shimbun*, 1 Aug. 1984.
34 Personal interview, March 1985.
35 This account of the creation of the Fukuoka Part-Timers' Hot-Line is based on a personal interview with officials of the Fukuoka Chiku Rōdō Kumiai Kyōgikai, Feb. 1985.
36 Fukuoka Chiku Shuntō Kyōtō Kaigi, *1985-nendo Fukuoka Chiku Shuntō Hōshin*, An, p. 11.
37 Gōka Rōren/Kagaku Ippan, *Dakara Ima, Komyunitī Yunion*, Pamphlet produced by the Gōka Rōren/Kagaku Ippan Total Community Union, Tokyo.
38 Zenkoku Ippan Rōdō Kumiai, *Hataraku Nakama o Zenkoku Ippan e*, Pamphlet produced by the regional branch of Zenkoku Ippan, Fukuoka; *Yomiuri Shimbun*, 30 Dec. 1984.
39 *Asahi Shimbun*, 24 Feb. 1985.

11 Towards an Alternative Utopia

> Is it not our main task now – as it always was – to resuscitate
> social relations, opposition, defiance, struggle and hope
> wherever they have been crushed, distorted or stifled by order,
> which is always the order of the state? It is not enough simply
> to denounce the order; one must show that it is not all-powerful,
> one must discover the spring hidden beneath the cement, the
> word beneath the silence, the questioning beneath the ideology.
> (Alain Touraine, *The Voice and the Eye*)

Throughout history human beings have used their knowledge to
control and influence their environment, and so to secure the
necessities of existence. As this knowledge has accumulated, the
networks of our control over the natural world have become
stronger and more complex, and our ability to create and to
destroy more potent. At the same time, the ways in which this
knowledge is stored and applied have changed, evolving through
the development of language, tools, writing, the harnessing of
natural sources of energy, the diffusion of printing and the creation
of complex systems of machinery. The innovation which lies at
the source of contemporary technological change is a further step
is this process – one which makes it possible for stored knowledge
to be applied directly to production without the human being
acting as intermediary between the information and the machine.

As the ideologists of the information society correctly point out,
this development has enormous potential to free human beings
from physical toil and to allow them to devote more time to the
creative use of their intellectual capabilities. Any nostalgia that
we may feel for the age of simpler, pre-mechanised technologies
quickly dissolves when we read of the unremitting drudgery of the
pre-war Japanese peasant's life. And, however strongly we reject

the delusion that technology alone offers a sufficient solution to poverty in the contemporary world, we cannot deny that the stock of human knowledge can and should be used to prevent the disease, the malnutrition and the grinding labour which are still intrinsic elements in the lives of most of the human population.

The problem is that, the further technology progresses, the wider becomes the gap between potential and reality. In the words of Ernest Mandel, the worst waste

> lies in the *misuse* of existing material and human forces of production; instead of being used for the development of free men and women, they are increasingly employed in the production of useless and harmful things. All the historical contradictions of capitalism are concentrated in the twofold character of automation. On the one hand, it represents the perfected development of the material forces of production, which could in themselves potentially liberate mankind from the compulsion to perform mechanical, repetitive, dull and alienating labour. On the other hand, it represents a new threat to job and income, a new intensification of anxiety, insecurity, return to chronic mass unemployment, periodic losses of consumption and income, and intellectual and moral impoverishment.[1]

In Japan, the spread of information technology is *not* affording the majority of people more creative work or increased leisure. The most significant trends are, rather, the shift from routine manual production work to routine 'information transfer' work and from service work in the household to service work in the paid workforce; average working hours, meanwhile, are the same today as they were ten years ago. Though mass unemployment has so far been avoided (at a cost), insecure and transient employment in the peripheral workforce is expanding. Most importantly, Japanese people, while being promised greater opportunities for self-actualisation and for participation in voluntary communities, are at the same time experiencing increasing social atomisation and a growing sense of powerlessness to influence the organisational and technological forces which govern their lives. The intensifying reseach effort of this strongly knowledge-oriented society, meanwhile, is not being directed to finding practical solutions to the most urgent areas of human need, nor even, in any meaningful sense, to raising the quality of life of most Japanese people. Instead, it is concentrated on areas which will result in the creation of more sophisticated, more highly 'value-added' products for the prosperous minority of the world's population (and in so doing, will exacerbate the forces of protectionism and economic nationalism in Japan's developed trading partners).

What has gone wrong? One answer to this question might run something like this: technology is ethically neutral; it has both good and bad uses. Clearly, the uses to which computer-related technologies are being put in Japan are not the best possible ones. In the future, therefore, we must hope that more rational and far-sighted choices will be made.

But this answer seems to me an inadequate one. As long as the decision-making power remains in the hands of a small section of society, and the economic motivation of that section remains the same (long-run profits) the choices which are made will never become more rational or far-sighted. Changes in the use to which social knowledge is put must begin with changes in the structure of society itself.

In the last chapter I suggested that the agents of this change must be social movements which are not limited to the workplace, but extend into all areas of society: the household, the neighbour-hood, the school, local and central government. This may seem a somewhat ill-defined and insubstantial notion. But in fact such groups have appeared already, both in Japan and in other countries experiencing similar economic and social change. In Japan they have taken the form of anti-pollution groups, in which local residents, unionists, students, academics and others cooperated to combat the ravages of rapid industrialisation on environment; and, more recently, they have reappeared in the shape of the local and nationwide groups (often including rank-and-file workers rather than union hierarchies) created to oppose the centralised computer-isation of personal data and threat of the *kanri shakai* (controlled society).

It is characteristic of such groups that they draw their supporters from a wide stratum of social backgrounds but focus on relatively specific social issues – often upon an issue previously neglected both by government and by opposition parties, both by big business and by big unions. Because of their specific focus, they tend to be fragile and transient, appearing and disappearing as new social issues emerge, never having time to establish firm roots in a broader and more permanent critique of the technocratic system. Yet, as Alain Touraine suggests, they may be seen as precursors of the future, preparing the ground by sweeping away the fossilised traces of earlier modes of resistance and so enabling us to discover 'the path that leads towards the new social movements of the programmed society'.[2]

In this process of discovery it will be necessary to envisage new Utopias. These alternative Utopias will not be proffered to the populace by the elite as a reward for acquiescence to the 'forces of technological progress'. Instead, they will depict futures which can only be created by the determination of ordinary people at all costs to understand, to challenge and to control those technological forces themselves.

Some outlines of alternative Utopias are already emerging. In France, where official promotion of '*l'informisation de la société*' is almost as enthusiastic as it is in Japan, André Gorz, theorist of post-industrial socialism, writes of a world where pay will no longer be related to labour, and where heteronomous work (work performed for society) will be kept to a minimum, allowing the maximum expansion of autonomous work: 'activities performed for their own sake – for love, pleasure or satisfaction, following personal passions, preferences and vocations'.[3]

Though this vision of the future may appear to contain echoes of the images of the information society which we examined in Chapter 2, its philosophical foundations are quite different, for Gorz recognises that it can only be attained by a radical transformation of society (including the socialisation of the sphere of heteronomous work). Unless this occurs, he believes, the progress of automation, and even the distribution of its products to non-workers, can only result in technocratic domination and the expansion of a stratum of socially marginalised unemployed.[4]

In Japan, too, Hidaka Rokurō criticises technocratic society with its soft but pervasive controls imposed by 'integration through induced spontaneity (even if false spontaneity) rather than by coercive, authoritarian means'.[5] Against this he counterposes the concept of an alternative society, characterised by

> centralised, regulated administration shifting to a dispersed,
> decentralised, self-management type of socialist
> administration; the mass production system becoming a small-
> scale production system; the overcoming of the division of

labor as a new goal; a significant shortening in working hours;
. . . elimination of the distinction between work and leisure;
a fresh estimation of the skills of the people as something
more important than those of specialists.[6]

Although the analyses of contemporary society presented by
Gorz and Hidaka are far from identical, and differ also from the
analysis which I have outlined in this book, both contribute in
important ways to the complex and difficult exploration of the
contours of technocratic society and to the discovery of its potential
for transformation. I shall conclude this book by combining some
elements of their thought with some of my own to provide a sketch
of an alternative Utopia, which I shall name not 'information
society' but 'information democracy'.

Because the central element in information capitalism is the
private appropriation of social knowledge and its conversion into
a source of corporate profit, the key to information democracy
must be the re-socialisation of knowledge; that is, the return of
knowledge to every member of society. This simple statement,
however, involves a mass of complex implications, of which some
of the most important are listed below.

I The dismantling of the legal and institutional systems which convert knowledge into private property

Copyrights and patents are no longer simply devices to reward the
ingenuity of the creative thinker. Most patents, in any case, are
not held by individual inventors but by large corporations for
whom they are a crucial source of wealth and power.[7] The private
ownership of knowledge is presented by its proponents as being
an essential means of rewarding, and so encouraging, human
creativity. But, even assuming that creativity can only be stimulated
by material rewards, there are many possible forms of reward
(such as grants and prizes) which do not involve the conferring of
property rights on the producer of knowledge. As Kenneth Arrow
convincingly argues: 'for optimal allocation to invention it would
be necessary for the government or some other agency not
governed by profit-and-loss criteria to finance research and invention'.[8]

The harnessing of knowledge creation to profit-making not only
implies that human talents are increasingly directed to trivial

activities (market research, the composition of advertising copy, the re-styling of consumer products and so on), but it also tends to divert resources from basic research to more immediately profitable applied research, and to create artificial barriers to the diffusion of ideas.[9] In this sense it can be said to be a hindrance rather than an impetus to the creation of a genuine 'information society'.

The private appropriation of knowledge, however, is supported not only by the framework of law but also by institutional structures: the size of research establishments, the scale of production and the power of brand names all enable large corporations to profit from monopolies of knowledge. These monopolies too must be broken down if the social potential of new technologies is to be realised. The productive organisations of information socialism are therefore envisaged as being relatively small-scale, non-profit-oriented, and, most importantly, owned and controlled by their workforces.

II Workers' control of technological change

This implies not simply the right of union leaders to be consulted before new technologies are introduced, but the right of all workers to participate in the selection of the technologies and products which are to be developed. Workers' participation in decision making at this level can obviously only occur in a situation in which the ownership of capital has been socialised. However, as Bahro so eloquently demonstrates, the abolition of the private ownership of corporations does not in itself reduce the subordination of workers to the technocratic system. Where organisational and decision-making structures remain centralised, the consequence of socialisation is only a shift from the private control of knowledge by the corporation to the monopolisation of knowledge by the state.[10] The position of the majority of the population continues to be one of 'subalternity', a situation (similar to that criticised by Hidaka in contemporary Japan) in which individuals regard themselves as 'little people', lacking all power to influence the wider society, and therefore devoid of all responsibility for the outcome of social change.[11]

Information democracy, therefore, can only be achieved when the workforce takes control both of the economic and political power to make decisions and of the knowledge necessary to exercise that power effectively.

III Education for self-determination

One of the greatest difficulties encountered by experiments in self-management has always been the lack of decision-making expertise among the workforce. As the mass of human knowledge becomes greater, so this problem might be expected to become more severe. The age of the Leonardo da Vinci, of the universal genius, has long passed. How can an ordinary working person possibly be expected to have the knowledge necessary to decide upon the complex issues surrounding the development and introduction of new technologies? And yet, in everyday life, we constantly entrust such decisions to non-experts: to managers, to politicians and to bureaucrats, many of whom may have only the most rudimentary understanding of the technical details of an innovation or a scientific research project (and little concept of its social implications).

What has happened, in fact, is not simply that various branches of knowledge have come to be the domain of the specialist, but that decision making itself – the ability to collect and analyse information and to form and express one's own judgement – has become a speciality in which only a small elite receive training. And because our hierarchical society *requires* that decision making be confined to an elite, the education system has become a mechanism not only for teaching the minority to make decisions, but also for teaching the majority *not* to make decisions. When individuals are educated from their earliest childhood to accept the views of elders and superiors, to listen to the wisdom of experts, and to mistrust their own judgement, it is not surprising that they should grow into adults who lack the ability even to form their own opinions on matters of social significance. (A very capable second-year university student was distressed when I told him that the main purpose of an assignment was to enable him to express his own opinion on a particular question. 'We don't have to have opinions in my other courses,' he said.)

The Japanese education system exemplifies this selection of decision-makers in a particularly clear-cut way. Until graduation from high school, the curriculum is a relatively intensive and inflexible one centring on the memorisation of large amounts of data. At university, however, and particularly at the elite ex-Imperial universities, the system of study is considerably more relaxed, and much wider scope is given to the pursuit of individual interests and ideas. It is for this reason that the high-status universities have frequently become a focus of opposition to the existing political and social order. Yet the establishment has generally tolerated this criticism because of the overall advantages of an education system whose lower levels inculcate information rather than intellectual autonomy, and whose higher levels produce a small, articulate and self-confident decision-making elite.

At present, the Japanese education system is under review. The Temporary Education Council (*Rinji Kyōiku Iinkai*), set up by the government in 1984 to conduct this review, has produced a number of interim reports which emphasise the need for liberalisation, diversification and the promotion of individual creativity.[12] But while these sentiments appear on the surface to be admirable ones, a closer examination of the Education Council's approach reveals a different reality. As Koyama Kenichi, a prominent member of the Council, makes clear in his writings on the subject, 'liberalisation' implies a redistribution of resources away from public and towards private education.[13] Likewise, 'diversification' in practice means a shift from the present single-track system (where all students study the same curriculum) to a multi-track system with separate curricula for high achievers and low achievers.[13] In short, the 'liberalisation' proposed by the more conservative members of the Council is nothing other than a further extension of the conversion of knowledge into a commodity to be sold to children by educational corporations, with a concomitant widening of inequalities between the disadvantaged and the elite.

The creation of information democracy, on the contrary, depends, not simply on the reform of the school and college system, but on that transformation which Bahro describes as 'the humanisation of childhood'.[14] It depends, in other words, upon an open and egalitarian approach to the up-bringing of children, in which the development of work-related skills is associated with the development of the skills of criticism and decision making, the ability to search for information, to form one's own judgements and to participate actively in the making of society.

IV The restructuring of the division of labour

The processes of automation, by promoting a shift of human labour from the production of goods to the production of information, have had two important effects on the structure and distribution of social knowledge. Firstly, procedural knowledge has become relatively less important, and propositional knowledge more important; and secondly, the sorts of procedural knowledge required in production have become less diverse: as we have seen, automation tends to convert both manufacturing and office work into information transfer work, involving the reading of video screens, the entry of data into computer terminals and so on.

These developments provide the opportunity for a radical reshaping of the division of labour. Propositional knowledge – whether of electronics or biochemistry, linguistics or design – will have to remain specialised, since the scale and complexity of human knowledge is now far too great to allow the individual to master more than a fragment. But the declining specialisation of procedural knowledge removes the logical basis for the existence of a class of workers whose entire working life is devoted to routine manual tasks. Instead, it should be increasingly possible for routine tasks such as data entry or programming to be shared evenly among the whole workforce, allowing all workers also to participate in the production of knowledge and the management of the enterprise in which they are employed. It is only with this radical reorganisation of work structures that the spread of information technology can really come to be a source of more creative work for all, rather than of intellectual work for the few and routine, uncreative employment for a growing peripheral workforce.

V The expansion of free time

Automation makes it possible for the goods which a society requires for survival to be produced with a small amount of human labour. At the same time, it also enables human beings to devote a greater proportion of their working hours to the production of new knowledge. At present, however, a large part of this know-ledge-producing labour is devoted either to the administrative tasks involved in running large, bureaucratic organisations, or to the frenzied pursuit of the perpetual stream of innovations necessary to maintain corporate profitability. With information democracy, however, much of this labour would become superfluous, and it would be possible *both* for knowledge creation to be directed to more socially useful ends *and* for paid employment (what Gorz calls 'heteronomous work') to consume less of an individual's active life. The result would be an expansion of free time, not just in its popular sense of 'time not devoted to paid work', but in its literal sense of time in which one is free to do as one chooses.

However, for expanding periods of time outside paid working hours to become genuine free time it is necessary to reverse the process by which leisure itself has come to be a commodity, purchasable ready-made, at a price. This requires a fundamental reorientation of the structures and spaces of life, which at present are centred on paid work. The choice of a place to live, for example, might be determined by the proximity of friends, of people who share common interests, rather than by proximity to commuter routes to work. The home itself could be transformed from its present status as a dormitory for the paid worker and a prison for the unpaid housekeeper to a place whose design was conducive to participation in activities – whether silent or noisy, messy or orderly, sports or music, craft or contemplation.

New technologies make all of these things possible. Computers, by providing a means for the automation of small-scale, variable production, increase the potential for reducing the size of productive enterprises. Smaller enterprises enhance the viability of workers' participation in decision making. Automation makes the sharing of routine tasks easier and erodes the economic logic which underlies the division between mental and manual labour. New information networks create new opportunities for flexibility in the location of work.

But technology by itself makes none of these things inevitable, nor even particularly likely. Instead, applied within the existing political and social structure, it threatens to produce unstable employment, widening social inequalities, a sense of individual isolation and powerlessness and a worsening of international economic tensions. It might be comforting to conclude, in the tradition of millenarianism (to which Utopianism is closely related) that these problems will inevitably lead to the collapse of the technocratic system and its replacement by a new and just society. But the study of Japan and of other technologically advanced societies gives little basis for such a conclusion. Information democracy will be created neither by the forces of technological progress nor by the unfolding of historical inevitability, but only by people's determination to seize control of social knowledge and make it a source not of technocratic domination but of human liberation.

Notes

1   E. Mandel, *Late Capitalism*, London, Verso Press, 1978, p. 216.
2   A. Touraine, *The Voice and the Eye: an Analysis of Social Movements*, Cambridge, Cambridge University Press, and Paris, Editions de la Maison des Sciences de l'Homme, 1981, pp. 17–19.
3   A. Gorz, *Paths to Paradise: On the Liberation from Work*, London and Sydney, Pluto Press, 1985, p. 53.
4   Ibid., pp. 36 and 57–8.
5   Rokurō Hidaka, *The Price of Affluence: Dilemmas of Contemporary Japan*, Harmondsworth (UK) and Ringwood (Australia), Penguin Books 1985, p. 90.
6   Ibid., pp. 101–2.
7   In the United States, the percentage of patents held by individuals fell from 81.7% at the beginning of the century to 23.2% in the first half of the 1970s; G. Rosegger, *The Economics of Production and Innovation: an Industrial Perspective*, Oxford, Pergamon Press, 1980, p. 175.
8   K. J. Arrow, 'Economic Welfare and the Allocation of Resources for Invention' in D. M. Lamberton (ed.), *Economics of Information and Knowledge*, Harmondsworth, Penguin Books, 1971, p. 156.
9   Ibid., pp. 151–2.
10 R. Bahro, *The Alternative in Eastern Europe*, London, New Left Books/Verso, 1978.
11 Ibid. pp. 146–7.
12 Takeuchi Yasuo, 'In Pursuit of Educational Reform', *Japan Echo*, vol. xii, no. 2, 1985, 41–2.
13 Koyama Kenichi, 'An End to Uniformity in Education', *Japan Echo*, vol. xii, no. 2, 1985, 41–9.
14 Bahro, *The Alternative in Eastern Europe*, p. 291.

Appendix Categorisation of the Occupational Structure (see Chapter 8)

The data in Figures 8.1 to 8.3 are derived from tables in the Employment Status Survey showing employment by types of activity, industry (intermediate groups) and occupation.

In Figure 8.1 I have tried to relate the categories as closely as possible to those used in M. U. Porat's *Information Economy*, although this has not always been possible because of the lack of detail in the source material. The categories used in Figure 8.1 are as follows:

    I *Agriculture*: Farmers, lumbermen and fishermen (all industries); labourers (agriculture and fisheries);

    II *Industry*: Workers in mining and quarrying occupations (all industries); craftsmen and production process workers (all industries except printing and publishing); labourers (mining, construction and manufacturing);

    III *Services*: Professional and technical workers (personal services); half of all managers in retail trade; sales workers (all industries except finance, insurance and real estate); workers in transport and communications occupations (all industries except communications); labourers (retail and wholesale trade; transport and communications; electricity, gas and water supply; services; public employment); protective services workers (all industries); service workers (all industries except finance, insurance and real estate);

    IV *Information*: Professional and technical workers (all industries except personal services); managers and officials (all industries except retail trade, where half have been counted as service workers); clerical and related workers (all industries); sales workers (finance, insurance and real estate); workers in transport and communications (communications industry); labourers (finance, insurance real estate); service workers (finance, insurance and real estate).

In Figures 8.2 and 8.3 the classifications 'agriculture' and 'industry' are unchanged, and the remaining categories are defined as follows:

III *Transfer of goods*: Half of all managers in retail trade; sales workers (all industries except eating and drinking places, finance, insurance and real estate); workers in transport and communications occupations (all industries except communications); labourers (wholesale and retail trade; transport and communications; electricity, gas and water supply);

IV *Information production*: Professional and technical workers (all industries except personal services); managers and officials (all industries except retail trade, where half have been counted as service workers).

V *Transfer of information*: Clerical and related workers (all industries); sales workers (finance, insurance and real estate); workers in transport and communications occupations (communications industry); craftsmen and production service workers (printing and publishing); labourers (finance, insurance and real estate); service workers (finance, insurance and real estate);

VI *Services*: Professional and technical workers (personal services); sales workers (eating and drinking places); labourers (services, public employment); protective service workers (all industries). Service workers (all industries except finance, insurance real estate). In Figure 8.3 this category also includes non-participants in the workforce listed by the Statistics Bureau as 'engaged in housework' (15,870,000 in 1977 and 15,550,000 in 1982).

Index